Claude

for dummies®
A Wiley Brand

Claude

by Stephanie Diamond

for dummies®
A Wiley Brand

Claude For Dummies®

Published by: **John Wiley & Sons, Inc.**, 111 River Street, Hoboken, NJ 07030-5774, www.wiley.com

For general information on our other products and services, please contact our Customer Care Department within the U.S. at 877-762-2974, outside the U.S. at 317-572-3993, or fax 317-572-4002. For technical support, please visit https://hub.wiley.com/community/support/dummies.

Wiley publishes in a variety of print and electronic formats and by print-on-demand. Some material included with standard print versions of this book may not be included in e-books or in print-on-demand. If this book refers to media that is not included in the version you purchased, you may download this material at http://booksupport.wiley.com. For more information about Wiley products, visit www.wiley.com.

Library of Congress Control Number is available from the publisher.

ISBN 978-1-394-42573-0 (pbk); ISBN 978-1-394-42575-4 (ebk); ISBN 978-1-394-42574-7 (ebk)

SKY10161686_070726

Table of Contents

Introduction

Every week, millions of people type questions into artificial intelligence (AI) tools and get back answers that range from baffling to brilliant. If you've ever wondered how to reliably land on the brilliant end of that spectrum, or if you're just curious what this whole Claude thing is about, this book is for you.

Claude is an AI assistant built by Anthropic, an AI development company. You can have a conversation with Claude, asking it to write or edit a document or help you research a topic, analyze a spreadsheet, generate code, brainstorm ideas, or prepare for an important meeting. Using Claude doesn't require technical expertise, and this book shows you how to get useful results from your first session.

Claude AI For Dummies isn't about theory or hype. It's a practical, hands-on guide to using Claude as a tool you'll reach for every day for work, learning, creative projects, and everything in between. Whether you type your first prompt in the next five minutes or you've already dabbled with AI and want to go deeper, this book gives you the foundation, the techniques, and the confidence to get value from Claude.

About This Book

You can read this book cover-to-cover or jump straight to whatever you need right now. Each chapter stands on its own, so feel free to skip around based on what's most useful to you today.

Here's a quick map of what's inside.

Part 1 (Chapters 1–6) introduces Claude and shows you how to set up an account and pick the right plan, have your first conversation, write prompts that work, use Projects and Memory to organize your work across sessions, and customize Claude with Skills and Connectors.

Part 2 (Chapters 7–9) goes deeper into the craft of the prompt. You start with proven templates you can use immediately, then learn how to understand and evaluate Claude's responses, and finally combine techniques to get consistently first-rate results.

Part 3 (Chapters 10–15) shows Claude in action across everyday tasks: writing and editing faster, learning new subjects, solving problems and making decisions, working with data and documents, creating content, and following complete start-to-finish workflow examples.

Part 4 (Chapters 16–20) covers Artifacts (Claude's way of packaging shareable, reusable content), pulling in current information from the web, using extended thinking and research mode for your most complex questions and projects, putting Cowork to work as your desktop agent, and diagnosing and fixing the most common problems you'll run into.

Part 5 (Chapters 21 and 22) delivers the classic *Dummies* quick-reference pair: ten ways you can save time every day with Claude and ten signs your prompt needs a rewrite.

Foolish Assumptions

Every author makes a few assumptions about readers, and here are mine about you:

- You have internet access and a device (desktop, laptop, tablet, or phone) with a web browser.
- You've heard of AI. You don't need a background in artificial intelligence, machine learning, or computer science.
- You're not a developer looking for the Claude API or deep technical documentation. (Those resources exist, but this isn't that book.)
- You want to accomplish real things (write better, learn faster, solve problems, save time), not just experiment with a chatbot.

Icons Used in This Book

Throughout these pages, small icons appear in the margin to flag different types of information. Here's what each one means:

TIP

The Tip icon highlights shortcuts, best practices, and insider advice that save you time or help you get better results. These are the things an experienced user would tell you.

REMEMBER

The Remember icon highlights key ideas worth keeping in mind as you work with Claude. You don't have to memorize everything, but this stuff is worth a second glance.

TECHNICAL STUFF

The Technical Stuff icon flags deeper technical details for readers who want to understand the "why" behind the "what."

WARNING

The Warning icon alerts you to common mistakes, pitfalls, and situations where things can go sideways. Pay attention to these.

Beyond the Book

I have included a few useful bits online in a cheat sheet for your enjoyment and edification. To find the cheat sheet, go to `www.dummies.com` and search for *Claude For Dummies cheat sheet*. You'll find information on the four main ways prompts fail and advanced tips for power users. In addition, visit `www.dummies.com/go/claudefd` for a bonus chapter on how to use Claude responsibly.

Where to Go from Here

You can start anywhere in this book, but if you're new to Claude, Chapter 1 is the best place to begin. It covers the big picture: what Claude is, how it works, and why it's different from other AI tools you may have tried. Chapter 2 walks you through setting up your account and choosing the right plan, and Chapter 3 has you up and running with your first real conversation.

If you've already explored Claude a bit and want to get better results fast, jump straight to Chapter 4 or Chapter 7. Either one will give you an immediate payoff.

And if you hit a snag at any point, Chapter 20 is your troubleshooting home base. The table of contents and the index are there to help you find what you're looking for as well.

The goal of this book is simple: by the time you're done, you should feel comfortable using Claude to make your work and life easier, faster, and a lot more interesting.

1

Getting Started with Claude

IN THIS PART . . .

Meet Claude and discover what makes it special.

Pick the right plan and get set up fast.

Ask your first question and get a great answer.

Learn what makes a prompt work.

Give Claude context once and let it remember the rest.

Make Claude your own with Skills, Connectors, and Cowork.

IN THIS CHAPTER

» Finding out how Claude works

» Discovering what makes Claude different

» Knowing when to double-check Claude's responses

Chapter 1
Introducing Claude

You've been hearing about AI assistants. Perhaps your colleagues rave about using them, or you've seen articles about how they change the way people work. But what exactly is Claude, and what can it do for you?

In this chapter, you discover what Claude is without getting buried in technical jargon. You find out how Claude differs from search engines and other tools you might already use. You then discover the types of tasks that are best suited for Claude. Finally, and most importantly, you find out when you should verify its responses and when it's best to use another tool. By the end of this chapter, you'll have a clear understanding of how to start using Claude effectively.

Describing Claude

Claude is available in several plans to fit different needs. The Free plan gives you access to core features at no cost. Pro and Max are paid plans that unlock higher usage limits, priority access, and advanced features. Team and Enterprise plans are designed for organizations that need collaboration tools, administrative controls, and security guarantees.

Throughout this chapter, features that require a specific plan are noted so you always know what's available to you. For a detailed list for each plan, see Chapter 2.

Claude is an AI assistant created by Anthropic, a leading AI software development company. Think of Claude as a well-informed partner who's always available to help you write, think through problems, learn new topics, and get things done. You can have conversations with Claude through an app or a browser on a smartphone or tablet; a laptop; or a desktop computer (see Chapter 2 for details). Claude responds in natural language. It's just like texting with a knowledgeable colleague who's always available.

TIP

For more information about Anthropic's mission and approach to building Claude, see `https://anthropic.com/company`.

Defining AI without the jargon

AI (artificial intelligence) may sound intimidating, but at its core, it's just software that can understand and respond to your questions and requests in a way that feels natural and helpful.

Claude is what's called a *large language model* (LLM). In plain English, this means that Claude has been trained on a mixture of licensed data, data created by human trainers, and text from the internet. Through this training, Claude learned patterns about how language works and how to answer questions, explain concepts, write different types of content, and reason through problems.

TIP

You don't need to understand the technical details of how Claude works any more than you need to understand how your car engine works to drive it. What matters is knowing what you can do with Claude and how to use it effectively.

REMEMBER

Unlike traditional software that follows rigid software rules ("if this, then that"), Claude is designed to understand context and ambiguity. If you ask, "Make this email friendlier," Claude understands what *friendlier* means and how to adjust the tone. If you say, "Explain quantum physics like I'm 12 not 20," Claude knows to simplify the language and use relatable examples.

Understanding how Claude differs from search engines

Today's search engines, like Google AI Mode (`https://google.com/aimode`) and Copilot (`https://copilot.com/`), use advanced AI. They now feature conversational answers, summaries, and direct recommendations, instead of just producing lists of links based on keywords. This blurs the lines between web search and generative AI, but it's important to understand where Claude stands apart. Here are several of Claude's distinct strengths. Claude can:

- **Process and synthesize extremely large documents or datasets:** Claude can work with full ebooks, manuals, and multipage reports in a single conversation. Most AI search engines, even with recent upgrades, are limited to medium-size document analysis.
- **Engage in deep, multiturn interactions:** These interactions include nuanced reasoning, brainstorming, planning, and extended dialogue, well beyond the short conversational memory of even the most advanced AI-driven search platforms.

  REMEMBER

  Deep multiturn conversations are extended back-and-forth exchanges where each message builds on the previous ones. Claude maintains the full context of what you've discussed in each conversation. This is in contrast to AI search engines, which typically handle one to three exchanges before losing context or requiring you to start over.
- **Generate, structure, and refine original content:** This content includes emails, documents, creative writing, and executive summaries tailored to your unique prompts, context, and files.

Knowing what makes Claude special

Several AI assistants exist today, so what makes Claude different? Here are some key characteristics that set Claude apart. Claude:

- **Has a natural conversation style:** Claude responds in a conversational rather than a robotic or overly formal way. The tone can adapt to your needs: professional for business writing, collaborative for brainstorming, and helpful for learning.
- **Excels at complex thinking:** Claude performs well at tasks that require reasoning and analysis. Whether you're working through a business decision or understanding a complicated concept, Claude can break down complex problems into manageable pieces.
- **Is an effective writing assistant:** From emails to reports to creative content, Claude helps improve your writing. It can match specific tones and styles, and many users find it particularly good at editing and refining drafts.
- **Is honest about its limitations:** Claude is often more transparent about limitations than many AIs, but it still sometimes provide incorrect or outdated information without explicit warning, especially for recent events. The model attempts to tell you when it doesn't know, but it doesn't always do so. You should always verify important or high-stakes information.

- **Focuses on safety and helpfulness:** Anthropic built safety into Claude from the ground up. They say that "Claude is designed to be helpful, harmless, and honest." It declines requests that could cause harm while remaining genuinely useful.
- **Provides a long context window:** Claude can work with large amounts of text at once. You can upload entire documents, share long context, and have extended conversations without Claude forgetting what you discussed earlier. (See Chapter 5 for information about Claude's Memory settings.)

TIP

Claude's maximum context window varies by version, but your actual limits depend also on versions and subscription tiers. As of April, 2026, Claude Opus 4.7 and Sonnet 4.6 support 1 million tokens (2,500 pages of text) and are available at no extra cost on Pro and Max. Claude Haiku 4.5 remains at 200,000 tokens (500 pages).

- **Creates artifacts:** When you ask Claude to create substantial content like documents, code, or web pages, it generates these as separate artifacts (windows) you can easily view, edit, and download, not just as text in a chat. (Check out Chapter 16 for more about using artifacts.)

Discovering How Best to Use Claude

Like any tool, Claude has its sweet spots. It shines when performing some tasks, but also has its limitations. Knowing both will help you use Claude effectively and avoid frustration. In this section, you discover the areas in which Claude excels.

Writing and thinking

Writing and thinking are widely considered Claude's superpowers. You can use Claude for writing and thinking tasks such as the following:

- **Draft creation and polish:** Claude excels at first drafts of emails, reports, blog posts, and social media content. It can take your rough draft and suggest improvements in clarity, tone, and structure.
- **Tone and format transformation:** Claude adapts to your audience, whether the tone needs to be formal or casual. It distills long documents into summaries and transforms formats, such as turning meeting notes into action items or technical specs into easy-to-understand explanations.

- **Problem-solving and analysis:** Claude breaks down complex problems, compares options, finds pros and cons, and helps you think through implications from several perspectives.
- **Idea generation and planning:** Claude generates options quickly and creates outlines, frameworks, and step-by-step plans to help organize your thinking.

REMEMBER

Most tasks that AI can help with involve language, reasoning, and creativity. If you can describe what you need in words, Claude can probably help you.

Learning complex topics

One of Claude's most valuable capabilities is helping you learn. If you're trying to understand a new concept or master a skill, Claude can be a patient tutor.

Consider what makes Claude effective for learning:

- **Explanations at your level:** Tell Claude your background knowledge ("I'm new to this" or "I have a basic understanding of economics"), and it adjusts its explanations accordingly. No more getting lost in jargon or feeling talked down to.
- **Complexity simplified:** Complex topics become digestible when Claude breaks them into smaller concepts, explains connections, and builds understanding step by step.
- **Multiple perspectives and analogies:** If one explanation doesn't click, ask Claude to try a different approach. It can use analogies, examples from different domains, or alternative frameworks until something resonates.
- **No judgment:** Feel free to ask "dumb questions" or ask the same thing multiple ways. Claude never makes you feel bad for not understanding something, which is important when you want to learn.
- **Interactive learning:** You can ask follow-up questions, request clarification, or dig deeper. The conversation adapts to your learning pace and interests.
- **Practice and examples:** When you're learning a skill, ask Claude for practice problems, examples, or exercises. It can check your work and explain where you went wrong. You can be specific about exactly what's tripping you up.

To get started, here's how to think about constructing a prompt:

- **Understanding technical concepts:** "Explain blockchain like I'm an artist, not a programmer."

» **Learning new professional skills:** "Teach me the basics of project management."

» **Making sense of documents:** "Summarize this legal contract in plain English."

» **Preparing for challenges:** "Help me understand this topic for my presentation."

» **Filling knowledge gaps:** "I understand X and Z, but what's Y?"

TIP

You start using prompts in Chapter 3, and I cover creating prompts in depth in Parts 3 and 4.

Recognizing What to Verify

Claude is very capable, but it's not perfect. Understanding when to verify Claude's responses is crucial for using it effectively and responsibly. Verification matters most for high-stakes decisions, specific facts, and time-sensitive topics.

REMEMBER

Verification is not a failure of Claude but rather a smart practice when using any information source.

Always verify the following types of information:

» **Specific facts and figures:** Claude generally provides accurate information, but errors, hallucinations (confident but incorrect statements), and outdated information can occur, especially for highly specific or recent data. Verification is critical for important use across all content.

» **Current events and recent information:** Claude's knowledge has a cutoff of early-to-mid 2025, depending on the model you're using. To find the exact date for your model, ask Claude directly: "What is your knowledge cutoff date?" For anything more recent, use Claude's web search. Note that web search is available on all plans, including Free, so you can use it to supplement Claude's knowledge for time-sensitive topics.

» **Medical, legal, or financial advice:** Claude can provide general information and help you understand concepts, but never rely on it for professional advice in these critical areas. Always consult appropriate professionals.

» **Citations and sources:** If Claude mentions a study, quote, or specific source, verify that it exists and says what Claude claims it does. Claude sometimes gets sources wrong or combines information from multiple sources.

- **Code and technical implementation:** Claude is competent at writing code, but the code may have bugs or security issues. Always test and vet code thoroughly before use.

When verifying information, watch for these red flags:

- **The answer seems too convenient:** If Claude's response aligns perfectly with what you hoped to hear, verify that it's accurate, not just what you want to be true.
- **The information is unusually specific:** Highly detailed statistics or specific technical specifications require verification.
- **The stakes are high:** For important decisions, significant financial implications, or situations where errors could cause problems, always verify.
- **Something feels off:** Trust your instincts. If something in Claude's response doesn't seem quite right, investigate further.
- **You need to cite the information:** If you're writing an academic paper, professional report, or anything that requires citations, verify the information through primary sources.

VERIFY ANYTHING THAT MATTERS TO YOU

To always be confident in the information you use, build these good verification practices:

- Cross-check important facts with authoritative sources.
- Ask Claude to explain its reasoning or provide the basis for claims.
- Use Claude's web search feature for time-sensitive information.
- Consult subject matter experts, if possible, for critical decisions.
- Test code in a safe environment before production use.
- Use a second AI tool (such as Gemini or ChatGPT) to independently check critical claims.

The goal isn't to distrust Claude; it's to use it wisely. Think of verification as part of good information hygiene, whether you're getting information from Claude, search engines, or anywhere else. Claude is a powerful tool that works best when combined with human judgment and appropriate verification.

Understanding When to Use a Different Tool

Claude is versatile, but it's not the only tool for every job. Knowing when to use another tool alongside or instead of Claude saves you time and frustration. Consider using search engines when you need the following:

- **The absolute latest information:** For breaking news, current stock prices, today's weather, or anything happening right now, search engines are faster and more up-to-date. (Pro and Max users can enable Claude's web search for current information.)
- **Multiple perspectives:** If you want to explore various viewpoints on a controversial topic or compare different sources, search engines let you see the range of opinions and sources directly.
- **Specific websites or resources:** Need to find a particular company's contact information or access a specific government form? Search engines excel at finding and accessing specific web resources.

Use specialized software for the following:

- **Doing complex calculations:** For financial modeling, statistical analysis, or scientific calculations, use Excel, specialized calculators, or analytical software. Although Claude can help explain formulas or troubleshoot spreadsheet errors, it's not designed for computation.
- **Creating visual designs:** For graphic design, photo editing, or complex visual projects, use dedicated design software. Claude can create simple diagrams and write HTML/CSS (the code that creates web pages) for web design, but it's not a replacement for image-generation applications such as Midjourney (`https://midjourney.com/`) or DALL·E 3 (`https://openai.com/dall-e-3/`).
- **Managing structured data:** Databases, spreadsheets, and data management tools are better for organizing, querying, and analyzing large datasets. You can integrate Microsoft Excel into Claude to create and revise spreadsheets along with other capabilities. (This function is available only for Pro and Max plans.)
- **Working with real-time collaboration:** For team projects that require simultaneous editing, use collaborative tools such as Google Docs or Microsoft Teams. Claude works with only one person at a time in each conversation.

Consult human experts for the following:

- Medical diagnosis and treatment plans
- Legal advice and contract review
- Licensed professional services (for example, accounting or engineering)
- Critical safety decisions
- Personal counseling

Understanding how to strategically combine tools makes you more effective than relying on any single tool. Here are some combinations to consider:

- **Start with an AI tool like Perplexity (`www.perplexity.ai`) for search, and then analyze with Claude.** When researching a topic, use search engines to gather current sources and specific information. Then paste that information into Claude and ask it to analyze, compare, or synthesize what you found. A search gives you the raw materials. Claude helps you understand what they mean and how to use them. This approach combines the strengths of both: current information from search with analysis and explanation from Claude.
- **Draft with Claude, refine with specialized tools.** Claude excels at quickly turning your ideas into a first draft. Once you have that draft, move it into your word processor for detailed formatting, spell-checking with proper context, and collaboration with colleagues. Use presentation software to design slides after Claude helps you outline your structure and key points. The specialized tools handle the final polish and format, while Claude handles the heavy lifting of getting started and organizing your thinking.
- **Let Claude explain what experts tell you.** After consulting a doctor, lawyer, or financial advisor, you might have questions about what they said or need help understanding the implications. Ask Claude to explain medical terms, break down legal concepts, or help you think through financial decisions. Claude can't replace professional advice, but it's excellent at helping you understand and apply what the experts told you. This approach works particularly well when you need to make informed decisions based on professional guidance.
- **Use Claude to write better search queries.** If you're not finding what you need through a search, ask Claude to help you refine your search strategy. Describe what you're looking for and what you've tried. Claude can suggest alternative keywords, explain search techniques, and help you frame your question more effectively. Then use those improved searches to find what you need. This method creates a feedback loop where each tool makes the other more useful.

» **Don't expect Claude to remember information from one conversation to another.** Each new discussion starts fresh. If you need Claude to remember context across sessions, either keep working in the same conversation or provide the context again. (Pro and Max users should see Chapter 5 for information about Claude's Memory features.)

» **Don't use Claude for formal documentation or official records.** For legal documents, medical records, financial statements, or official correspondence that require compliance with specific regulatory requirements, work with the appropriate professionals and use established systems. Claude can help you understand these documents or draft initial versions but shouldn't create the official versions.

Still unsure which tool to use? Ask yourself whether you need current, real-time information. If yes, start with search engines or specialized real-time tools. Are you making a decision with serious legal, medical, or financial consequences? If yes, consult appropriate professionals. Do you need to understand, create, or think through something? If yes, Claude is likely a good fit.

REMEMBER

Often, you'll answer yes to more than one question. That's when combining tools makes sense. Search for current facts, consult experts for critical decisions, and then use Claude to help you understand and apply what you've learned. The goal isn't to choose one perfect tool. It's about combining the right tools for your situation.

IN THIS CHAPTER

» Setting up your account and understanding your choices

» Choosing the right plan for your needs

» Managing your subscription, security, and account details

» Touring the Claude interface

Chapter 2

Setting Up and Managing Your Account

Most people start using Claude because they need to accomplish a specific task, such as writing an email, analyzing data, or brainstorming ideas. They create an account, type a question, and get a response. But the choices you make when first setting up Claude can determine how smoothly everything works from then on.

This chapter walks you through setting up your account properly from the start. You'll understand which plan fits your needs, how to work across devices, and how to configure your subscription and security settings. Then you can focus on getting things done rather than wrestling with how it all works.

Creating Your Account in Five Minutes

Getting started with Claude is easy. You need only an email address and a web browser. After the signup process guides you through a few simple steps, you'll have immediate access to Claude.

Signing up at claude.ai

Visit `https://claude.ai` in any web browser. You'll see a signup screen with options to Continue with Google or Continue with email, as shown in Figure 2-1.

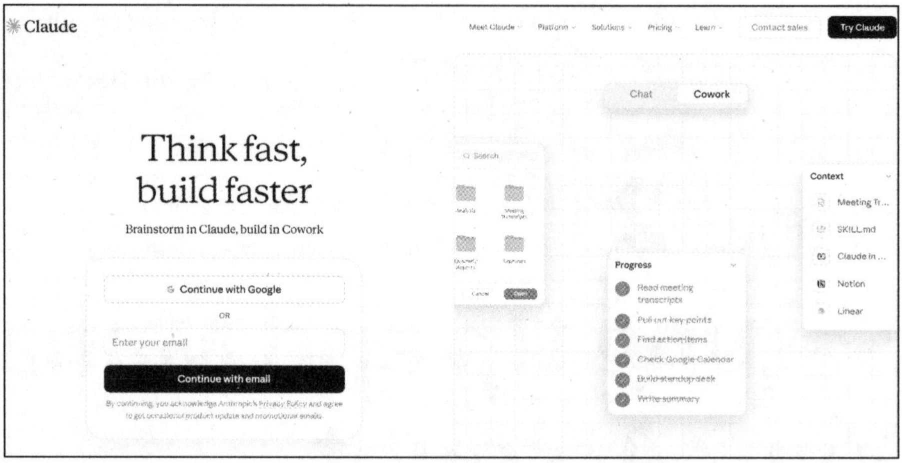

FIGURE 2-1: The claude.ai signup screen.

REMEMBER

On iOS, you can also sign up using Apple's Hide My Email feature, which creates a private relay address.

TIP

If you already use Gmail for work, the Google sign-in option lets you connect your account with a single click. It's the fastest way to get started.

The email option works differently. Claude uses passwordless authentication. You enter your email address and click or tap Continue with Email, and Anthropic sends you a secure login link. Click or tap the link in that email to authenticate. You don't create a password. If you request the link on one device and click or tap it from another, Claude generates a verification code to enter on the original device instead.

Organizations with Team or Enterprise plans use single sign-on (SSO), which lets employees access Claude through their company's existing authentication system. If your organization offers this, you'll receive setup instructions from your IT department. SSO is not available as a general signup option for individual accounts.

Choosing between web, desktop, and mobile

After signing up, you can access Claude in three ways: through your web browser at claude.ai, through desktop apps for Windows and Mac, or through mobile apps for iOS and Android. All three connect to the same account and conversations.

Your Claude account automatically syncs conversations, Projects, Memory, and preferences across all devices. So you can start a discussion on your phone during your commute, continue it on your desktop at work, and finish on the web version from a conference room. Each device shows the same conversation history and, on paid plans, gives you access to the same Projects.

The web version works immediately. Open `https://claude.ai` in any browser, sign in, and start working. No installation required, and updates happen automatically. This option is the best when you're using a shared or borrowed computer. It also serves as a reliable backup if the desktop app encounters issues.

The desktop app adds convenience. Download it from `https://claude.com/download`. The app launches and runs in the background, integrating with your operating system. A keyboard shortcut can bring Claude up instantly while you're working in another application. The desktop app provides the best experience for substantive work. The desktop's large screen lets you view conversations and artifacts side by side, and seamlessly copy and paste between Claude and other applications. Use the desktop app for document creation, complex analysis, and any task that requires seeing both the conversation and the output simultaneously.

The mobile app (iOS, iPadOS, and Android) lets you work anywhere. You can dictate prompts using voice input, snap photos of documents to analyze, and continue conversations you started on your computer. To get the mobile app, open the App Store on iOS or iPadOS, or open Google Play on Android, and search for *Claude by Anthropic.*

The mobile app adds voice input and camera capabilities not found in the desktop app, as shown in Figure 2-2, left. To dictate prompts instead of typing, tap the microphone icon. To add an image to a chat, tap + (plus sign); you see the camera as one of the options, as shown in Figure 2-2, right. Tap the Camera icon to photograph documents, whiteboards, receipts, or handwritten notes for Claude to analyze. These features make your phone a powerful information capture tool, especially useful when you're away from your desk.

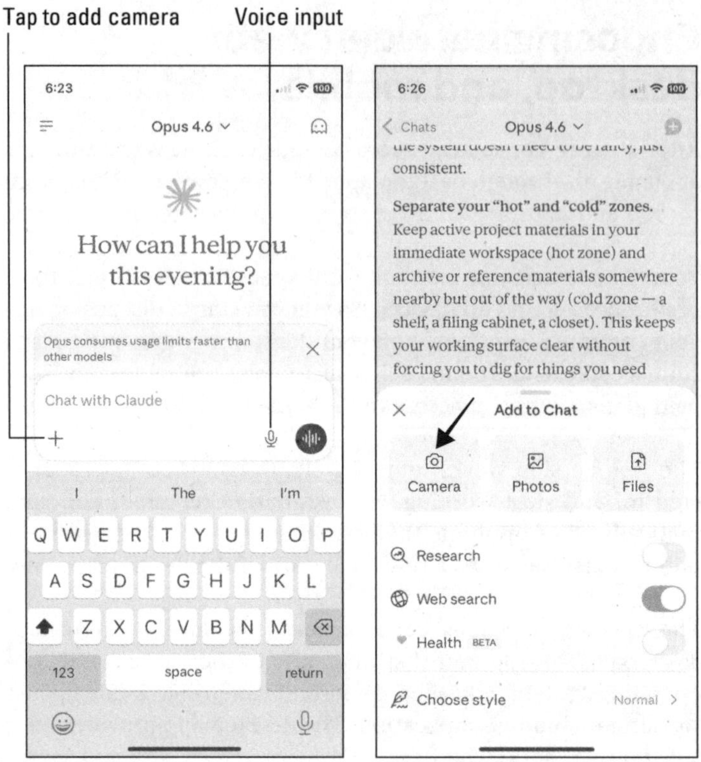

FIGURE 2-2: Camera and voice input options for capturing information on the go (left) and the option to add a camera (right).

REMEMBER

In the mobile app, you will see either the conversation or the *artifact* (a document, chart, or other output Claude creates for you), not both simultaneously. (On the iPad, both may appear simultaneously.) When an artifact is open, the Chat and Artifact tabs appear at the top of the screen; tap them to switch views.

Understanding what happens to your data

When you send a message to Claude, it travels from your device to Anthropic's servers. The servers process your request, send back a response, and store the conversation in your account so you can return to it later. Anthropic protects this data using industry-standard security measures.

WARNING

Anthropic updated its data usage policy in late 2025. When you first sign in, you'll see a pop-up with a Help Improve Claude toggle that defaults to on. To opt out, switch the toggle off before accepting. You can also change this setting later in Settings under Privacy, as shown in Figure 2-3.

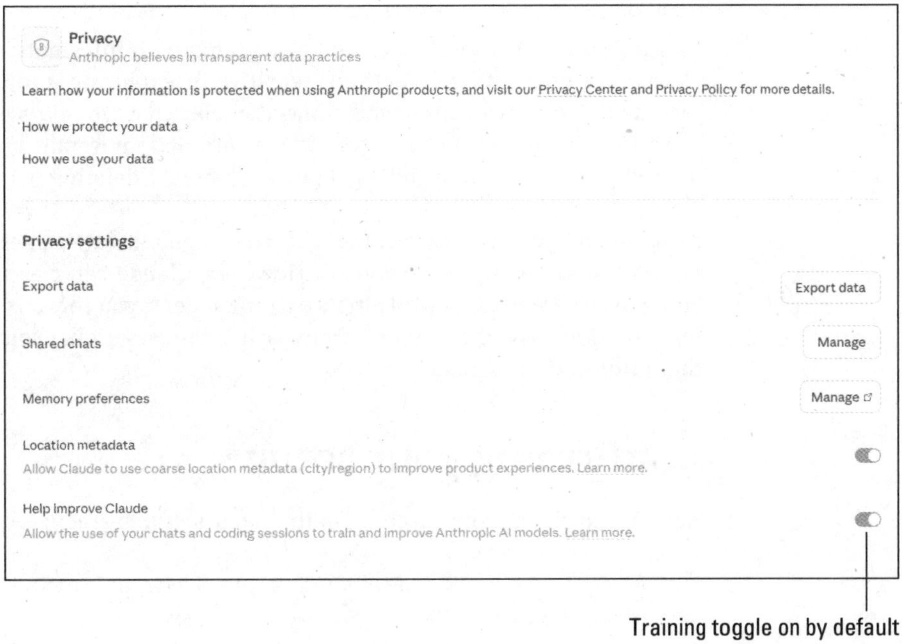

FIGURE 2-3: The data training toggle defaults to on.

Even if you opt out of model improvement, Anthropic may still review conversations flagged for safety or trust purposes. This practice is standard across AI platforms and helps prevent misuse.

You can control your data beyond the training toggle. You can delete individual conversations or your entire account whenever you want. (See "Downloading and deleting your data," later in the chapter.) The Settings menu includes options to export all your data before deletion.

Team and Enterprise plans add additional controls. Administrators can set data retention policies, control which features are available, and review usage patterns without accessing conversation content.

Using incognito conversations for extra privacy

If you want to create a conversation that Claude doesn't save, use incognito mode. Simply click or tap the ghost icon in the upper-right corner of the screen when starting a new chat. (Incognito chats are not available in Projects.) Incognito conversations don't appear in your chat history, aren't searchable after the session ends, aren't used to generate Memories, and aren't used for model improvement even if you've opted in to that setting.

Incognito mode is useful when you're working with information you'd rather not store, such as drafting something sensitive or exploring a topic you don't want recorded. The conversation works like a regular chat while it's open, but once you close it, you can no longer access it. (Anthropic may retain incognito data for a limited period for safety and legal purposes before deleting it.)

TIP

Incognito mode doesn't affect Claude's core capabilities. You get the same models, features, and quality of responses. However, Claude can't access its Memory of your past conversations while in incognito mode. If you rely on Claude remembering your preferences or context from earlier conversations, you'll need to provide that information manually.

Confirming your setup

Here's a quick checklist to confirm that your setup is ready:

1. Account created at claude.ai with your preferred sign-in method (Google, email, or Apple on iOS).
2. Privacy toggle reviewed. Open Settings, go to Privacy, and confirm that the Model Improvement toggle is set to your preference. Remember that the toggle defaults to on.
3. Login security confirmed. Verify that the email or Google account you use to sign in to Claude is secure.
4. Apps installed on the devices where you'll use Claude most. Use the desktop app for substantive work and the mobile app to capture ideas and quick questions.

Choosing a Plan

Claude offers several subscription tiers. Free gets you started with core capabilities. Pro unlocks professional features and higher usage limits. Max provides extensive capacity for power users.

The Team plan is designed for groups of 5 to 150 members. It adds shared Projects that your entire team can access, SSO for company authentication, centralized admin controls, and Connectors for Microsoft 365 and Slack. Standard seats are priced at $25 per person per month (billed annually).

HOW THREE WORKFLOWS COMPARE

Not sure which plan fits? Here are three common user patterns and the plan that suits each one:

- **Occasional brainstormer:** Uses Claude three to four times a week for idea generation and quick questions. Rarely hits usage limits. Doesn't need research mode or extended thinking. Verdict: Free will work fine.
- **Daily drafter:** Uses Claude every workday for writing, editing, and light analysis. Hits usage limits once or twice a week during busy periods. Wants Memory so Claude remembers their style and role. Verdict: Pro may pay for itself in saved time.
- **All-day power user:** Uses Claude constantly for client work, coding, research, and document creation. Hits Pro's limits multiple times per week. Needs maximum throughput. Verdict: Max 5× will eliminate the bottleneck.

The Enterprise plan supports organizations with more than 150 members, adds compliance features such as audit logs, and offers usage-based billing rather than per-seat limits. Enterprise pricing requires working with Anthropic's sales team.

The difference between plans isn't just about how many messages you can send. Each tier unlocks specific capabilities that change what Claude can help you accomplish, as shown in Table 2-1.

TABLE 2-1 Claude Plan Comparison

Feature	Free	Pro	Max	Team and Enterprise
Price per month	Free	$20	$100 (Max 5×) $200 (Max 20×)	Varies by contract
Default model	Sonnet 4.6	All models included; Opus 4.7	All models included; Opus 4.7	All models included; Opus 4.7
Usage capacity	Basic (rolling limits)	5× more than Free	5× or 20× more than Pro	Varies by contract
File uploads and analysis	✓	✓	✓	✓
Web search	✓	✓	✓	✓

(continued)

TABLE 2-1 ***(continued)***

Feature	Free	Pro	Max	Team and Enterprise
Artifacts	✓	✓	✓	✓
Code execution and file creation	✓	✓	✓	✓
Projects	Up to 5	Unlimited (with knowledge base)	Unlimited (with knowledge base)	Unlimited (with knowledge base)
Connectors (Google Workspace and others)	✓	✓	✓	✓
Microsoft 365	✓	✓	✓	✓
Enterprise search	—	—	—	✓
Extended thinking/ adaptive thinking	—	✓	✓	✓
Research mode	—	✓	✓	✓
Memory (cross-conversation)	—	✓	✓	✓
Cowork (desktop agent)	—	✓ (Mac and Windows)	✓ (Mac and Windows)	✓ (Mac and Windows)
Claude in Excel	—	✓	✓	✓
Skills	✓	✓	✓	✓
Claude in PowerPoint	—	—	✓	✓
SSO and admin controls	—	—	—	✓ Enterprise only

REMEMBER

Opus 4.7 features adaptive thinking, which automatically adjusts how deeply the model reasons based on the task's complexity. No manual setup is required.

REMEMBER

Plan names, included features, and prices can change. Use this table as a guide to how the tiers differ and confirm the latest specifics on the Claude pricing page before you decide.

TIP

To switch between models on a paid plan, click or tap the model name at the bottom of the conversation area. Click or tap More Models from the menu that appears, as shown in Figure 2-4, and select a model.

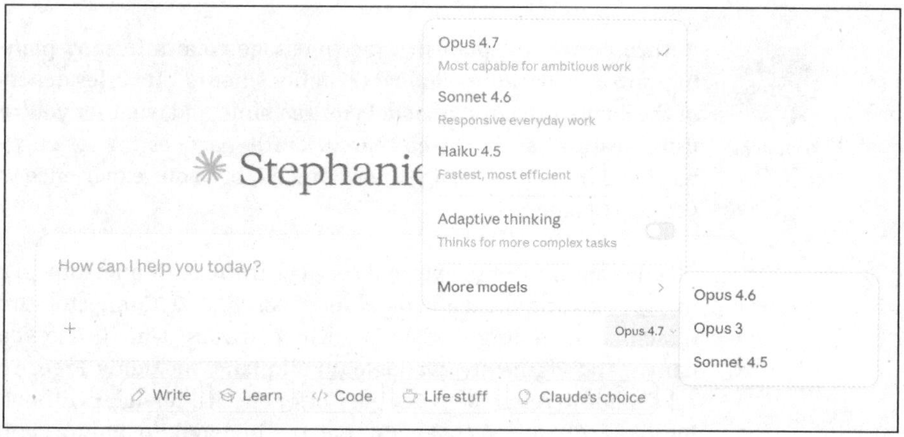

FIGURE 2-4: If you have a Pro or Max plan, click or tap More Models for additional options.

Starting with the Free plan

The Free plan lets you explore Claude without a financial commitment. You can discover whether Claude's approach matches your needs, test it with real work tasks, and determine which features matter most before spending anything. You can also compare it to other AI tools like ChatGPT and Gemini.

For example, a content creator spent two weeks on the Free plan before upgrading. They used it to brainstorm article ideas, refine headlines, and review drafts. Those two weeks showed them that Claude's writing assistance justified a paid subscription.

The Free plan gives you access to Claude Sonnet 4.6, Anthropic's balanced model that handles most tasks well. You can upload files, use web search, and create artifacts such as charts and interactive content.

Free accounts have a usage window. When you hit the cap, Claude displays a message telling you that you've reached your current limit and shows an approximate time when you can send messages again. You aren't locked out of the interface. You can still browse your conversation history, copy previous responses, and access your Projects.

The limit resets on a rolling basis, so spacing your usage throughout the day helps. However, you might hit the usage cap while deep in analysis or run out of messages during a creative surge. These moments clarify whether upgrading makes financial sense for your workflow.

TECHNICAL STUFF

Anthropic doesn't publish exact message counts for any plan. Instead, usage is measured in a rolling window (roughly 5 hours). It varies depending on the length of the conversation, the model you're using, and whether you're uploading files or using features such as web search. Third-party estimates suggest that Free users receive dozens of messages per window, but your experience will depend on how you use Claude.

Claude can connect to external services through Connectors, giving it direct access to your existing tools and data. As of early 2026, Connectors from the Connectors directory, including Google Workspace (Docs, Gmail, Calendar), Slack, Notion, Canva, and Figma are available on all plans, including Free. That means you can ask Claude to reference a Google Doc or check a calendar without manually uploading files. (Chapter 6 covers Connectors in detail, including setup steps, supported integrations, and practical workflows.)

The Free plan works well for occasional users. If you need Claude a few times per week for discrete tasks, Free access may suffice indefinitely. Think of it as both a permanent option for light users and a trial period for everyone else.

TIP

Track your usage patterns for a week or two before deciding to upgrade. Note how often you hit limits, which features you wish you had, and whether the restrictions disrupt your work or require minor adjustments to your schedule.

Upgrading to Pro for everyday power users

The Pro plan makes sense when Claude becomes part of your regular workflow: you use it multiple times daily, want access to Claude's most capable models, or need certain features. Most Pro users report saving several hours monthly through faster research, automated document creation, and reduced back-and-forth on complex tasks.

For some users, the research feature alone justifies purchasing Pro. Research mode sends multiple Claude agents to investigate topics in parallel, delivering comprehensive reports with citations. You can create unlimited Projects with full knowledge base capabilities, meaning Claude can search through your uploaded reference documents using advanced retrieval. Memory and extended thinking become available, allowing Claude to recall information about you across conversations and reason more deeply through complex problems before responding, respectively.

The Pro plan costs $20 per month (or $17 per month if you pay annually) and significantly expands your capabilities. The Pro plan gives you access to all current Claude models beyond including Haiku 4.5, Sonnet 4.6, and Opus 4.7. Opus handles the most complex reasoning but uses more of your usage allocation per message. Using Opus in Claude Code requires enabling extra usage at additional cost. Haiku responds fastest and uses the least. Sonnet balances capability and efficiency for most everyday tasks.

Pro also unlocks the capability to create custom Connectors using Model Context Protocol (MCP), which lets you connect Claude to your own tools and internal data sources beyond the prebuilt options in the Connectors directory.

The Cowork desktop agent (currently in research preview, available on macOS and Windows) allows Claude to work with files on your local computer. And Claude in Excel lets you work with spreadsheets directly.

Choosing Max for professional and advanced work

Max serves users who integrate Claude deeply into their professional workflows — writers, analysts, developers, and researchers running extremely intensive workflows, such as day-long coding sessions, extensive research, or managing multiple, simultaneous client Projects.

It comes in two tiers: Max 5× ($100/month) gives you five times the message capacity of Pro, and Max 20× ($200/month) gives you twenty times. Both include everything in Pro with substantially higher usage capacity.

REMEMBER

Memory, which lets Claude remember your preferences, role, and context across every conversation, is available starting with the Pro plan. You don't need Max for this feature.

The primary distinction between Max and Pro is how many messages you can send before hitting a usage limit. If you consistently run up against Pro's limits mid-project, Max gives you the breathing room to work through the day without interruption. For example, a freelance consultant chose Max 5× after repeatedly exhausting Pro's limits during client engagements. The consultant worked with four clients a week, each requiring extensive back-and-forth with Claude for analysis, document creation, and strategy development. Max let them work continuously without tracking message counts.

Max also unlocks Claude in PowerPoint, a feature available on Max, Team, and Enterprise plans but not on Pro. If creating and editing presentation files directly in Claude is important to your work, this may be another reason to consider Max.

Like Pro, Max supports custom MCP Connectors, which are useful for power users running complex workflows that pull from multiple data sources simultaneously.

TIP

Before upgrading from Pro ($20/month) to Max ($100 or $200/month), track your Pro usage for two weeks. Note when you hit limits and how frequently you need to wait. If you're consistently maxing out Pro's capacity, Max becomes worthwhile. If you occasionally hit limits but can work around them, stick with Pro.

Situation: A freelance graphic designer used Claude a few times a week for copywriting and concept brainstorming. Although they have never hit the Free plan's limits, they wonder whether Pro's features would help.

What they tried: They tracked their usage for two weeks. They averaged eight messages per day, never hit limits, and didn't need research mode because their work relies on creative generation rather than deep investigation. They didn't need extended thinking because their requests are creative rather than analytically complex.

Result: The Free plan covered their needs. They saved $20 per month by not upgrading prematurely. They bookmarked the upgrade path and planned to revisit their decision when client volume increased.

Why this matters: Not everyone needs a paid plan. Tracking your usage before upgrading prevents paying for capabilities you don't use. Track your Claude usage for one to two weeks before choosing a plan. Note how often you hit limits, which features you wish you had, and whether restrictions disrupt your productivity.

Comparing capabilities and knowing when to upgrade

Upgrade signals will appear through your daily experience. Perhaps you're hitting usage limits more than once a week. Or you need a feature that's unavailable on your current plan. Or you're spending time working around restrictions rather than focusing on the task at hand.

Consider downgrading just as actively as upgrading. If you subscribed to Pro but rarely use it, drop to Free to save money. If Max's capacity exceeds your needs, Pro might suffice. A researcher downgraded from Max to Pro when their intensive Project ended, keeping Pro's features while reducing costs by $80 a month.

Your decision about which plan to use comes down to three factors: how often you use Claude, which features your work requires, and whether usage limits disrupt your productivity. Free works for light, occasional use. Pro serves regular users who need professional capabilities and Memory. Max fits intensive professional workflows where Claude functions as a core, all-day tool.

Managing Your Plan and Account

You can manage your account in Settings. It houses your subscription tier, billing and payment information, security settings, and your personal data.

Do the following:

1. **If you're using the web or desktop app and the sidebar is hidden, display it by clicking or tapping the sidebar icon (shown in the margin).**

   The sidebar icon appears in the upper-left corner of the screen.

2. **Click or tap your profile icon (initials).**

   Your profile icon is in the lower-left corner in the web and desktop apps and the upper-left corner in the mobile app.

3. **Select Settings in the menu that appears, as shown in Figure 2-5.**

   This central location handles subscriptions, security, data controls, and account details.

Upgrading or downgrading your subscription

You may want to upgrade or downgrade your subscription after using Claude for a while. Note that nothing is deleted if you downgrade: your conversations, uploaded files, and Project contents all remain intact and accessible. What changes is which features you can use going forward.

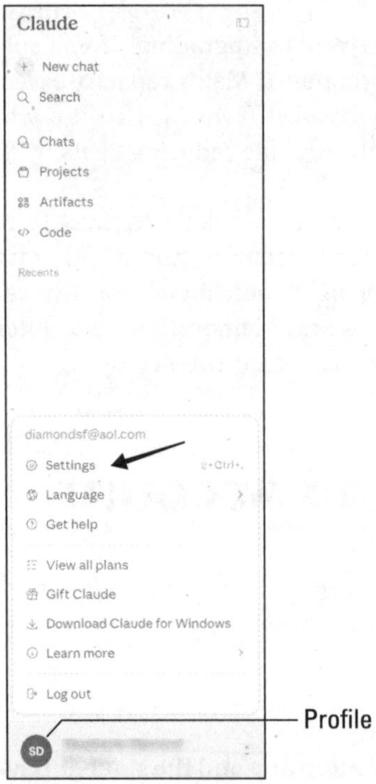

FIGURE 2-5: Click or tap your initials to access Settings.

If you drop from Pro to Free, you retain access to up to five Projects, but any beyond that limit become inaccessible until you resubscribe. You won't be able to choose which ones, so consider archiving or deleting Projects you no longer need before downgrading. The data inside all Projects is preserved regardless. Memory stops generating new entries, though your existing Memories remain visible in Settings.

You also lose access to research mode, extended thinking, and the ability to choose between models such as Opus 4.7, Haiku 4.5, or the previous Sonnet 4.5. The Free plan uses Sonnet 4.6 as its default model. Any files Claude created for you (spreadsheets, documents, presentations) are still in your conversation history and can still be downloaded.

To upgrade or downgrade, follow these steps:

1. **In Settings, click or tap Billing.**

   Your current plan appears at the top.

2. **Click or tap the Adjust Plan button, as shown in Figure 2-6.**

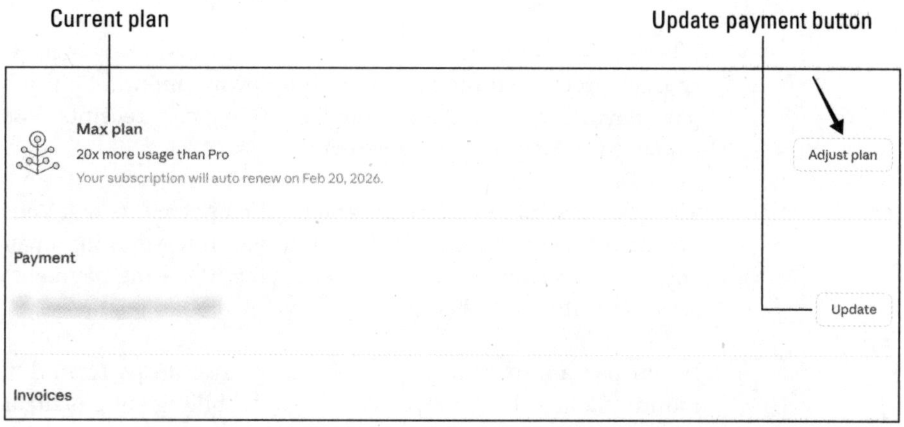

FIGURE 2-6: Make changes to your current plan.

3. **Select your desired tier and confirm your payment details.**

   If you upgrade, the change takes effect immediately, and you gain access to new features and higher limits right away.

   If you downgrade, the change takes effect at the end of your current billing period. You keep your current plan's benefits until then.

When upgrading before the end of a billing period, you pay a prorated amount for the remaining days. If you upgrade to Pro on the 15th of the month, you pay approximately half the monthly rate to cover the rest of that billing cycle. Your next full billing cycle charges the standard amount.

You can cancel a subscription by using the same menu. You revert to the Free plan at your next billing date. Your data and conversation history remain accessible, but paid features become unavailable.

Adjusting billing and payment methods

Claude accepts credit cards and debit cards for payment. The Billing section in Settings shows your current payment method and billing history.

PayPal and other payment services may be available through specific integrations or regional offerings, so check the current pricing page for supported options. If you see conflicting information elsewhere, rely on the latest details in the Billing section and on the Claude pricing page.

To update payment information, open the Billing section, click or tap the Update button next to Payment (refer to Figure 2-6), and enter the new card's details. Changes apply to future billing cycles.

Billing recurs monthly on your signup anniversary. Subscribe on March 10, and charges process on the 10th of each following month. Your billing history shows past payments, dates, and amounts. Download receipts from this section for expense tracking or reimbursement.

The system sends email notifications when payments fail. You get several days to update payment information before service interruption. If payment fails repeatedly, your account reverts to the Free plan. Updating payment details and resubscribing restores paid access.

TIP

If you pay annually instead of monthly, Pro drops from $20 to about $17 per month ($204 billed once per year). Annual billing isn't available for all plan tiers, so check the pricing page at `https://claude.com/pricing` for current options.

Keeping your account secure

Claude uses passwordless authentication, so traditional two-factor authentication (2FA) with authenticator apps or SMS codes is not available for individual accounts. Instead, your account security depends on the security of your email account or Google account.

WARNING

Since Claude relies on your email or Google account for authentication, losing access to that account means losing access to Claude. Make sure you have configured recovery options for your email account, such as a backup email address or phone number. If you use a Google account for authentication, save your Google account recovery codes in a secure location, such as a password manager.

Downloading and deleting your data

Your conversations belong to you. You can export all your data or permanently delete your account and associated information.

To download your data, navigate to Settings, select Privacy, and then click or tap Export Data. The export function creates a ZIP file containing JSON files with all your conversations, Projects, and settings. The process takes a few minutes for accounts with an extensive history. When ready, Claude sends a download link to your email that remains valid for 24 hours. Deleted conversations are not included in exports.

To delete your account, go to Settings and then the Account section. Click or tap Delete Account and follow the prompts. Claude removes access to your conversations, Projects, settings, and account details. This action is permanent; you can't recover deleted data. Before deletion, always export your data if you want a record of your work.

WARNING

Account deletion does not automatically cancel active subscriptions. You must manually cancel your subscription in the Billing section first, wait for your current billing period to end, and then proceed with account deletion. Skipping this step could result in continued charges even after your account is deleted.

TIP

Deleting your account removes your conversations and profile, but two things remain outside your control. First, Anthropic may retain some data as required by law or for policy enforcement. Second, if Anthropic previously incorporated any of your data into trained models, that data can't be removed after the fact. If you don't want your data used for model training, turn off the Help Improve Claude in the Privacy settings before that data is processed. Opting out later won't undo earlier use.

Touring the Interface

Claude's interface prioritizes simplicity. The main elements remain consistent across the web, desktop, and mobile versions. In this section, you see how to navigate the interface efficiently and find the features you need.

Finding your way around the main screen

The main Claude screen is divided into three areas: the sidebar on the left, the conversation area in the center, and account controls in the corners, as shown in Figure 2-7.

The sidebar lists your recent conversations and Projects. The conversation area is where you type prompts and read Claude's responses. Each response includes options to copy text, provide feedback, or retry the answer.

TIP

Your profile icon (name or initials) appears in the lower-left corner in the web and desktop apps and in the upper-right corner in the mobile app. Click or tap your profile icon to access Settings, which controls your subscription, security, preferences, and data.

Locating the controls you'll use most

The message input box sits at the bottom center of the conversation area. Click or tap inside and start typing. Press Enter or Shift+Return to send your message. or press Shift+Enter to add a new line without sending. On a touchscreen keyboard, tap the Enter key to send the message.

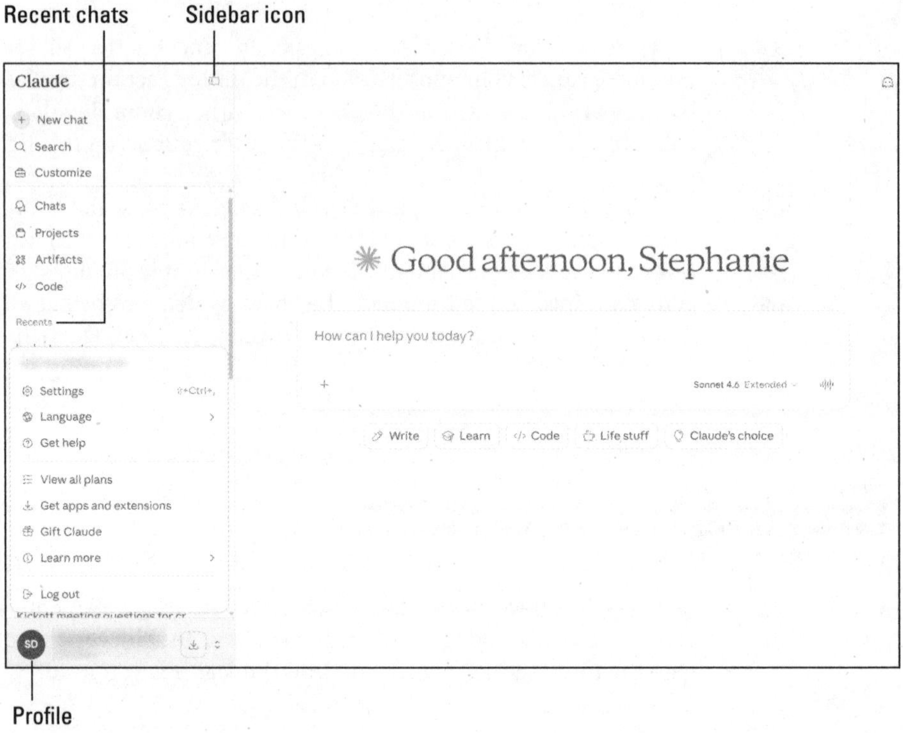

FIGURE 2-7: The main Claude interface showing the sidebar, conversation area, and account controls.

To the left of the input box is a + (plus sign). Click or tap it to see attachment options for uploading files. Depending on your plan, you can upload PDFs, Word documents, spreadsheets, images, and other file types. The system confirms when files are ready for Claude to analyze.

Below Claude's response are a row of icons, as shown in Figure 2-8:

- **Copy:** Grab the response text to paste elsewhere.
- **Thumbs up and thumbs down:** Send feedback on the response's quality.
- **Retry:** Ask Claude to generate a new response. (Retry is called regenerate in some AI tools.)

TIP

Copying a response is one of the most commonly used features. Claude drafts content, and you copy the text into your writing software, email client, or messaging app.

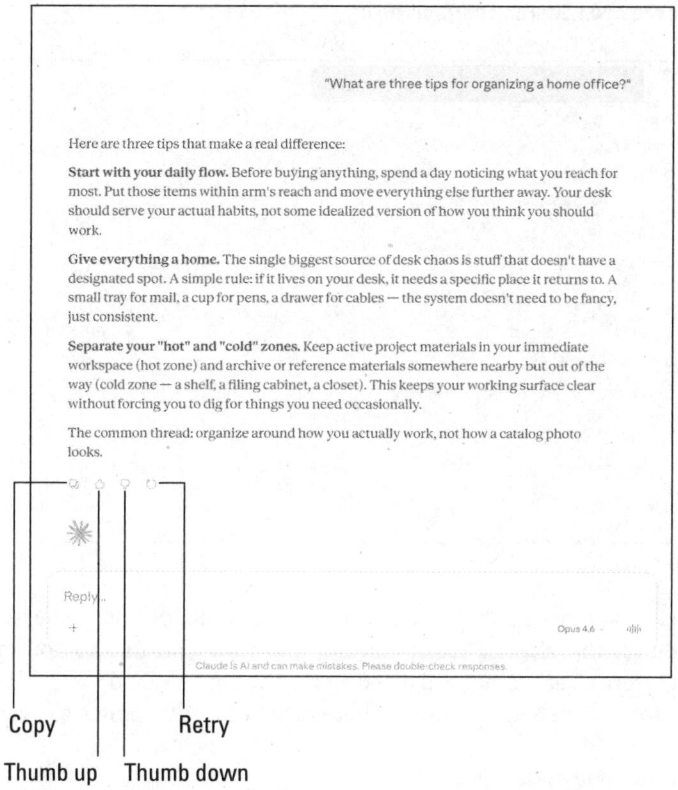

FIGURE 2-8: Icons below Claude's response.

Customizing Claude with Styles and Preferences

The Styles and Preferences settings let you adjust how Claude communicates with you across all conversations, not just the current one.

Styles control Claude's writing voice. Five presets give you quick starting points: Normal (Claude's default), Learning (part of Claude for Education), Concise (shorter, more direct), Formal (clear polished responses), and Explanatory (thorough, educational responses). If none of those quite fit, you can describe the style you want or upload samples of your own writing. Claude will analyze them and generate a matching style.

To access styles, click or tap + in the lower-left corner of the chat interface and select Use Style, as shown in Figure 2-9.

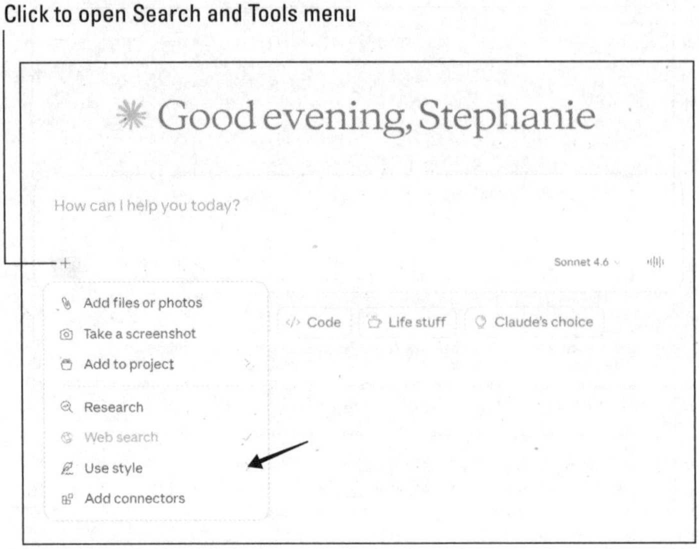

FIGURE 2-9: This menu gives you access to styles and other features.

The Preferences settings are where you tell Claude about yourself. Add your background, the kind of work you do, and how you like to communicate. Think of preferences as a standard briefing that you give Claude once, so you never have to repeat it. Whatever you share here automatically applies to every conversation.

To set your preferences:

1. **If the sidebar is hidden, display it by clicking or tapping the sidebar icon in the upper-left corner of the screen (and shown in the margin).**
2. **Click or tap your profile icon (your initials) and select Settings.**

   Your profile icon is in the lower-left corner in the web and desktop apps and in the upper-right corner in the mobile app.
3. **Select General.**
4. **In the text box under What Preferences Should Claude Consider in Responses? (see Figure 2-10), type whatever context you'd like Claude to keep in mind.**

You can update your preferences anytime.

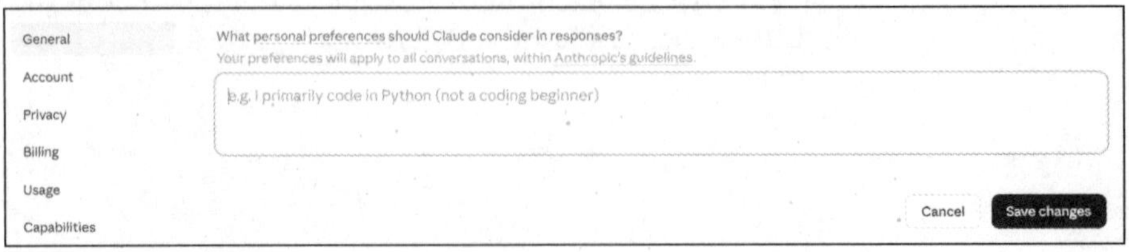

FIGURE 2-10: Tell Claude your preferences here.

Together, styles and preferences do different jobs. Preferences give Claude context about who you are and what you need; styles tell it how to format and deliver what it says. You can use one, both, or neither. Following are some examples.

For styles:

- A marketing professional set their style to Concise and added a preference, noting that they work in B2B SaaS. Now every conversation starts with Claude calibrated to deliver brief, industry-aware responses.
- A technical writer working on software documentation switched to the Formal style. Claude stopped using casual phrases and structured every response with clear terminology.
- A graduate student studying for exams chose the Explanatory style and found that Claude automatically added relevant examples and background context without being asked.

For references:

- A freelance translator added a preference noting: "I specialize in legal documents and work between Spanish and English. Always use precise legal terminology and flag any terms that may not translate directly." Now every conversation starts with that context already loaded so they never have to explain their work to Claude again.
- A home baker turned food blogger added a preference noting: "I write recipe posts for beginner bakers. Always explain techniques in plain terms and assume readers don't own specialty equipment." Now when the baker asks Claude to help write up a new recipe, it automatically skips references to stand mixers and pastry weights and explains folding or crimping as if for the first time.

IN THIS CHAPTER

» Starting with clear, specific requests

» Getting started with voice input

» Customizing Claude to work your way

Chapter 3
Having a Successful First Conversation

The first time you type something to Claude, you may feel uncertain. You might wonder what to ask, how to phrase it, or whether you're doing it right. The good news is that Claude responds to natural language.

This chapter walks you through your first successful conversations with Claude, showing you the essential features you'll use every day and helping you customize the experience to match how you work.

Starting with a Clear Request

The way you begin a conversation shapes everything that follows. A clear, specific request gives Claude the information it needs to provide useful responses. A vague request forces Claude to guess what you mean, often requiring that you spend more time clarifying your request than getting work done.

Understanding what makes a request clear

Clear requests share three qualities: they specify what you want, they provide relevant context, and they indicate what success looks like. You don't need all three for every request, but the more clarity you provide, the better Claude's first response will be.

Here's an example in practice:

> **Situation:** A marketing consultant wanted help preparing for a difficult client conversation.
>
> **First prompt:** "Help me with a client meeting."
>
> **Claude's first response:** It offered generic advice on meeting preparation, which was useful but not specific to the situation.
>
> **Second prompt:** "I need to explain a four-week project delay to a frustrated client. The delay happened because our vendor, not our team, missed deadlines. Help me frame this conversation to maintain trust while being honest about what happened."
>
> **Claude's second response:** It addressed the specific situation. It suggested acknowledging the client's frustration, explaining the vendor issue without making excuses, outlining concrete steps to prevent future delays, and offering options to accelerate remaining work.
>
> **Result:** In minutes, the consultant had a clear framework for the conversation.
>
> **Why this worked:** The difference between the two prompts was their specificity. The second request told Claude the situation (project delay), the cause (vendor issues), the challenge (maintaining trust), and what success looked like (honest framing that preserves the relationship). When you provide this context, Claude can tailor responses to your needs rather than offering general advice.

Think about what Claude needs to know to help you effectively. When:

- **Asking for writing help:** Who is the audience, and what is the purpose?
- **Solving a problem:** What have you already tried?
- **Making a decision:** Which factors matter most?

REMEMBER

You don't need to write a novel-length prompt. A few specific details can make the difference between generic advice and genuinely useful guidance.

Reading and using Claude's response

Claude's responses appear gradually as they're generated, streaming in from left to right. You'll see text appear in real time, so you can start reading before the full response appears. Short responses appear quickly. For longer, more detailed responses, you might read the first paragraph while Claude is still writing the third.

Once Claude finishes responding, you have several options. You can:

- Read and implement Claude's suggestions without any further interaction.
- Ask a follow-up question to refine or expand on what Claude provided.
- Tell Claude what worked and what didn't, guiding the next response.
- Start a new conversation if you want to tackle a different topic.

REMEMBER

Resist the urge to tack on a new topic to an existing conversation. When you do, Claude keeps the earlier context in its response whether you want it to or not. Always keep separate topics in separate conversations. (See "Managing your conversation history," later in this chapter, for tips on staying organized.)

For example, a project manager asked Claude to help draft a status update email. Claude provided a draft, but it felt too formal for the team culture. Instead of starting over, the project manager said, "Make this more casual because we're a relaxed team and this sounds like corporate-speak." Claude revised the email to match the team's tone. The project manager made one small edit and sent it.

REMEMBER

This back-and-forth feels natural because that's how conversations work. You don't need to get everything perfect in your first message. You can adjust and refine as you go. Claude uses the context of your conversation, so each exchange builds on what came before.

Asking follow-up questions that improve results

Follow-up questions let you refine responses without starting from scratch. Claude uses the context from earlier messages in the same conversation to inform its responses, which means you can build on previous responses, ask for variations, or zero in on specific parts that need more development.

The most effective follow-ups either clarify what wasn't quite right or expand on something useful, such as the following:

- **"Can you explain the second point in more detail?"** focuses Claude on the most relevant part.
- **"Can you make this shorter and more action-oriented?"** keeps the good elements while adjusting the style.
- **"What if we approached this from a different angle?"** suggests that Claude reconsider the problem.

For example, an event planner used Claude to brainstorm venue ideas for a corporate retreat. Claude's first response included hotels, conference centers, and outdoor spaces. The planner said, "Focus on outdoor options within two hours of Boston that can accommodate 75 people." Claude narrowed the suggestions to specific parks, retreat centers, and estates in the area, with details about capacity, amenities, and typical costs. Another follow-up could be: "Which of these works for October weather?" This prompt would further refine the list.

TIP

Each question was built on the previous response, creating increasingly useful information. This iterative approach often works better than trying to pack every detail into your first request. You can start with a broad prompt and then narrow down, or start with a specific prompt and then expand. The conversation flows in whatever direction serves your needs.

When responses aren't quite right, be direct about what's missing. Here are some prompts you can try:

- **"Explain it like I'm new to the topic"** tells Claude to adjust the expertise level.
- **"Focus more on quality than cost"** redirects the priorities.
- **"Give me three options instead of one approach"** changes the format.

Claude responds well to clear feedback because it clarifies what you need.

Trying Essential Features Right Away

Claude's interface includes several features that make conversations more efficient. You don't need to memorize shortcuts or commands because these features appear as simple buttons and options.

Regenerating responses when needed

Sometimes Claude's first response doesn't quite hit the mark. Maybe it misunderstood your request, took an approach you didn't want, or wasn't what you needed. The regenerate feature gives you a fresh response to the same request without editing your original message. (See Chapters 2 and 8 for a detailed explanation of the regenerate feature.)

You'll find the regenerate icon near Claude's response, as shown in Figure 3-1. When you click or tap it, Claude generates a new response to your same request. This response might take a different approach, emphasize other aspects, or interpret your request differently. You're not revising anything; you're simply asking Claude to try again.

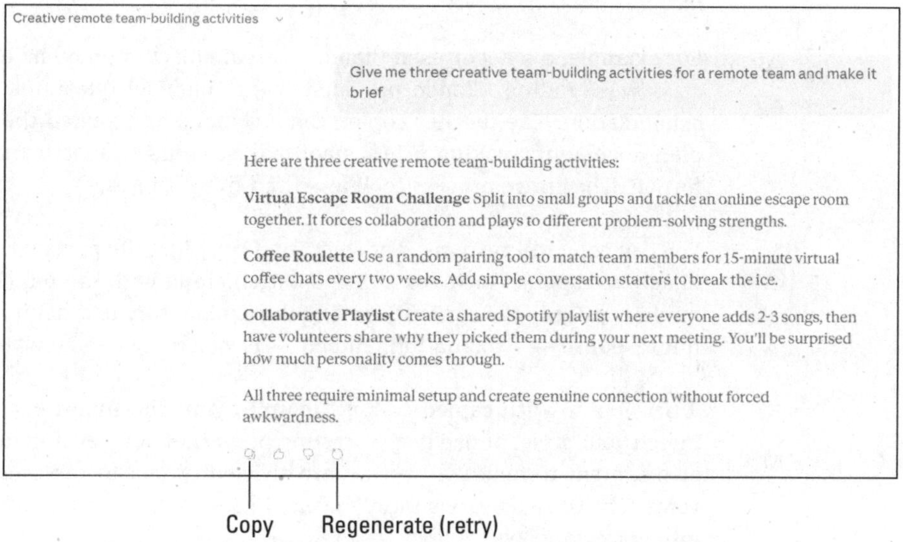

FIGURE 3-1: The regenerate function.

Here's an example. A consultant asked Claude for icebreaker questions for a workshop. Claude's first response included questions that felt too formal for the casual atmosphere. Instead of trying to explain what was wrong, the consultant clicked the regenerate icon. The questions in the second response had a different tone and were more conversational and approachable, and one those questions was perfect for the workshop.

TIP

Regenerate works well when you know Claude can help, but the first attempt missed. You might regenerate to see different options, to get a fresh perspective on a problem, or simply because the first response didn't resonate. There's no penalty for regenerating; it's a quick way to explore different possibilities without crafting a new request.

Sometimes you'll regenerate several times as Claude approaches your request from multiple angles. Other times, the first response works perfectly, and you never need the feature. Either way is fine. Regenerate is an option when you need it; not something you must use.

Copying and sharing what Claude creates

When Claude creates something useful, you can use it elsewhere: in an email, a document, a presentation, or anywhere else you work. The copy feature makes using material straightforward.

Near Claude's response, you'll see an option to copy the text (refer to Figure 3-1). Click or tap it, and the response is copied to your clipboard. You can then paste it into any application, just like text you've copied from anywhere else.

For example, a teacher used Claude to create discussion questions for a novel the class was reading. Claude provided five thoughtful questions that would spark conversation. The teacher copied the questions and pasted them into the lesson plan document, making a few small adjustments to match the class discussion format. The entire process took less than five minutes.

REMEMBER

You can copy full responses or select and copy just the parts you need. Sometimes Claude's response includes an explanation along with the requested content. You might copy only the content, leaving the explanatory text behind. Other times, the full response — explanation, and all — is exactly what you want.

What you do with copied content is up to you. You might use it as-is, edit it to match your style, or use it as a starting point that you develop further. Claude creates content to help you work more efficiently, not to replace your judgment or voice. The copy feature simply makes it easy to move useful content from Claude into your workflow.

Managing your conversation history

Every conversation you have with Claude is saved automatically. You'll find your conversation history in a list on the right when you click or tap Chats, as shown in Figure 3-2. Each conversation shows a brief preview of what you discussed, making it easy to find and return to previous work.

REMEMBER

When you start a new conversation, Claude begins fresh with no memory of previous discussions. This clean slate helps when you're tackling different topics. If you want Claude to remember the earlier context, continue the existing conversation rather than starting a new one.

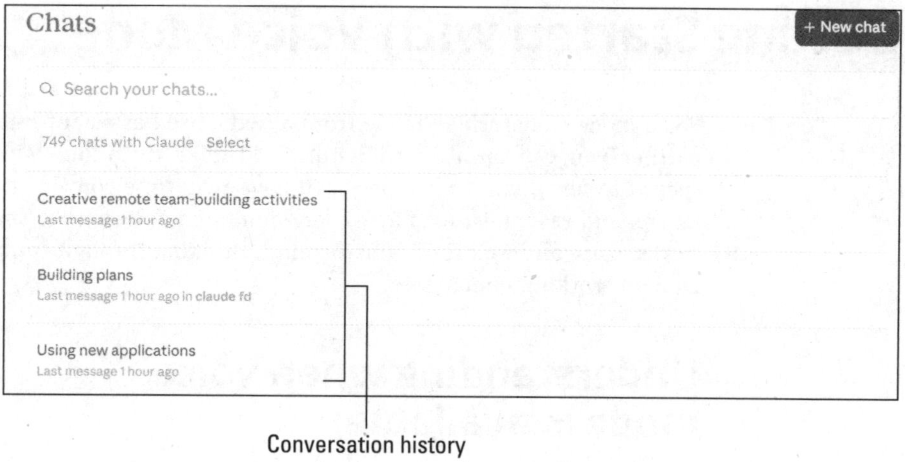

FIGURE 3-2: Your conversation history.

For example, a freelance writer kept separate conversations for different clients. One conversation contained all the work for a technology blog, another for a healthcare newsletter, and another for marketing materials. This organization made it easy to return to the right context when working on each project. Within that conversation, Claude can take earlier messages into account, including previously stated preferences, requirements, and examples.

TIP

You can rename conversations to make them easier to identify later. Instead of letting Claude's automatic preview determine how a conversation appears in your history, you can give it a specific name that makes sense to you. You can also delete conversations you no longer need, keeping your history focused on current work.

The key to managing conversation history is recognizing when to continue a conversation versus when to start afresh. Continue conversations when:

- Claude needs to remember what you've discussed
- Claude should understand the ongoing project
- You need consistency with previous work

Start new discussions when:

- You're shifting to completely different topics
- Previous context would be irrelevant or potentially confusing

Getting Started with Voice Mode

Voice mode transforms Claude from a text-based assistant into a conversational partner you can speak with naturally. Unlike dictation (which converts your speech to text), voice mode lets you have real-time conversations where Claude listens and responds, displaying key points on screen as it speaks. This feature works especially well for brainstorming, thinking through complex problems out loud, or working hands-free.

Understanding when voice mode is available

At the time of this writing, voice mode is available in Claude's iOS and Android apps, so you'll find it in the Claude app on your phone or tablet. Voice mode isn't available on the desktop (Mac or Windows) or web version. This mobile-only approach makes sense for a feature designed for on-the-go conversations.

The Claude mobile app is available for download in the Apple App Store at `www.apple.com/us/search/claude?src=globalnav`. The Android version of the Claude app is available for download on Google Play at `https://play.google.com/store/search?q=claude+for+android&c=apps&hl=en_US`. Alternatively, you can open the App Store app on your iPhone or iPad or the Google Play Store app on your Android device, and search for *Claude by Anthropic*.

It's worth clarifying what voice mode is and isn't, since Claude has multiple voice-related features. The mobile app also has a dictation feature (the microphone icon), which converts your speech to text. That feature is useful, but it's not voice mode; dictation is a one-way transcription. Voice mode is a two-way conversation where Claude responds with audio, not just text. To enable voice mode, tap the sound wave icon in the chat interface, as shown in Figure 3-3.

The microphone icon activates dictation, which converts your speech to text that appears in the chat box. The sound wave icon activates voice mode, which starts a real-time conversation where Claude speaks back to you.

For this section, we're focusing on voice mode. It's the conversational feature that makes Claude feel more like talking to a colleague than typing to an assistant.

REMEMBER

Voice mode works with all Claude subscription tiers, though usage limits and features may vary by plan. Also, at the time of this writing, voice mode currently supports only English, although additional languages are expected as the feature develops.

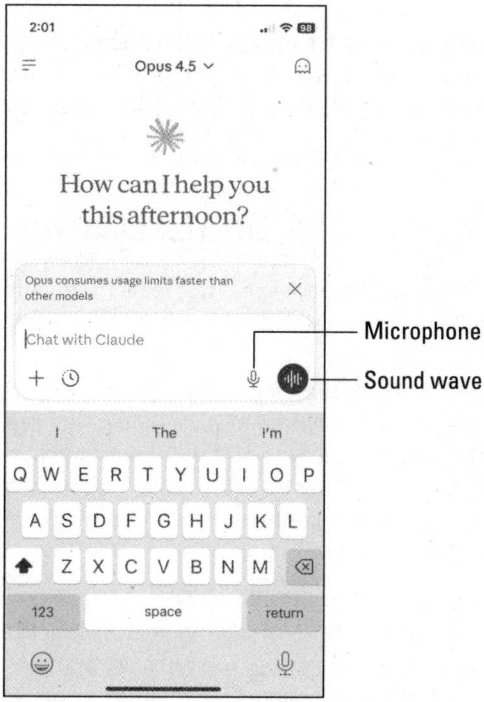

FIGURE 3-3: Tap the sound wave icon to activate voice mode versus the microphone icon for dictation.

Once voice mode is active, you simply start talking. Claude listens to what you say and begins responding out loud when you pause. As Claude speaks, key points appear on the screen so you can follow along visually while hearing the response. This dual presentation — audio plus text highlights — helps you absorb information better than either mode alone.

For example, a product manager discovered voice mode while preparing for a difficult client meeting. Instead of typing notes, they opened Claude's app during their commute and said, "I need to explain why we're delaying the product launch by six weeks. The client is frustrated. Help me think through how to frame this conversation." Claude responded verbally, talking through positioning strategies while displaying the main points on screen. The manager could listen while watching the road, glancing at the phone when the car was stopped to see the key points Claude was highlighting.

The conversation flowed naturally. The product manager interrupted Claude mid-response to add context: "The delay is because of vendor issues, not our team." Claude acknowledged this and adjusted its suggestions in real-time. By the time the manager reached their destination, they had a complete communication strategy developed through conversation rather than typing.

This approach worked because voice mode can handle interruptions in a way that feels similar to human conversations. You often don't need to wait for a response before adding context or clarification. The interaction feels conversational rather than transactional.

Knowing when voice beats typing

Voice mode excels in situations where speaking feels more natural than typing or where your hands and eyes are occupied with other tasks. For example:

- **When you're physically moving:** Walking, commuting, or pacing while thinking all become productive time with voice mode. Your brain often works differently when your body is in motion. Many people find that walking helps them think through problems, but they lose those insights when they stop to type, which disrupts the flow. Voice mode captures thoughts as they form without breaking your stride.
- **When you're doing exploratory thinking:** When you're not sure exactly what you want to ask or how to frame a problem, speaking lets you work through ideas more fluidly than typing. You can start with a vague question, hear Claude's response, and pivot based on what resonates. The conversational back-and-forth helps you discover what you're really trying to figure out.
- **When working through complex scenarios:** Explaining nuanced situations with multiple factors often flows more naturally through speech. You can describe context, add qualifiers, and adjust your explanation mid-sentence in ways that would feel awkward when typing. Voice mode lets you talk through complexity without worrying about sentence structure or organization — Claude follows your train of thought.
- **When accessibility matters:** Voice mode provides genuine hands-free access for people with injuries, mobility limitations, or conditions that make typing difficult or painful. Unlike dictation, which still requires you to read and send text, voice mode creates a complete conversational loop without needing to interact with the screen beyond initial activation.

A consultant used voice mode exclusively for two weeks due to a wrist injury. They initially worried that this would limit productivity but discovered the opposite. They could brainstorm strategy documents, work through client analysis, and develop presentation outlines entirely through conversation. The lack of typing removed the habit of editing while drafting, which helped their initial thinking flow more freely. Claude's verbal responses felt like having a thinking partner rather than using a tool.

TIP

Voice mode isn't a replacement for all interactions with Claude. When you need precise formatting, want to craft specific wording, or are working with code or technical syntax, typing gives you more control. Many people develop a natural rhythm, using voice for exploration and brainstorming, and text for refinement and precision work.

Quick tips for voice accuracy and editing

Voice mode handles natural conversation remarkably well, but a few practical considerations improve the experience and reduce frustration:

- **Choose quiet environments when possible.** Background noise can interfere with voice recognition or cause Claude to miss parts of what you say. While voice mode works in various settings, you'll get the best results in quieter spaces. If you're in a noisier environment, speak slightly more deliberately without becoming unnatural or robotic. You can also use a head or throat mic to reduce background noise.
- **Speak naturally at your normal pace.** Voice mode is designed for conversational speech, not dictation. You don't need to speak slowly, overenunciate, or pause artificially between words. Talk the way you would to a colleague sitting across from you. Claude handles natural pauses, filler words (like *um* or *you know*), and the slight messiness of spontaneous speech.
- **Break complex queries into smaller pieces.** If you're working through a complicated request with multiple layers, pause occasionally to let Claude respond to one piece before adding more. This approach creates more natural conversation flow and helps Claude organize its responses around distinct questions rather than trying to address everything simultaneously.
- **Watch the screen periodically.** While voice mode is hands-free, glancing at the screen helps you track the key points Claude highlights. These visual summaries capture the core ideas even if you miss something in the audio response. The combination of audio and visual presentation reinforces understanding better than either alone.
- **Interrupt when you need to add context.** If Claude's response goes in an unexpected direction or you realize you need to add context, you can interrupt by speaking. Claude will stop and listen to your additional input. This interruption capability makes conversations feel natural rather than forcing you to wait through responses that aren't quite right.
- **Monitor battery and data usage.** Voice mode processes audio in real-time, which uses more battery than text conversations. If you're planning an extended voice session, make sure your device is sufficiently charged.

A marketing director developed a habit of using voice mode during morning walks. They found that a 20-minute walk gave enough time to work through one major challenge, a campaign strategy, a difficult email, or a project plan. The physical movement help their thinking, and they had a clear direction for the day by the time they returned home. They kept the phone in a pocket with earbuds, glancing at the screen only when Claude mentioned something that they wanted to note visually.

TIP

Voice mode changes your relationship with Claude from "using a tool" to "having a conversation." The distinction might seem subtle, but it affects how you think and how you approach problems. When you're typing, you tend to formulate complete thoughts before expressing them. When you're speaking, you can think out loud, discover ideas as you articulate them, and adjust your direction based on what you hear yourself say. Voice mode enables a different kind of thinking — more exploratory, more spontaneous, and often more creative than the structured approach that typing encourages.

Customizing Claude to Work Your Way

Claude's default settings work well for most people, but you can adjust several options to match your needs and preferences. These customizations apply across all your conversations, creating a consistent experience that feels tailored to how you work.

Setting up custom instructions that apply everywhere

Custom instructions let you give Claude context that applies to every conversation automatically. Instead of repeating the same information, you set it once, and Claude uses this information as background context in future conversations until you change or remove it.

You might share your role, audience, or preferences with Claude. A teacher could specify: "I teach high school English. When I ask for lesson plans or discussion questions, aim for a 10th-grade reading level and include diverse perspectives." A small business owner might say, "I run a bakery with three employees. When discussing business topics, keep advice practical for small operations with limited budgets."

These instructions save time and improve consistency. Claude doesn't need to guess your context or expertise level; you've told it upfront. This information means fewer clarifying questions, better-matched responses, and less repetition across conversations.

To access personal preferences:

1. **If the sidebar is hidden, display it by clicking or tapping the sidebar icon in the upper-left corner of the screen (and shown in the margin).**
2. **Click or tap your profile icon (your initials).**

   Your profile icon is in the lower-left corner in the web and desktop apps and in the upper-right corner in the mobile app.
3. **Click or tap Settings and then General.**
4. **Scroll down to the What Personal Preferences Should Claude Consider in Responses? text box, as shown in Figure 3-4.**

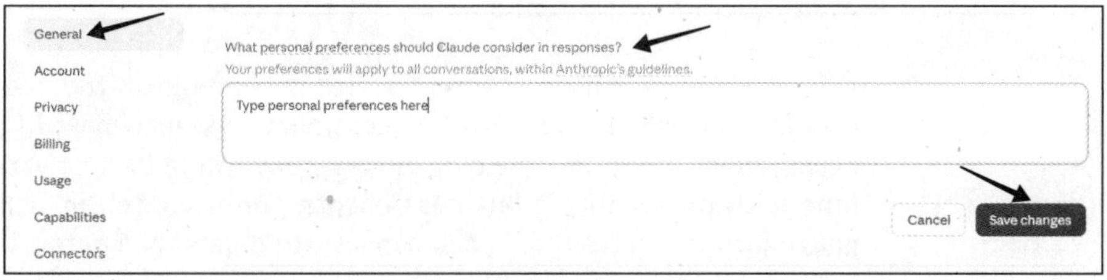

FIGURE 3-4: Access personal preferences in Settings to add context that applies to every conversation.

You can edit these instructions anytime they need updating, and you can clear them if your needs change.

For example, an independent consultant set custom instructions explaining their work: "I help manufacturing companies improve production efficiency. My clients are typically operations managers who understand their processes but want fresh perspectives on optimization." Now when the consultant asks about strategy frameworks, case studies, or client communication, Claude automatically tailors responses to that context.

TIP

Personal preferences work best when they're concise and focused on information that's universal to your Claude usage. Your role, audience, industry, and consistent preferences all make good custom instructions. Specific project details or one-time requests don't belong here; save those for relevant individual conversations or Projects.

Creating different styles for different purposes

Beyond personal preferences, you can guide how Claude communicates with you. Some people prefer concise, bullet-point responses. Others want detailed explanations with examples. Some need formal language for professional contexts, while others work better with casual, conversational tones.

You don't need special settings to adjust style; you can tell Claude what you want. "Keep responses short and action-oriented" gives Claude clear guidance. "Explain things thoroughly with examples" sets a different expectation. "Use a professional tone suitable for client-facing materials" defines the communication style you need.

These style preferences can vary from conversation to conversation. You might want detailed, thorough responses when you're learning something new but quick, concise answers when you're looking up specific information. You might need formal language for one project and casual language for another. Tell Claude what style fits each situation.

A freelance writer used different styles depending on the client. For healthcare clients, they asked Claude for "professional, evidence-based language with clear explanations." For lifestyle blog clients, they wanted a "conversational, engaging tone with personality." Business clients preferred "clear, action-oriented language focused on results." Each conversation gets the appropriate style by simply stating the preference at the start.

The flexibility matters because the same information can sound very different depending on how it's communicated. Claude can be technical or accessible, brief or thorough, formal or casual.

REMEMBER

Knowing how to adjust the style when needed enables you to get content that matches your needs, not some default that might or might not work for your situation.

Adjusting display and language preferences

Your account settings include options for how Claude's interface appears and what language it uses. These preferences affect your experience across all devices where you use Claude. Follow these steps to change your display:

1. **If the sidebar is hidden, display it by clicking or tapping the sidebar icon in the upper-left corner of the screen (and shown in the margin).**
2. **Click or tap your profile icon (your initials) and select Settings.**
3. **Click or tap Settings and then General.**
4. **Scroll to Appearance, as shown in Figure 3-5.**
5. **Click or tap an option under Color Mode and Chat Font.**

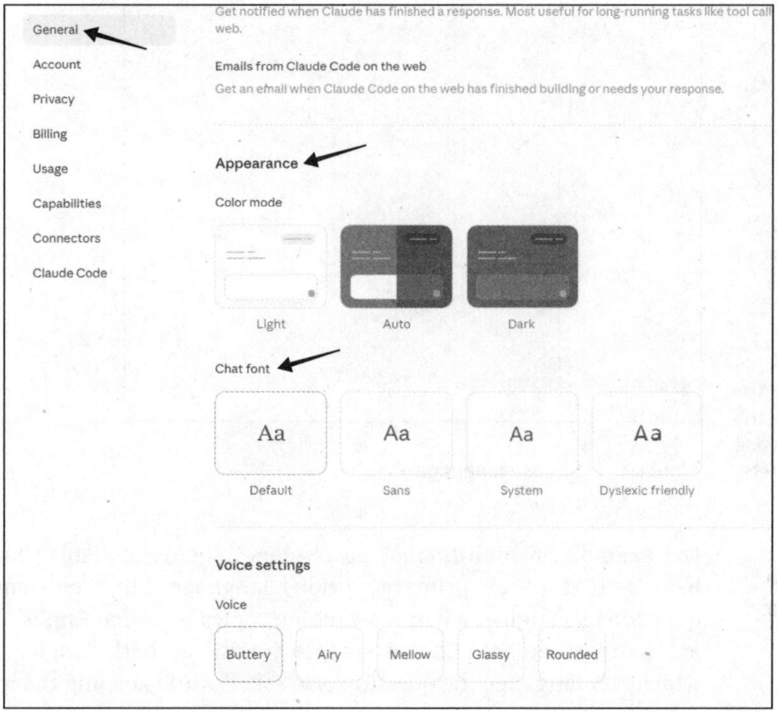

FIGURE 3-5: Adjust text size, theme, and display preferences to match your comfort level.

To choose a language:

1. **Open the sidebar if it's closed.**
2. **Click or tap your profile icon.**
3. **Click or tap Language, as shown in Figure 3-6.**
4. **Click or tap a language in the menu that appears.**

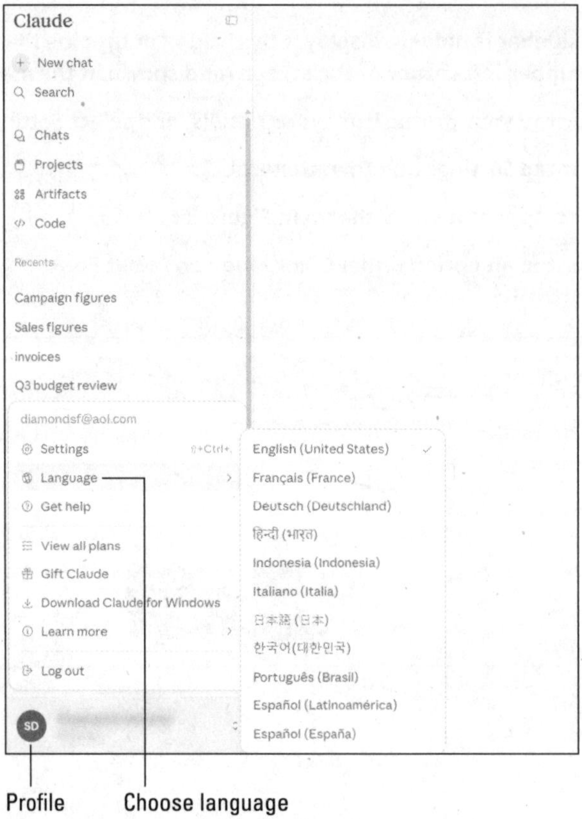

FIGURE 3-6: Change the language Claude uses here.

For example, a multilingual professional set their display language to French because that's their primary working language, but they frequently ask Claude questions in English when researching topics in which English-language sources are more abundant. Claude smoothly handles both languages, responding in whichever language the question was asked while keeping the interface in French.

REMEMBER

The larger point about customization is that Claude should adapt to you, not the other way around. Whether through custom instructions, style preferences, or display settings, you're creating an experience that matches how you work and what you need. This flexibility means Claude becomes more useful over time as you discover what works best for your situation.

IN THIS CHAPTER

- » Using examples to guide results
- » Building your example library (Pro and Max)
- » Working through complex requests step by step

Chapter 4
Crafting Prompts That Get Results

Modern search engines are powerful, but they still focus on finding and ranking existing web pages for your query. Claude, by contrast, holds an ongoing conversation with you, using your words, examples, and follow-up questions to generate new, tailored responses rather than just pointing you to links.

TIP

The fancy term for this process is *prompt engineering*, but that makes it sound more complicated than it is. You're not engineering anything. You're communicating clearly, the same way you'd explain something to a smart colleague who wants to help but needs to understand what you're working on.

In this chapter, you learn the core principles that make conversations with Claude work, such as being specific, providing context, using examples, and asking for exactly what you want. These aren't tricks or hacks. They're the same communication skills that help you get what you need from any conversation. The difference shows up immediately in real conversations. Here's how this plays out in practice:

Situation: A marketing manager needs help with a presentation.

First prompt: "Help me with my presentation."

Claude's response: Claude responded with generic advice about slide structure and speaking tips. Useful, but not what was needed.

Second prompt: "Review my ten-slide sales presentation for a skeptical CFO audience and identify the three weakest arguments." The marketing manager attaches the presentation file with this second prompt.

Claude's response: Claude dove into specific slides, pointed out where their ROI calculations lacked supporting data, and suggested how to strengthen their cost-benefit analysis.

Why this worked: The difference was clarity. The second prompt told Claude who the audience was, what kind of help they needed, and what success looked like. That's what you learn to do in this chapter.

This framework applies throughout the chapter. When we talk about being specific, we're closing the translation gap around what you want. When we discuss context we're closing the gap around your situation. When we use examples, we're focusing on quality and style. The mental picture in your head becomes visible to Claude.

Being Clear and Specific

The single biggest factor in getting good results from Claude is specificity. Vague requests force Claude to guess what you mean, and those guesses often miss the mark. Specific requests eliminate the guesswork and get you answers you can use.

Understanding why clarity matters

When you ask something vague, Claude has to make assumptions. It might assume you want beginner-level information when you're an expert. It might assume you want a formal tone when you need something casual.

These assumptions aren't wrong. They're reasonable guesses based on what most people want. But they're still guesses. And guesses often mean you spend time clarifying, asking follow-up questions, or starting over entirely.

CLOSING THE TRANSLATION GAP

When you ask Claude for help, you have a mental picture of what a good response looks like, but Claude can't see that picture. It sees only the words you type.

The *translation gap* is the distance between what you imagine and what you write. Vague prompts have a wide gap. Specific prompts close it. If you ask a colleague for help, they'd ask clarifying questions. "Who's this for?" "What have you already tried?" "What format do you need?"

Claude can ask clarifying questions, too, but it's more efficient to anticipate them. When you catch yourself thinking, "Claude should know what I mean," that's a signal to spell it out.

Are you curious about why people write vague prompts in the first place? When you know what you want, it feels obvious. You can picture the perfect response in your head. The gap between that mental picture and the words you type is where vagueness creeps in. You assume Claude can see what you see. It can't. The discipline of prompting well is the discipline of translating your mental picture into explicit words.

REMEMBER

Spending thirty extra seconds making your prompt specific will save you ten minutes of back-and-forth later. The investment in clarity pays off immediately. That said, sometimes starting broad and refining through conversation is the right approach, especially when you're not yet sure what you need. You see both strategies in this chapter.

These prompt techniques work because Claude processes language through pattern matching and context analysis, not keyword searches. Vague prompts leave multiple interpretation paths open, so Claude picks the most common one, which often misses your specific needs. Specific nouns, verbs, and constraints narrow those paths to match your intent exactly. You need to include:

- **Examples** work especially well because Claude excels at recognizing patterns in structure, tone, and style from samples. A good example captures nuances that descriptions alone can't fully convey.
- **Background context** fills in your situation so Claude doesn't fall back on generic defaults. The more relevant detail you provide, the more tailored the response.
- **Constraints** act like guardrails, focusing Claude's output within practical boundaries instead of attempting complete coverage of a topic.

Why does this approach work? Large language models generate responses based on patterns from their training. When you communicate clearly using examples, context, and constraints, you're positioning your request with those patterns, which means more precise, useful results. A director experienced this firsthand:

Situation: A nonprofit director who runs an animal shelter wanted help improving donor communication.

First prompt: "Help me write to donors."

Claude's response: Claude sent a generic fundraising letter template, complete with bracketed placeholders such as "[Organization Name]" and "[Specific Impact]." This response is technically helpful, but the director could have found similar templates with a Google search.

Second prompt: They tried again, this time with more detail. "Write a thank-you email to first-time donors who gave under $100 to our animal shelter during our December campaign. Warm, personal tone. Mention their gift made a difference without being over-the-top."

Claude's response: This time, Claude produced an email that felt genuine. It thanked donors for joining the shelter's community, mentioned that December gifts helped cover unexpected veterinary costs during the cold months, and invited them to visit and meet the animals they'd helped.

Result: The director used the email with minimal editing.

Why this worked: The difference came from eliminating guesswork. The second prompt specified the audience (first-time donors, smaller gifts), the occasion (December campaign), the purpose (thank-you, not solicitation), and the tone (warm but not excessive). Claude didn't have to guess any of that.

Template: "Write a [type of message] to [specific audience] who [their situation/action]. [Tone description]. [What to include or emphasize]."

Knowing how much detail to include

You need to strike a balance: too little detail and Claude guesses but too much detail and Claude gets overwhelmed or focuses on the wrong things. The goal is just enough context to eliminate ambiguity without drowning the request in information. Consider these signs that you've included too little:

- » Claude asks clarifying questions before answering.
- » The response feels generic, like it could apply to anyone.
- » You find yourself thinking, "That's not quite what I meant."
- » The answer covers basics you already know.

Here are signs you've included too much:

- » Claude seems confused or addresses minor details while missing the main point.
- » The response is much longer than you need.
- » Claude focuses on the backstory instead of the question.
- » You spent five minutes writing a prompt for a simple question.

Here's a good test: Ask yourself, "Would the average person understand what I need from this prompt?" If a capable person who knows nothing about your situation could understand what you're asking for, you've probably included the right amount of detail.

Here's what too vague looks like: "Edit this email." Claude doesn't know if you want grammar fixes, tone adjustments, length changes, or something else entirely.

Better: "Edit this email to sound more confident and cut it to under 150 words." Now Claude knows exactly what kind of editing you need.

Here's what too much looks like: a 500-word prompt explaining your company's history, your relationship with the email recipient, three previous emails in the thread, and your personal communication style preferences, all to ask for help shortening a two-paragraph message.

Better: "Shorten this email to the key points. Keep it professional but friendly." Include only details that directly affect what you're asking for.

Being specific about what you want

Specificity shows up in three places: your nouns, your verbs, and your constraints. Getting specific in all three areas substantially improves results.

Specific nouns beat vague categories. "Marketing strategies" could mean anything. "Three email subject lines for a flash sale on winter coats" tells Claude exactly what you need.

REMEMBER

Specific verbs beat general actions. "Help me with" is vague. "Write," "compare," "analyze," "summarize," "critique" tell Claude exactly what action to take. Numbers and constraints focus on results. "Give me some ideas" opens the floodgates. "Give me five ideas, each under $500 to implement," creates useful boundaries.

In Table 4-1, we see how vague and specific prompts compare side by side:

TABLE 4-1 Vague versus Specific Prompts

Vague Prompt	Specific Prompt
"Make it better."	"Make it more persuasive for skeptics."
"Write something about marketing."	"Write a 200-word LinkedIn post about email marketing mistakes."
"Give me some ideas."	"Give me five ideas under $500 each for reducing customer wait times."

Template: "[Specific action verb] [specific output] about [specific topic] for [specific audience/use case]. [Specific constraints: length, number, format]."

REMEMBER

Specificity tells Claude what you want. But Claude also needs to understand your situation to tailor their response. That's where context comes in.

Providing the Context Claude Needs

Claude doesn't know anything about you, your situation, or your goals unless you share that information. Context helps Claude understand not just what you're asking, but why you're asking and what kind of answer will help.

Adding background

Three types of background (context) matter the most. They are:

- **Who you are or your situation:** Are you a beginner or an expert? A student or a professional? Someone exploring options or someone ready to act? The answer shapes how Claude frames its response.

- **Who the output is for:** Is this for your manager, your customers, or your five-year-old? The audience changes everything about tone, detail level, and what to emphasize.
- **What you've already tried or know:** If you've already read the basics, you don't need them repeated. If you've tried something that didn't work, Claude can suggest alternatives.

These details transform generic responses into targeted ones. A real example makes this clearer:

Situation: A fourth-grade teacher wanted help explaining fractions.

First prompt: A fourth-grade teacher wanted help explaining fractions.

Claude's response: Without context, the teacher received a generic explanation that began with "A fraction represents a part of a whole" and proceeded through standard textbook material. Accurate but not useful for the specific classroom challenge.

Second prompt: They added background. "I'm a 4th-grade teacher. My students understand multiplication but struggle with the concept that fractions represent parts of a whole. They keep trying to multiply numerators and denominators separately. Help me explain why 1/2 + 1/3 doesn't equal 2/5."

Claude's response: Now Claude understood the problem. It suggested using pizza slices to show why you can't just add across. It created an analogy about why half a pizza plus a third of a pizza can't equal two-fifths of a pizza (the slices aren't the same size).

Why this worked: The background on what students already understood (multiplication) and where they were going wrong (adding across) let Claude target the specific misunderstanding rather than starting from scratch.

Template: "I'm a [your role/situation]. [What you/your audience already knows]. [The specific challenge or confusion]. Help me [specific goal]."

Using examples

Examples in your prompt provide context. When you show Claude what you're working with or what you've seen before, you give it reference points that shape the response. Without reference points, Claude has to guess what matters to you. Here's what providing an example looks like in real work:

Situation: A consultant needed a competitive analysis for a client.

First prompt: Their first attempt was broad. They wrote, "Tell me about my competitors."

Claude's response: Claude had no idea who their competitors were or what aspects mattered. Its answer was generic.

Second prompt: The consultant added an example of what they were looking for. "I'm comparing email marketing platforms for a solopreneur client. Here's an example of the comparison format I need. Product one: Strengths include a user-friendly interface and good templates. Weaknesses are that it gets expensive as the list grows. Now do this comparison for Product one and Product two, focusing on ease of use, pricing for under 1,000 subscribers, and automation capabilities."

Why this worked: The example demonstrated to Claude the format, depth of analysis, and structure. Claude matched that pattern perfectly, making it easy for the consultant to compile client recommendations.

Template: "Here's an example of [what I need/the format I want]: [your example]. Now [do a similar task] for [your specific situation]."

Including relevant context and constraints

Constraints are not limitations that make Claude's job harder but guidance that makes results more useful. Think of constraints as guides that keep the answer relevant to your needs.

Here are some common constraints that improve results:

- **Length:** "In under 100 words," "in three paragraphs," "as a one-page summary"
- **Audience level:** "For someone who's never coded," "for an expert audience," "for a 10-year-old"
- **Tone:** "Formal and professional," "casual and friendly," "enthusiastic but not salesy"

HARNESSING THE CONSTRAINT PARADOX

Here's an interesting principle. Contrary to what most people think, constraints don't limit creativity. They enable it. When you give Claude an open-ended request like "write something interesting about productivity," the possibilities are infinite. Infinite possibilities create paralysis. Claude has to guess which direction you prefer, and that guess often produces something generic, the safest path through unlimited options.

Add constraints, and something shifts. "Write 200 words about one productivity myth, in a conversational tone, for people who've tried everything and are skeptical of advice." Now Claude has boundaries to push against. The constraints create a specific shape to fill rather than an endless void to wander.

The *constraint paradox* says that the more specific your boundaries, the more creative the response within them. The form focuses creative energy instead of dispersing it. Apply this by thinking of constraints not as limitations but as definitions. You're not restricting Claude; you're defining what success looks like.

- **What to avoid:** "Without jargon," "don't mention competitors," "avoid clichés"
- **What to emphasize:** "Focus on cost savings," "emphasize ease of use," "highlight the risks"

It's easy to underestimate the power of "don't" statements. Telling Claude what to avoid can be just as useful as telling it what to include. Consider these examples:

- **For a product description:** "Write this product description without using the words 'innovative' or 'revolutionary.'" This prompt forces fresher language.
- **For a meal plan:** "Create a meal plan for someone who can't eat gluten and dislikes seafood." The constraints define what success looks like.

Template: "[Task]. Constraints: [length], [audience level], [tone], [what to avoid], [what to emphasize]."

Using Examples to Guide Results

Examples are the most powerful tool you have for shaping Claude's output. When you show Claude what you want, it understands at a level that descriptions alone can't capture.

Seeing why examples make a difference

Claude excels at pattern matching. When you show it an example, it picks up on structure, tone, length, word choice, and dozens of subtle elements that would take paragraphs to describe. An example communicates style and quality in ways that instructions can't.

For example, think about trying to describe a particular writing voice. You might say "conversational but professional, with short sentences and occasional humor." That's helpful, but it still leaves room for interpretation. Show a paragraph in that voice, and suddenly Claude knows exactly what you mean.

Understanding the show-versus-tell principle

The show-versus-tell principle is one of the most important concepts for working with Claude effectively. Descriptions are translations of what you want. Examples are the thing itself. When you describe "warm and friendly," you're hoping Claude's definition matches yours. When you show a paragraph that feels warm and friendly to you, there's no translation needed.

TIP

You can think of the difference between showing and telling this way: describing is like giving directions using landmarks, but showing is like handing someone a GPS with the destination already entered. Both can work, but one eliminates the need for additional interpretation.

The show-versus-tell principle applies beyond tone and style. You can show:

- **Format:** An example of how you want information structured
- **Depth:** A sample that demonstrates the level of detail you need
- **Approach:** A previous solution that worked for a similar problem
- **Quality:** An output that meets your standards

Whenever you find yourself writing a long description of what you want, instead ask: "Could I just show this instead?" If the answer is yes, you can save words while improving results. One professional discovered this shortcut by accident:

Situation: A real estate agent was trying to standardize their property descriptions. They wanted a specific tone: warm and inviting, focused on lifestyle rather than square footage, with vivid but not flowery language.

Description: They started by describing the style, "Write in a warm, inviting tone that emphasizes lifestyle over features." Claude produced descriptions that were pleasant but generic. Words like "charming" and "delightful" appeared everywhere. It wasn't wrong, but it just wasn't their voice. Then they tried to show instead of tell. They included one of their favorite descriptions they'd written: "Morning light floods the kitchen, where wide counters have hosted everything from Tuesday homework sessions to Saturday morning pancakes."

Prompt: "They asked Claude to write a similar description for a different property. The result captured their voice: specific moments instead of generic praise, sensory details that created scenes, the feeling of life being lived in a space. Claude had absorbed not just the tone but the technique."

Template: "Here's an example of the style I want: [your example]. Now write a similar [type of content] for [your specific subject]."

Showing what you want (and don't want)

Examples work in two directions. Positive examples show Claude what to aim for. Negative examples show what to avoid. Using both is even more powerful than either one alone. Here are two examples:

- **For email subject lines:** "Write subject lines like 'Your weekend plans just got better' NOT like 'Newsletter #47: March Updates.'" The positive example shows energy and benefit; the negative shows boring and generic. Claude now has a clear target and a clear warning.
- **For a report structure:** "Structure the report like the attached example but with shorter paragraphs." This tells Claude to follow the overall pattern while adjusting one specific element.

TIP

How many examples do you need? Usually, one to three is enough. One clear example often works for simple tasks. Two or three examples help when you want to show variety within a style or when the pattern is more complex. More than three examples rarely help and sometimes can confuse Claude.

Template: "[Task]. Style should be like this example: [good example]. Avoid this style: [example of what you don't want]."

Setting quality standards with your examples

Your example defines the ceiling. If you provide a weak example, you'll get mediocre output. If you give a really good example, Claude aims for excellence. Choose your examples carefully because they set the standard Claude aims for. See how this works in practice:

> **Situation:** A manager needed help writing performance reviews. They grabbed a quick example from last year's files, something they wrote in a hurry.
>
> **First prompt:** "Good team player. Meets expectations. Should work on communication." This prompt was obviously vague and unhelpful.
>
> **Claude's response:** Claude produced reviews in that same style: generic praise, unclear feedback, nothing an employee could act on.
>
> **Second prompt:** The manager tried again with a better example, one where they'd taken time to be specific. "Led the Q3 migration project, coordinating across three teams and bringing the project in two weeks ahead of schedule. The strongest contribution was translating technical requirements for non-technical stakeholders. Growth area: delegate more effectively when workload spikes. Specific suggestion: identify one task per week that could develop a junior team member's skill."
>
> **Claude's second response:** The reviews Claude produced now included specific achievements, concrete feedback, and actionable growth suggestions. The example set the standard.

Knowing when to show versus when to tell

Showing works powerfully, but it's not always the right choice. Sometimes a clear description gets you there faster. The key is knowing which situation you're in before you invest time in either approach. Here are some guidelines. Show when:

- You've tried describing, and Claude keeps missing the mark.
- The quality you want is hard to articulate. ("I'll know it when I see it.")
- Consistency matters, and you'll make similar requests repeatedly.
- The style, format, or structure is unusual or specific to you.

Tell when:

- The request is straightforward and standard (a professional email, a bulleted list).
- You don't have a good example handy.
- You want Claude to surprise you with fresh approaches.
- Speed matters more than precision.

Most people default to telling when they should be showing. If you've sent two or three follow-ups trying to describe what you want and Claude still isn't getting it, that's your signal. Stop describing. Find or create an example.

Distinguishing between essential and optional examples

Examples aren't always necessary. Sometimes they add overhead without adding value. Knowing when to use them saves time. Examples are essential when:

- You need to match a specific voice or style.
- You want to replicate a particular format.
- You want quality and consistency more than speed.
- You used previous attempts without examples that missed the mark.

Examples are optional when:

- You want Claude's best judgment on the approach.
- The format is standard, like email, a list, or a summary.
- You're generating rough drafts for heavy editing.
- Your first attempts work without examples.

WARNING

Consider the trade-offs. If you want Claude to give you fresh approaches, too many examples can limit that. If you want consistency and control, examples are essential. A marketing team exploring new campaign directions might skip examples to see what Claude generates. That same team executing on an approved brand voice needs examples every time.

Building your example library

If you use Claude regularly for similar tasks, building a library of go-to examples and reference documents saves time and improves consistency.

Saving your best examples

When Claude produces something that perfectly captures your voice or meets your standards, save it. These successful outputs become your examples for future requests. This habit compounds over time. An example makes this clearer:

> **Situation:** A freelance writer works with multiple clients, each with a distinct voice. The writer keeps a folder of "good examples" for each client. This folder includes the blog posts they loved, the email newsletters that got high engagement, and the product descriptions that converted well.
>
> **Prompt:** When they start a new piece for any client, they include the relevant examples in their prompt. Instead of re-explaining each client's voice every time, they show Claude: "Match the tone and style of these examples." Their first drafts now require far less revision.

TIP

Start simple. After a conversation in which Claude delivers exactly what you want, copy that output into a document labeled "Examples That Work." Also, you should organize by type. These might include email, report, or social media examples, or whatever categories match your regular needs.

What makes an example worth saving? Look for outputs where you thought "Yes, that's exactly right." Pay attention to responses that captured a tone you struggled to describe, solved a formatting challenge, or nailed a tricky balance like "professional but warm." These good examples teach Claude what success looks like faster than any description.

Over time, you'll notice patterns in your saved examples. A consultant realized that all their best proposal examples shared a specific structure: problem statement, proposed approach, expected outcomes, and required investment. They hadn't consciously chosen this structure, but now they include it in their prompts, and their first drafts need far less revision.

REMEMBER

Don't limit yourself to final outputs. Sometimes a conversation includes a moment where Claude's response shifted from generic to perfect after you provided a key piece of context. Save that exchange, too. It will remind you of information that matters for that type of task.

Using uploaded documents for reference

All Claude plans, including Free, let you upload documents directly to your conversations. This feature transforms how you can work with examples and reference material. Instead of copying and pasting text from a style guide into every prompt, you upload the style guide once. Claude can reference it throughout the conversation. This approach works especially well for brand consistency:

Situation: A marketing team uploaded its 20-page document on their brand's voice.

Prompt: Now they can say, "Write a press release for our product launch following our brand guidelines in the uploaded document."

Claude's response: Claude reads the guidelines and applies them without the team having to summarize or excerpt.

The following documents work well as references:

- Brand voice and style guides
- Templates and format specifications
- Collections of examples that show the requested output
- Background information Claude should know
- Previous work you want Claude to build on or match

The key is choosing documents that help. A 50-page employee handbook might seem useful for writing HR communications, but Claude will work better with a 2-page excerpt covering tone guidelines and key terminology.

REMEMBER

Dense documents with lots of irrelevant information slow things down and can pull Claude's attention to details that don't matter for your task.

Think of uploaded documents as reference materials, not required reading. Claude draws from them when relevant, but you still need to point to what matters. For example, "Write a product announcement following our brand guidelines" works better than just uploading the guidelines and hoping Claude figures out what you need.

Organizing reusable materials in Projects

Projects in Claude let you create persistent workspaces with their own instructions and knowledge. For anyone who does similar work repeatedly, Projects transform the experience. Here's what using Projects looks like for someone who writes regularly:

Situation: A content creator set up Projects for each type of work they do. Their Newsletter Project contains their brand voice guide, examples of successful past newsletters, and custom instructions about their typical audience and goals. Their Client Proposals Project has their standard proposal format, pricing guidelines, and examples of winning proposals.

Prompt: When they start a new newsletter, they open that Project. Claude already knows their voice, format, and standards. They don't need to re-explain anything. They can simply say, "Write this week's newsletter about productivity tips," and Claude starts from exactly the right place.

TIP

Chapter 5 covers Projects in detail, including step-by-step setup and advanced organization strategies.

Asking for the Output You Want

The final piece of a strong prompt is specifying what you want back. Format, structure, length, and tone all affect whether Claude's response actually benefits you.

Specifying format, tone, and structure

Format tells Claude how to organize the response. For example, you can tell Claude that you want the following:

- Bullet points or paragraphs
- A table or a narrative
- Sections with headers or continuous text

By giving explicit instructions, you can avoid having to reformat the output later. Consider that you can say:

- "Give me this as a numbered list with one sentence per item."
- "Present this as a two-column table comparing features and drawbacks."
- "Write this as three short paragraphs, no bullet points."

Tone tells Claude how to sound. You can tell Claude that you want, professional or casual, enthusiastic or measured, technical or accessible. For example, you can say:

- "Write in a conversational tone like you're explaining to a colleague, not a formal report."
- "Keep it professional but warm, not stiff or corporate."

Structure tells Claude what comes first and how ideas connect. This matters especially for longer responses. Consider these examples:

- "Structure this with the recommendation first, then the reasoning."
- "Start with the bottom line, then provide supporting details."

Setting clear expectations

Telling Claude your length and completeness expectations prevents mismatches between what you wanted and what you got.

For length, be as specific as practical. You can prompt the following:

- "In about 200 words"
- "No more than one page"

- "Brief, just 2 to 3 sentences"
- "Comprehensive, covering all major aspects"

For completeness, be explicit about what you want the output to be. For example, say:

- "Outline" when you want structure and key points only
- "Draft" when you want a rough version, expecting revision
- "Write" when you want something polished and complete
- "Skeleton" when you want a bare framework to build on

Using the three-part prompt formula

For most requests, a simple three-part structure works remarkably well: task plus context plus format. This formula handles about 80 percent of what you'll ask Claude to do. Here's an example:

- **Task:** What action do you want Claude to take? What should it produce?
- **Context:** Who is it for? What's the situation? What background matters?
- **Format:** How should it be structured? How long? What tone?

Here's how the formula works in practice:

Situation: A project manager needed to update their manager on a delayed website launch.

Prompt: The manager started building the prompt piece by piece:

- **Task:** "Write a project update email."
- **Add context:** ". . . for my manager who asked about the delayed website launch."
- **Add format:** "Three short paragraphs: what happened, current status, next steps. Professional but not stiff."

The combined prompt was "Write a project update email for my manager who asked about the delayed website launch. Three short paragraphs: what happened, current status, next steps. Professional but not stiff."

Claude's response: It produced an email that acknowledged the delay, explained the cause (a third-party integration issue), outlined the current status (dev team working with the vendor), and provided next steps (a revised timeline by Friday).

Result: The project manager sent it with minor tweaks.

Template: "[Task: specific action + specific output] [Context: who it's for, situation, relevant background] [Format: length, structure, tone, any constraints]."

Working through Complex Requests

Not everything fits in a single prompt. Some requests are too big, too complex, or too nuanced to handle all at once. Knowing when and how to break things apart, use follow-ups, or start afresh makes you more effective.

REVIEWING THE ITERATIVE MINDSET

Many people approach Claude like a search engine. They type a query, get an answer, and stop. This one-shot prompt works for simple requests but fails for more complex ones.

The iterative mindset treats prompts as conversations, not commands. You don't need to get everything right in one prompt. You can:

- Start rough and refine.
- Ask for one piece, and then build on it.
- Get feedback before committing to a direction.
- Explore options before choosing.

(continued)

(continued)

This mindset change can be liberating. You don't need to craft the perfect prompt. You need a good enough starting point and the willingness to iterate. A mediocre first prompt followed by two smart follow-ups often beats an elaborate first prompt that you agonized over.

The iterative mindset also means viewing failures differently. A response that misses the mark isn't a waste. It's information. It tells you what Claude needs to hear to get it right. Each iteration closes the gap between what you wanted and what you got.

TIP

Think of complex requests as sculpting rather than ordering. A sculptor doesn't create the final form in one motion. They rough out the shape, refine it, and then polish it. Your conversation with Claude works the same way: rough draft, targeted refinement, final polish.

Breaking big requests into steps

Some requests fail not because the prompt is unclear but because the ask is too big. Claude might try to do everything at once and end up doing nothing particularly well.

Here are some signs your request might be too big:

- Results feel shallow, even though the topic is deep.
- Important pieces are missing.
- Claude seems to lose focus partway through.
- You're asking for multiple distinct deliverables in one prompt.

Here's what happens when you ignore these signs:

Situation: While creating a business plan, an entrepreneur learned the hard way about the pitfalls of making a prompt too encompassing.

First prompt: The entrepreneur asked Claude to create a complete plan covering market analysis, competitive positioning, financial projections, marketing strategy, and operational requirements.

Claude's response: The result was a surface-level overview of everything and a deep treatment of nothing. Each section got a few sentences when it needed pages.

Second prompt: They broke it into sequential prompts. First: "Analyze the market for premium pet food delivery in the Seattle metro area. Focus on market size, growth trends, and customer segments."

Claude's response: It produced three pages of useful analysis.

Third prompt: "Based on that market analysis, identify the top five competitors and their positioning. Where are the gaps?"

Claude's response: It built on the first answer, creating a competitive matrix that the entrepreneur could use.

Fourth prompt: "Given that competitive landscape, recommend a positioning strategy for a new entrant focusing on organic ingredients."

Why this worked: Each prompt was built on the previous one, creating depth that a single prompt couldn't achieve. You need one clear ask at a time. Use the output from each step as input for the next.

Recognizing where to break

The entrepreneur in the preceding section figured out their break points through trial and error. You can spot them faster by looking for these natural boundaries:

- **Break at transitions between thinking modes.** Research requires different processing than writing. Analysis differs from recommendation. When your request asks Claude to shift gears mid-task, that's a breakpoint. "Research competitors AND write the marketing copy" combines two modes. Split them.
- **Break at audience shifts.** Internal analysis looks different than client-facing summaries. A request that serves two audiences usually serves neither well. Get the analysis right first, and then translate it for the audience that needs it.
- **Break at decision points.** If later steps depend on choices made in earlier steps, break there. The entrepreneur's positioning strategy depended on which competitive gaps they found. Building everything at once meant Claude had to make decisions by guesswork that should have been made deliberately by the entrepreneur.

» **Break when depth matters more than breadth.** A shallow pass across five topics rarely helps. Deep treatment of one topic and then the next builds something you can use.

TIP

When you're unsure whether to break a request apart, ask yourself: "If Claude gets the first part wrong, does everything else fall apart?" If so, that's a breakpoint. Get the foundation right before building on it.

REMEMBER

The sequential approach has another benefit. You can course-correct early. If the first response heads in the wrong direction, you've invested one prompt, not ten. You can adjust your approach before building on a faulty foundation.

Using follow-up questions to refine results

Follow-ups aren't signs of failure. They're how conversations work. Sometimes the first response is close but needs adjustment. Sometimes it reveals that your original prompt was missing something. Either way, follow-ups are often the fastest path to what you need.

Effective follow-ups are specific about what to keep and what to change. For example, you can say:

» "Good start, now make the opening more attention-grabbing and cut the third paragraph."

» "Expand on point #2 with a specific example."

» "This is too formal. Rewrite with more contractions and shorter sentences."

» "The structure is perfect. Just make it about 30 percent shorter."

TIP

The pattern is to acknowledge what's working, and then specify what to change. This preserves the good parts while directing the revision.

Template: "Keep [what worked]. Change [what didn't] by [specific direction]."

Knowing when to start afresh

Sometimes a conversation has gone so far in the wrong direction that follow-ups can't fix it. The context has accumulated in ways that keep pulling Claude back to its original (wrong) interpretation.

Here are some signs it's time to start afresh:

- You've sent three or more follow-ups without getting closer to what you need.
- Claude keeps returning to an approach you've already rejected.
- You realize your original prompt was fundamentally flawed.
- The conversation has become confusing with multiple competing directions.

Starting afresh doesn't mean starting from scratch. Take what you learned from the failed attempt and build a better initial prompt. The failed conversation taught you something about what you actually needed. The failure itself reveals the real question. This truth became obvious to a writer who kept trying to fix the unfixable:

Situation: A writer spent ten messages refining the introduction of a blog post.

First attempt: Each revision addressed one problem while creating another. The conversation had accumulated so much context about what the writer didn't want that Claude couldn't find its way to what the person did want.

Second attempt: The writer started a new conversation with a better prompt: "Write an opening paragraph for a blog post about productivity myths. Hook readers by challenging the assumption that busy means productive. Conversational tone, under 100 words, don't mention hustle culture directly."

The fresh start, informed by what the writer had learned from the failed attempts, produced a usable introduction on the first try.

Starting fresh doesn't erase what you learned. Before abandoning a struggling conversation, take a moment to identify what went wrong. Was the original prompt missing key context? Did you ask for too much at once? Did Claude latch onto something you mentioned casually and treat it as a core requirement? These insights make your fresh start actually fresh, not just a repeat of the same mistakes.

TIP

Some people resist starting over because it feels like wasted effort. But a conversation that's gone sideways often wastes more time in continued attempts to fix it. Three focused follow-ups that don't improve results are a signal. Five is definitely too many. Cut your losses and apply what you learned to a better opening prompt.

Talking to Claude is a skill you develop through practice. The principles in this chapter work because they focus on clear communication, not tricks. You need to:

- Be specific about what you want.
- Provide context so Claude can tailor results.
- Show examples when descriptions aren't enough.
- Specify format and constraints to guide output.
- Iterate or restart when needed.

REMEMBER

When things aren't working, either refine with targeted follow-ups or start afresh with what you've learned.

Every technique in this chapter, including specificity, context, examples, constraints, and iteration, serves the same purpose: closing the translation gap between the picture in your head and the words Claude sees. The more you practice, the faster that gap shrinks. Soon, crafting effective prompts will feel as natural as explaining something to a colleague.

IN THIS CHAPTER

» Setting up Projects for organized, context-rich work

» Uploading reference documents to Projects

» Managing what Claude remembers about you

Chapter 5
Working with Projects and Memory

What if you had an assistant who already knew your business, remembered your preferences, and produced files you can use immediately? They are not someone you need to brief from scratch every morning, but a real partner who picks up where you left off. That's what Claude becomes with the features in this chapter.

Instead of starting fresh every time, Claude keeps your work context, creates real documents and spreadsheets, and learns what matters to you. If you've mainly used Claude for quick questions, you're about to see what it can really do.

Consider this example of a marketing consultant. They spent the first five minutes of every conversation with Claude re-explaining their business. They would paste their company description, target clients, service offerings, and preferred communication style every single time. Then they learned about three important Claude features:

- **Projects:** They set up their business context once and never repeated themselves.
- **Memory:** Claude remembered their preferences across all their work.

- **Skills:** Claude started producing presentation files instead of just describing what slides should contain.

REMEMBER

Skills work in all plans, including Free. Memory and full Projects require a paid plan (Pro, Max, Team, or Enterprise). Free users can create up to five basic Projects. Each of these features focuses on a different issue and makes Claude feel like a true assistant who knows your business. Projects organize your work with persistent context, the Memory feature maintains personal knowledge across everything you do, and Skills extend what Claude can create. These features work together to create something that is greater than the sum of their parts. We look at Projects and Memory in this chapter and Skills in the next chapter.

Understanding What Projects Are and When to Use Them

A *Project* is a dedicated workspace in Claude that maintains a consistent context for specific areas of your work. Think of it as a specialized room, designed for a particular task. When you enter a Project, Claude automatically applies the instructions and knowledge you've stored there.

TIP

A Project gives Claude a persistent (continuous) context for specific work. Instead of re-explaining your situation in every conversation, you set up a Project once with background materials and instructions. Every conversation within that Project starts with Claude already understanding what you're working on.

Learning how Projects differ from regular chats

In a regular chat, Claude starts fresh. It knows nothing about your business, your preferences, or your ongoing work until you explain. Each conversation is independent, which works fine for quick questions but becomes tedious for sustained work.

Projects change this dynamic. When you create a Project, you define the following:

- **Custom instructions:** Specific guidance that shapes Claude's responses
- **Reference documents:** Files that Claude can access when answering questions

- **A focused context:** Boundaries that keep conversations relevant to that domain

REMEMBER

Every conversation in a Project automatically inherits these settings. You don't need to repeat yourself. Claude already knows what you've told it about this area of your work.

Back to the freelance writer who experienced the frustration of having to repeat things daily. They had to write blog posts for three different clients, each with a distinct brand voice, target audience, and content guidelines. In regular chats, the writer would paste the relevant style guide at the start of every conversation. If they forgot a detail, Claude's output missed the mark. If they started a new chat to continue yesterday's work, they had to set up the context again.

Projects changed the freelance writer's workflow completely. They created three separate Projects, one for each client. Into each Project, they uploaded the client's style guide, sample posts they loved, audience demographics, and topics to avoid. Now, when the writer opens their TechStartup Client Project and asks Claude to draft a blog post, Claude already knows that the voice should be casual but authoritative, the audience is technical founders, and certain competitor names should never appear.

TIP

Regular chats require you to build context through conversation. Projects provide context before the conversation begins.

Deciding when to use a Project

Not every task needs a Project. Quick questions, one-time requests, and explorations work perfectly in regular chats. Projects shine when you have ongoing work with a consistent context.

Consider creating a Project when:

- **You repeat the same background information frequently:** If you find yourself pasting the same company description, style guidelines, or reference materials into multiple conversations, that's a signal to create a Project.
- **You work on something over multiple sessions:** A research paper, a marketing campaign, a software Project, or any sustained work benefits from persistent context.
- **Claude should always consider certain reference materials:** Documents, data files, guidelines, or examples that inform your work belong in a Project.

» **Multiple conversations relate to the same topic:** If you're having separate chats about different aspects of one initiative, a Project keeps them connected.

For example, a small business owner identified the natural dividing lines for their work: marketing campaigns, which contain their brand guidelines and audience research; product development, which includes feature specifications and customer feedback; and operations, which provides for their team structure and standard procedures. When they need help with a marketing email, they open the marketing Project. When they needed to draft a product announcement, they open the product development Project. Each Project gives Claude the right context for the right task.

TIP

Skip Projects when you have quick, unrelated questions. Asking Claude to convert a recipe measurement or explain a word doesn't need a dedicated workspace. Projects work best when you return to the same context repeatedly.

Setting Up Projects for Success

Now that you understand what Projects do, let's create one. The setup process takes just a few minutes, and a well-configured Project pays dividends across every conversation in it.

Creating your first Project

To create your first Project:

1. **If the sidebar is hidden, display it by clicking or tapping the sidebar icon in the upper-left corner of the screen (and shown in the margin).**
2. **In the left sidebar, click or tap Projects.**

   You see any existing Projects and an option to create one, as shown in Figure 5-1.
3. **In the upper right, click or tap New Project.**
4. **Give your Project a descriptive name, as shown in Figure 5-2.**
5. **Click or tap Create Project.**

   The Project workspace appears, with space for instructions and an area to upload reference materials, as shown in Figure 5-3.
6. **Click or tap Create Project.**

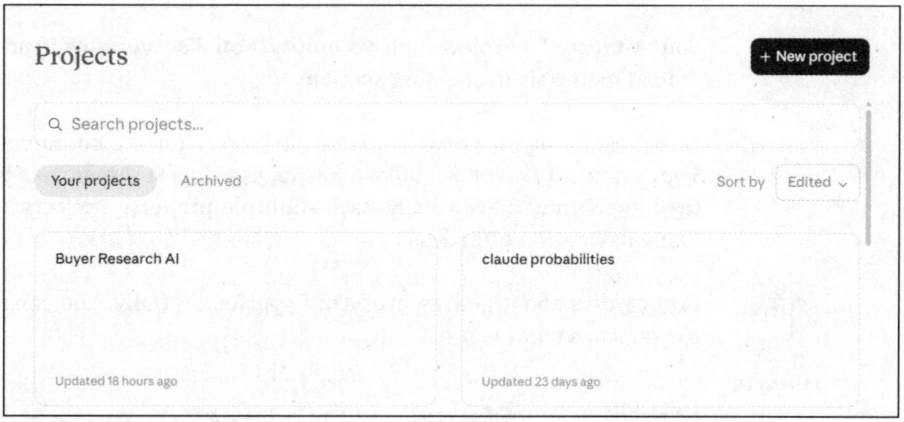

FIGURE 5-1: Choose your Project from the list.

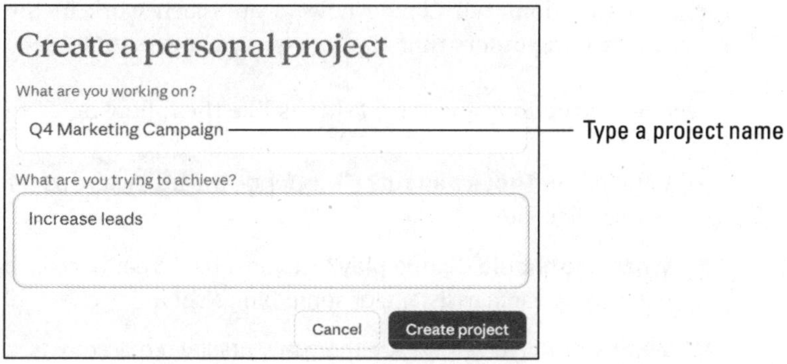

FIGURE 5-2: Name your Project.

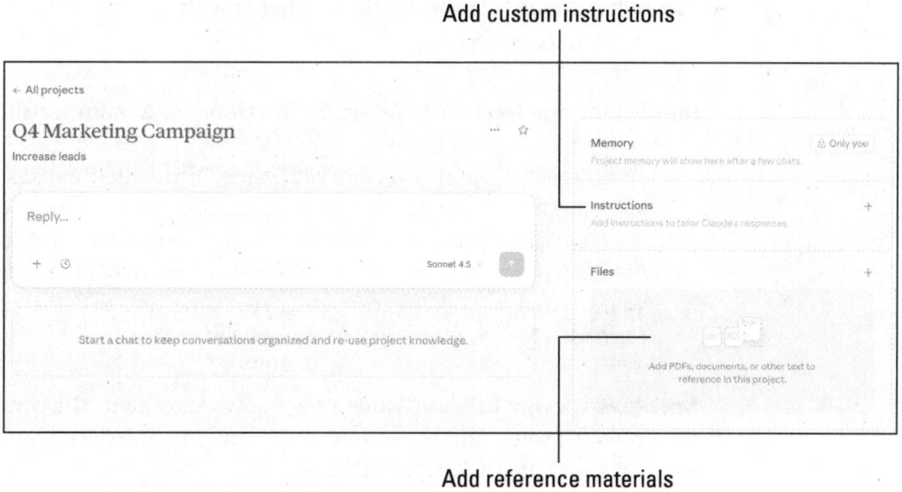

FIGURE 5-3: The Project workspace includes space for instructions and reference materials.

You've created a Project, but it's empty. You discover how to add instructions and upload materials in the next sections.

A real estate agent created their first Project for a commercial property listing. They named it *Downtown Office Complex, 555 Main St* rather than just *Listing* because they knew they'd eventually have multiple property Projects. The specific name made navigation effortless.

REMEMBER

Don't worry about getting everything perfect initially. You can refine your Project as you learn what works.

Writing effective Project instructions

Project instructions tell Claude how to approach work in the Project. Think of them as standing orders that apply to every conversation.

Effective instructions answer questions like the following:

- **What is this Project about?** Give Claude the big picture so that it understands the context.
- **What role should Claude play?** Should it be a creative collaborator, a careful editor, a research assistant, or something else?
- **What standards apply?** Are there any quality requirements, style guidelines, or constraints that Claude should know about?
- **What should Claude avoid?** Are there topics, approaches, or phrasings that don't fit this work?

Here's how one freelancer set up instructions for a manufacturing client:

> "This Project supports my work with Acme Corporation, a mid-size manufacturing company transitioning to sustainable practices. When helping with Acme work, maintain a professional but approachable tone suitable for their executive team. Focus on practical, actionable recommendations rather than theoretical frameworks. Avoid mentioning competitors by name, and all deliverables should be formatted for easy copying into PowerPoint or Word."

Note how specific this is. Claude now knows the client, the context, the audience, the preferred tone, and the output requirements. Every conversation in this Project starts with this understanding.

TIP

Start with a few essential instructions and add more as you discover what matters to you. Overly detailed instructions can needlessly constrain Claude. You can always refine your instructions based on experience.

Uploading reference documents and knowledge

Projects can hold documents that Claude references during your conversations. Upload materials that provide context, examples, or information Claude should consider.

Common uploads include the following:

- **Style guides and brand standards:** Documents that define voice, terminology, or formatting requirements
- **Background research:** Reports, articles, or data that inform your work
- **Examples of good work:** Samples that show Claude what you're aiming for
- **Specifications and requirements:** Documents defining what needs to be accomplished
- **Previous work:** Earlier versions or related materials that provide context

TECHNICAL STUFF

Projects accept files up to 30MB each. Supported formats are PDF, DOCX, TXT, CSV, HTML, RTF, ODT, and EPUB. (Open Document Text, or ODT, is an open-source file format used by free apps such as Google Docs that can be edited without proprietary software.)

What you see in the context window depends on the model you're using. Opus 4.7 and Sonnet 4.6 support up to 1 million tokens (roughly 2,500 pages of text). Haiku 4.5 supports 200,000 tokens (about 500 pages). If you hit limits, prioritize your most essential documents. Prioritize your most essential documents and consider splitting very large initiatives across multiple Projects. (For more information about tokens, see Chapter 2.)

REMEMBER

Because there are limits to how much you can upload, Claude works best when documents are relevant rather than exhaustive. Upload what Claude needs for this specific work, not everything tangentially related.

TIP

Documents in a Project stay available across all conversations in that Project. You upload the documents once, and Claude can reference the materials whenever relevant.

Comparing Projects and custom instructions

Custom instructions (covered in Chapter 2) apply to all your conversations with Claude. They're global preferences. Projects are local preferences that apply only in that specific workspace. Here's a practical way to think about the difference:

- **Custom instructions apply everywhere.** When you set preferences in a custom instruction, they affect every conversation across all of Claude. If you tell a custom instruction that you prefer concise responses with bullet points, every chat reflects that preference. Think of custom instructions as your general preferences and Projects as your work-specific knowledge bases. They layer together, with Project context adding to (and sometimes overriding) your general custom instructions within that Project's conversations.
- **Projects apply only within themselves.** When you add context to a Project, it affects only conversations in that Project. For example, your Legal Research Project might instruct Claude to cite sources formally, while your Creative Writing Project encourages experimental responses.

For example, a lawyer uses Claude's custom instructions to establish general preferences: formal language, thorough analysis, and clear structure. These apply whether the lawyer is working on a case, writing personal emails, or exploring new topics. The lawyer's individual Projects add case-specific context: client background, relevant statutes, prior rulings, and opposing counsel's arguments.

TIP

Put applicable preferences in custom instructions. Put context-specific details in Projects. This organization prevents you from cluttering Projects with information that should apply everywhere.

REMEMBER

Custom instructions shape how Claude communicates overall. Projects shape what Claude knows about each specific matter.

Using Projects for Different Purposes

Projects adapt to whatever you're working on. The following section shows how different types of work benefit from different Project setups.

Setting up Projects for work domains

Many professionals organize Projects around major areas of responsibility (domains) rather than individual tasks. For example, a marketing director created three domain Projects:

- Brand and Messaging contains brand guidelines, approved messaging, tone examples, competitor positioning, and any conversation about how to communicate using this Project.
- Campaign Management holds current campaign briefs, performance benchmarks, and templates. Planning and optimizing campaigns happen here.
- Team Development includes team structure, individual development goals, and feedback frameworks, as well as performance conversations and team planning used in the Project.

This domain approach means that the director rarely needs to explain context. Opening a particular Project gives Claude everything needed for that type of work.

TIP

Domain Projects work well when you have distinct areas of responsibility with different contexts, terminology, or standards. The boundaries between domains should feel natural based on how you organize your thinking.

Creating personal Projects

Projects aren't just for professional work. Personal Projects can help with hobbies, home management, learning goals, and life planning.

For example, a homeowner created a House Projects Project containing their home's layout, past renovation decisions, preferred contractors, and budget constraints. When planning a kitchen update, Claude already knew the home's style and the homeowner's previous choices and financial limits.

For another personal Project, a language student created a French Practice Project that included their current level, learning goals, topics they'd covered, and vocabulary they found difficult. Claude tailored every practice session to their specific progress.

REMEMBER

Personal Projects benefit from the same principles as professional ones. You need to upload relevant context, write clear instructions, and let Claude build on that foundation across multiple conversations.

Managing client or Project-specific knowledge

When you work with multiple clients or on distinct Projects, separate Projects prevent context from bleeding between them. For example, a writer maintains individual Projects for each client in the following way:

- Acme Corp — Digital Transformation contains Acme's organizational structure, current systems, project timeline, and stakeholder preferences.
- TechStart — Market Entry holds TechStart's product specifications, target market research, and competitive landscape.
- GlobalFirm — Process Optimization includes GlobalFirm's workflow documentation, pain points, and success metrics.

This separation ensured that advice for one client never accidentally referenced another client's information. Each Project was a clean, dedicated space.

REMEMBER

Client separation improves confidentiality and quality. Claude provides better help when the context is focused rather than cluttered with unrelated information from other engagements.

Managing Your Project Library

As you create more Projects, organization becomes important. This section covers keeping your Project library useful and easy to navigate.

Organizing multiple Projects

Projects appear in your sidebar, and you'll frequently need to scan this list. A few practices will keep the list manageable:

- **Use clear, specific names:** Q4 Marketing Campaign beats Marketing. Acme Corp Engagement beats Client Work.
- **Archive completed Projects:** When work concludes, archive the Project rather than deleting it. This approach preserves the context in case you need to reference it later without cluttering your active list.

- **Group related Projects visually:** While Claude doesn't offer folders for Projects, consistent naming conventions create visual grouping. For example, Client: Acme, Client: TechStart, and Client: GlobalFirm are alphabetized together.

TIP

A project manager with fifteen active Projects uses prefixes to stay organized: *Client:* for client work, *Internal:* for their own business development, and *Personal:* for non-work Projects. This simple convention makes navigation effortless.

Switching between Projects and regular chats

Not everything needs a Project. Quick questions, explorations, and one-off tasks work fine in regular chats. Here's how to do each one:

- **To start a regular chat:** Begin a new conversation without selecting a Project. Claude starts fresh without any Project context.
- **To work in a Project:** Select the Project from the sidebar before starting a conversation. Every chat in that Project shares the Project's context and instructions.

You can have multiple conversations in a single Project. Each conversation is separate but shares the Project's foundation. This approach works well when you're addressing different aspects of the same work.

For example, a product manager drew a clear line between when to use chats versus Projects. They use regular chats for quick research questions and general learning. They use their Product Projects for anything requiring product context, roadmaps, or specifications. This boundary felt natural. A question related to a specific product happened in a Project. A question about general knowledge happened in a regular chat.

Archiving and maintaining Projects

Archived Projects remain accessible but are no longer on your active list. Here's how to decide when to archive:

- **Archive:** The Project has concluded, the client engagement has ended, or you haven't used the Project in months and don't anticipate needing it

» **Keep active:** The work is ongoing, you reference the Project regularly, or you expect to need it again soon

TIP

Periodically review your active Projects and archive those you're no longer using. A clean Project list speeds up navigation and reduces the mental load of scanning outdated work.

When a Project wraps up, archiving is the smarter move over deleting. You have access to all the conversations and uploaded materials, but the Project moves out of your active list so it stops cluttering your workspace.

To archive a Project:

1. **Navigate to the Project you want to archive.**
2. **In the upper-right corner, click or tap the three-dot menu (. . .) and choose Archive, as shown in Figure 5-4.**

   A screen appears, asking you if you want to archive the project.
3. **To confirm, click or tap Archive.**

FIGURE 5-4: Archiving moves a Project off your active list without deleting it.

Archived Projects land in the Archived tab on your Projects page. They're not gone, just tucked away. You can still open them and read past conversations whenever you need to. To bring a Project back into active use:

1. **Go to your Projects page and click or tap the Archived tab, as shown in Figure 5-5.**
2. **Find the Project that you want to activate.**
3. **Click the Project's three-dot menu (. . .) and choose Unarchive.**

   The project returns to your active list, with all instructions, uploaded files, and conversation history intact.

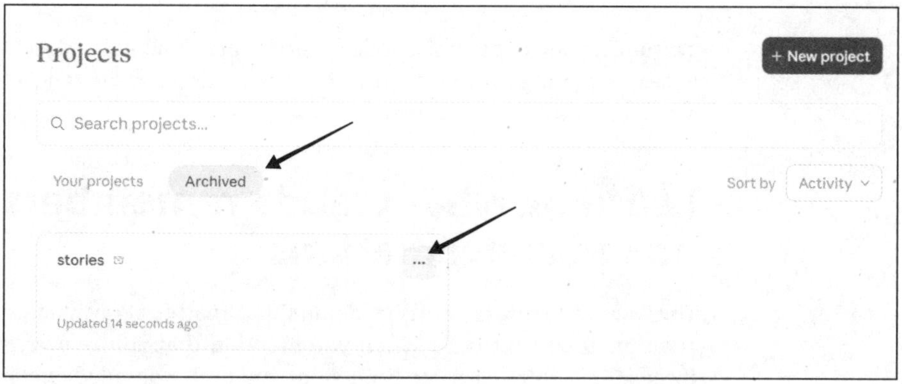

FIGURE 5-5: Unarchiving restores a Project to your active list.

REMEMBER

Archiving resets all sharing permissions to private. If you unarchive a Project you've shared with others, you'll need to invite them again.

Deleting a Project

If you've hit the Free plan's five-Project limit and need to make room, archiving is usually the smarter move. (I described archiving a Project shortly.) However, you can also delete a Project outright.

To delete a Project:

1. **On the Projects page, locate the Project you want to remove.**
2. **In the upper-right corner of the Project, click or tap the three-dot menu (. . .).**
3. **Select Delete from the menu (refer to Figure 5-4).**

   A screen appears, asking you if you're sure you want to delete the project.
4. **To confirm, click or tap Delete.**

WARNING

Deletion is permanent. All conversations, uploaded files, and instructions disappear immediately with no way to recover them. When in doubt, archive instead.

Understanding How Memory Works

The Memory feature allows Claude to remember information about you across all your conversations. (This feature is available on Pro, Max, Team, and Enterprise plans.) Unlike Projects, which hold context for specific work, Memory maintains personal knowledge that applies everywhere. Your name, your role, your preferences, your ongoing situations — you don't have to repeat them because the Memory feature keeps track.

Learning what Claude remembers across conversations

The Memory feature captures details that matter about you as a person, not just about your current task. When you mention that you're a veterinarian, you have three kids, you're learning French, or you prefer detailed explanations, the Memory feature can retain these facts for future conversations.

Here's how a teacher notices the difference the Memory option makes.

In their first conversation, a teacher mentioned that they taught fifth-grade science. In a later discussion a week afterward, they asked for help creating a lesson plan. Claude suggested age-appropriate activities and vocabulary, remembering the students' grade level without being reminded. The teacher didn't have to reestablish their context; Claude already knew.

TIP

The Memory feature works across all your Claude conversations, not just in a single Project. Whether you're in a Project, a regular chat, or switching between topics, the Memory option provides continuity about who you are and what matters to you.

Saving automatically versus manually

Claude can automatically save Memories as you chat, or you can explicitly tell it what to remember:

- **Automatic saving:** As you converse, Claude notices details that seem worth remembering. If you mention your job, location, preferences, or ongoing situations, Claude may store this information without your asking.
- **Manual saving:** You can directly tell Claude to remember something. For example, "Remember that I prefer responses in bullet points," or "Keep in mind that I'm allergic to shellfish when suggesting recipes." This approach ensures that important details don't get missed.

One financial advisor found that mixing both methods gave them the control they needed. They let Claude automatically capture details as they arise, but they stated critical preferences explicitly: "Always remember that my client work is confidential, and I never want you to reference one client's information when discussing another." Those instructions guide Claude's behavior in the future.

Comparing Memory, Projects, and custom instructions

Memory, Project, and custom instructions each solve a different problem:

- **Memory:** Stores facts about you as a person — your background, your preferences, your ongoing situations. Memory applies everywhere and updates as Claude learns more about you.
- **Project:** Stores context about specific work — your client's brand guidelines, your research sources, your Project specifications. Project information applies only within that Project.
- **Custom instructions:** Store preferences about how Claude should communicate your preferred format, tone, length, or style. Custom instructions apply everywhere but focus on Claude's behavior rather than its knowledge about you.

Table 5-1 compares Memory, Projects, and custom instructions.

TABLE 5-1 Comparison of Memory, Projects, and Custom Instructions

Feature	What It Stores	Where It Applies	Best For
Memory	Personal facts	All conversations	Universal personal context
Project	Work-specific context	Only that Project	Ongoing areas of work with reference materials
Custom Instructions	Communication and behavior preferences	All conversations	Consistent behavior

Here's how a marketing director uses all three. Claude's Memory feature knows that the person is a marketing director at a tech company, has a design background, and is currently planning their daughter's graduation party. Their Projects contain specific campaign briefs, brand assets, and competitor analysis for different initiatives. Their custom instructions specify that they prefer concise responses with clear action items.

When the director asks for help, the Memory feature provides personal context, the active Project provides work context, and custom instructions shape the response format. The three layers complement each other rather than compete.

Managing your privacy with Memory settings

You control what Claude remembers. Some people appreciate Claude's capability to build a rich understanding of their lives and work. Others prefer more privacy and less retention. Memory settings let you choose.

To set up Memory settings and see what Claude has stored in Memory, do the following:

1. **Click or tap your profile icon (your initials), and then click or tap Settings.**

   Your profile icon is in the lower-left corner in the web and desktop apps and in the upper-right corner in the mobile app.

2. **Select Capabilities from the menu.**
3. **Scroll down to Memory.**

   You can control two separate features, as shown in Figure 5-6:

   - *Search and reference chats:* Lets Claude search your past conversation history to find relevant context.
   - *Generate Memory from chat history:* Creates an ongoing summary of facts Claude learns about you.

4. **Enable one, both, or neither feature.**

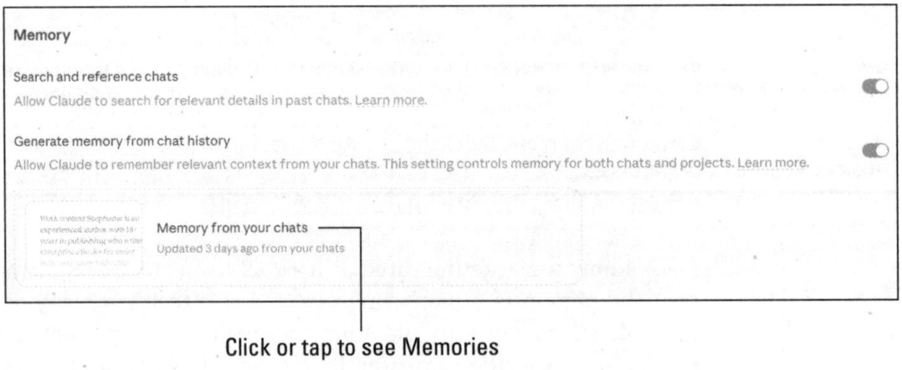

FIGURE 5-6: Managing Memories.

5. **To see what Claude has stored in Memory, click or tap Memory from Your Chats.**

   The window shown in Figure 5-7 appears, displaying Claude's complete Memory summary of you. You can review everything Claude remembers and make changes by clicking or tapping the pencil icon.

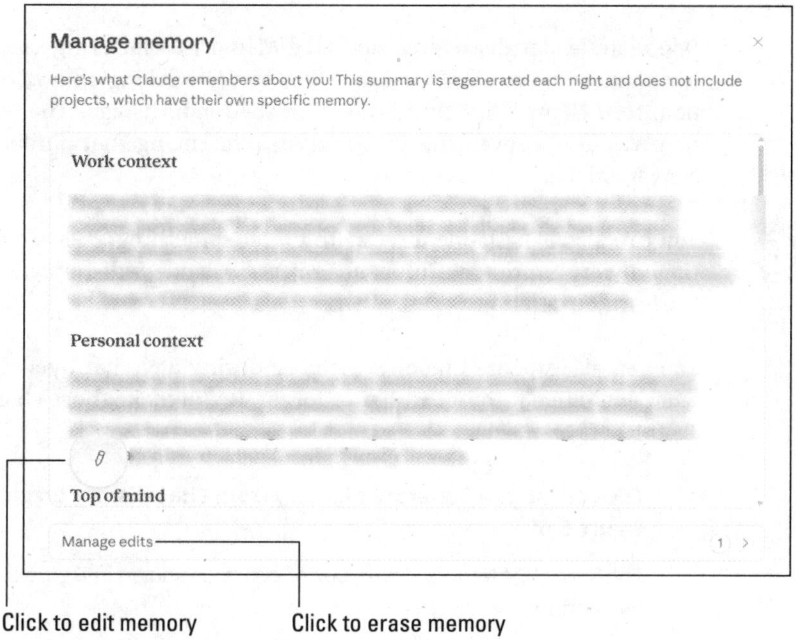

FIGURE 5-7: Your Memory summary.

Editing or deleting Memories

You can remove any Memory that's incorrect, outdated, or simply something you'd rather Claude not retain.

To delete a Memory, click or tap Manage Edits (refer to Figure 5-7). Then click or tap the trash can icon (delete), as shown in Figure 5-8. The Memory disappears immediately, and Claude will no longer reference that information.

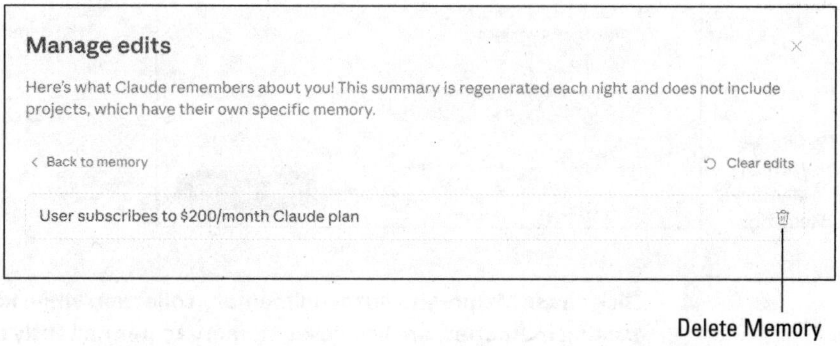

FIGURE 5-8: Deleting a Memory.

One team leader discovered outdated Memories cluttering Claude's understanding. Claude had remembered that they were "working on a website redesign for a nonprofit client," but that Project finished months ago. The team leader deleted that Memory, preventing Claude from referencing that outdated work in future conversations.

TIP

You can also ask Claude directly to forget something: "Please forget that I mentioned working on the Johnson Project." Claude will remove that Memory and confirm the deletion.

You can also update Claude's Memory during any chat by simply telling Claude what you'd like it to remember or forget. It will make those changes immediately. To turn off Memory:

1. **Click or tap the Generate Memory from Chat History toggle (refer to Figure 5-6).**

   The Turn Off Memory dialog box appears, as shown in Figure 5-9, with two options:

   - *Pause Memory:* Claude keeps its existing Memories but won't use them or create new ones. Conversations while paused won't be added to Memory even if you turn the feature back on.
   - *Reset Memory:* Claude permanently deletes all Memories, including Project Memories. You can't undo this action. If you reenable Memory later, Claude starts with a blank slate.

WARNING

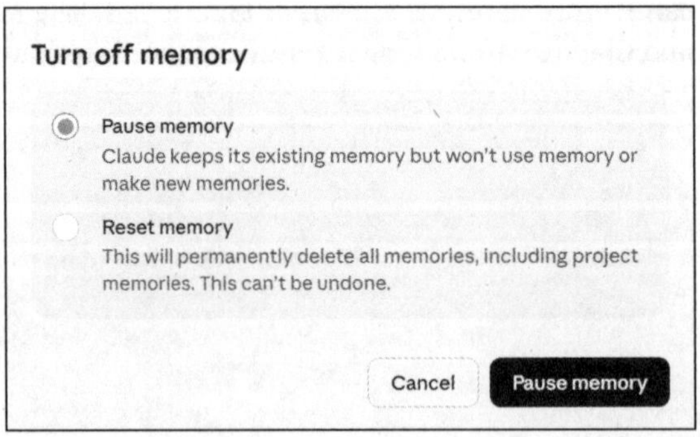

FIGURE 5-9: The Turn Off Memory dialog box.

2. **Click Pause Memory to suspend memory collection while keeping your existing memories, or click Reset Memory to permanently delete all memories and start afresh.**

   The setting takes effect immediately.

Managing What Claude Remembers

The Memory feature works automatically once enabled, but you maintain full control over what Claude retains. This section shows how to review, edit, and use the Memory feature strategically, so Claude remembers what helps you and forgets what does not.

REMEMBER

Check your Memories periodically, especially if Claude's responses seem outdated. Memories accumulate over time, and older entries might no longer apply.

If you value privacy, review your Memories periodically. Perhaps you appreciate Claude remembering your professional context but delete personal details. Or you might want to disable the Memory feature, preferring to start each conversation fresh. Both approaches work; choose whichever you're most comfortable with.

REMEMBER

The Memory feature is designed to help you, not to track you. Claude uses Memories to provide better, more personalized assistance. You maintain full control over what is retained and can delete anything at any time. You can also export your Claude Memories for backup, or import Memories from other AI services such as ChatGPT or Gemini.

Working incognito

For conversations you want to remain completely private, use incognito mode. This feature is available to all users, whether Free or paid.

To start an incognito conversation, click or tap New Chat in the left sidebar and then click or tap the faded ghost icon in the upper right, as shown in Figure 5-10. A screen with a black border appears, with the text You're incognito.

FIGURE 5-10: Click or tap the ghost icon for incognito mode.

Claude doesn't save new Memories or reference existing ones during an incognito session. This mode works well for sensitive topics or when asking a question for someone else.

Controlling what Claude should forget

You might have some information that should never be stored. If you're discussing something sensitive or temporary, you can tell Claude not to remember it. Here are suggested prompts you can use:

- "Don't remember anything from this conversation" prevents any new Memories from this chat.
- "Don't store any information about my medical situation" creates a standing instruction about what to exclude.

WARNING

These instructions guide Claude's Memory behavior, but you should avoid sharing sensitive information you don't want stored. Even individually harmless facts can combine into sensitive information. Your employer, neighborhood, daily schedule, and health habits are fine alone. But together they create a detailed profile. Be thoughtful about what you let Claude accumulate over time, and review your Memories periodically with this in mind.

For example, a user discussing a sensitive family matter asked Claude not to retain any details from that conversation. Claude helped with the immediate question, but didn't add anything to Memory. The user maintained their privacy while receiving assistance.

Using the Memory feature for better results

Memory works best when it contains accurate, current information about things that genuinely affect how Claude should help you.

Here are some good candidates for the Memory feature:

- Your profession and expertise level (so Claude calibrates explanations appropriately)
- Ongoing Projects or situations (so Claude can reference them naturally)

- Strong preferences about format or style (so every response matches your needs)
- Important constraints (dietary restrictions, accessibility needs, confidentiality requirements)

These are less useful for the Memory feature:

- Temporary tasks that will conclude soon
- Highly specific details are better suited to a Project
- Information that changes frequently

A business owner figured out exactly what belonged in Memory versus Projects. The owner let the Memory feature retain their role, industry, and communication preferences. But they kept client-specific details in Projects rather than in Memory, ensuring that Claude wouldn't accidentally mix up information between clients.

REMEMBER

Think of the Memory feature as your personal profile and Projects as your work files. Memory should contain things true about you, regardless of what you're working on. Projects should include items specific to a particular piece of work or client.

With Projects organizing your work context and the Memory feature maintaining your personal preferences across all conversations, you've built a strong foundation for working with Claude. But one more feature brings everything together.

In the next chapter, you discover how Skills extend what Claude can create, from documents and spreadsheets to presentations and more. You also see how Projects, Memory, and Skills work together to transform Claude from a helpful chatbot into something that feels like a true assistant that knows your business, remembers your preferences, and produces real work you can use immediately.

IN THIS CHAPTER

» Discovering the Customize hub where Skills and Connectors are located

» Setting up Skills to create polished documents from conversations

» Connecting Claude to the apps and services you use

Chapter 6

Customizing Claude with Skills and Connectors

Claude is a strong conversational partner. It helps you think, write, and shape ideas in real time. But conversation alone isn't where the biggest productivity gains happen. Claude has a full set of customization tools including Skills and Connectors, that let you move from discussing work to creating it.

This chapter shows you where those tools are located, what each one does, and how to put them to work. Skills let Claude give you a finished Word document or Excel spreadsheet instead of just describing it. Connectors give Claude access to the apps you already use, like Google Drive, Slack, and Canva.

Introducing the Customize Hub

Before diving into individual features, it helps to know where you can find each feature. Claude groups Skills and Connectors under a single sidebar called Customize, which serves as your command center for configuring how Claude works with you.

The Customize icon appears in the sidebar on the left side of the Claude interface. If the sidebar is hidden, display it by clicking or tapping the sidebar icon, which is in the upper-left corner of the screen (and shown in the margin). You see two main areas, as shown in Figure 6-1:

- **Skills** house the document-creation and task-specific capabilities you can toggle on. Anthropic builds a starter set of Skills for Word, Excel, PowerPoint, and PDF. Users of all plans, including Free, can browse example Skills and upload custom ones through the Customize sidebar.
- **Connectors** is where you browse and manage connections to external services such as Google Drive, Gmail, GitHub, Slack, Canva, Figma, and many more. Some Connectors are available on all plans, including Free. Others require a paid subscription.

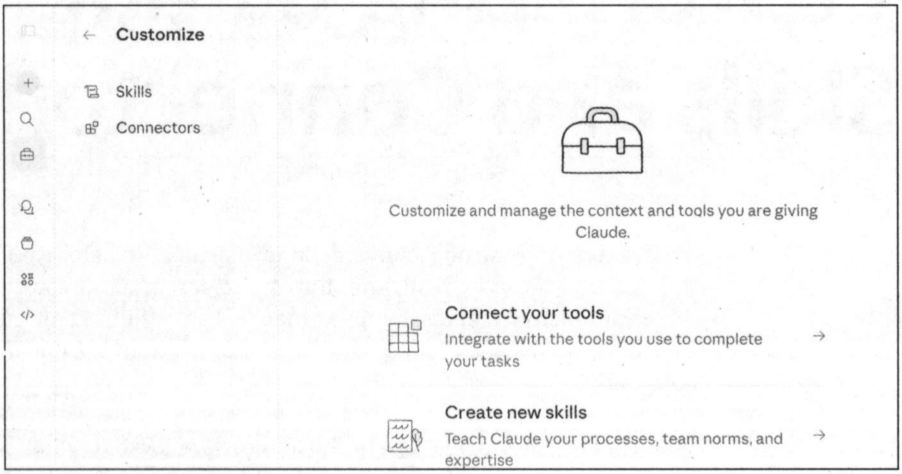

FIGURE 6-1: The Customize sidebar give you access to Skills and Connectors in one place.

TIP

Use the Customize sidebar to set up your choices. Claude carries those settings into all your conversations.

Learning How Skills Work

Skills are specialized capabilities that let Claude produce specific types of output. You don't need to understand the technical details to use Skills effectively, but a basic mental model will help you recognize when they will save time and when regular chat already gives you what you need.

Comparing Skills to a regular chat

In a regular chat, Claude communicates through text in the conversation window. It explains concepts, drafts content, and offers suggestions. Everything appears as text you can read and copy and paste elsewhere. That approach works perfectly for brainstorming, getting advice, answering questions, and exploring ideas.

With Skills activated, Claude produces tangible files. Instead of describing what a presentation should contain, Claude builds the presentation. Instead of writing spreadsheet formulas for you to copy into Excel, Claude creates the spreadsheet with those formulas already working. Consider this scenario:

Situation: A nonprofit director needed to prepare for a board meeting. They asked Claude: "Help me plan a board update presentation." Claude responded with a thorough text outline covering suggested slides, talking points, and time allocations. The outline was excellent, but the director still had to open PowerPoint and manually build every slide.

Prompt: The following month, the director tried a different approach: "Create a PowerPoint presentation for our quarterly board meeting covering program outcomes, financial summary, upcoming initiatives, and fundraising goals."

Claude's response: Claude produced a downloadable .pptx file with four content slides, each properly formatted with headings and bullet points.

Result: The director opened the file in PowerPoint, adjusted a few numbers, added their organization's logo, and finished in minutes instead of an hour.

Why this worked: The prompt specified both the format (PowerPoint) and the content structure (four named sections). Asking Claude to "create" rather than "help with" signaled that the director wanted a file, not a description.

Template: "Create a [file type] for [event/purpose] covering [topic 1], [topic 2], [topic 3], and [topic 4]."

If Claude responds with text instead of creating a file, be more explicit about the format. Phrases like "Create a downloadable Excel file" or "Build a PowerPoint I can edit" signal that you want a document, not just a description.

Knowing what Skills can and cannot do

Skills produce working documents, but they do have limits. They excel at

- » Creating properly formatted documents from your specifications
- » Building spreadsheets with working formulas and basic charts
- » Generating presentations with appropriate layouts and structure
- » Producing files you can immediately open in standard applications
- » Combining multiple file types when your task requires them

Their limitations include the following:

- » Complex visual design requires refinement in the native application.
- » Highly specialized formatting may need manual adjustment.
- » Large datasets may hit processing limits.
- » Brand-specific templates need to be applied after Claude creates the base document.

REMEMBER

Skill-created documents give you proper structure and accurate content. Think of them as strong first drafts that save you from having to start from scratch. You add the final polish.

For example, an event planner learned this balance through experience. Claude created excellent event run-of-show documents, but the planner always opened them in Word to add their company's header and color scheme. Claude handled the content and structure. The planner added the final branding touches. This division of labor still saved hours compared to building everything from scratch.

Not every task needs a downloadable file. Regular chat works perfectly when you want to:

- » Brainstorm ideas without committing to a format
- » Get quick answers to specific questions
- » Draft content you plan to paste into an existing document
- » Talk through a problem before deciding on a deliverable

For example, a teacher who uses Skills for creating lesson plan documents still uses regular chat to discuss classroom strategies and brainstorm activity ideas. Make sure to match the tool to the task.

Understanding Skill Types

Skills fall into two main buckets: Anthropic Skills, which are the ones Anthropic builds for you, and custom Skills, which are the ones you build yourself. Both types are available in all plans, including Free.

The built-in Anthropic Skills for Word, Excel, PowerPoint, and PDF activate automatically when code execution is enabled. (Code execution and file creation are available with all plans, including Free.) To browse Anthropic's example skills and upload custom skills, you use the Customize sidebar. The Skills Customize sidebar is available on all plans, including Free.

Anthropic Skills

Anthropic's team builds, tests, and maintains Anthropic Skills. Think of them as the starter toolkit that ships with your account. They work behind the scenes without any setup on your part. Four of them handle common file types:

- **Word (.docx):** Creates and edits documents with proper formatting, headings, and styles
- **Excel (.xlsx):** Builds spreadsheets with working formulas, charts, and data analysis
- **PowerPoint (.pptx):** Generates presentations with layouts and visual elements
- **PDF:** Creates formatted PDFs, extracts text from existing ones, and handles forms

These Skills activate automatically when your request calls for them. You don't toggle them on separately.

Custom Skills

Think of a custom Skill as a set of saved instructions that Claude follows every time you ask for a particular type of work. Instead of explaining your formatting rules, preferred terminology, or document structure in every conversation, you can save those instructions once and reuse them. From then on, Claude applies them automatically. To create or upload custom Skills, you must enable code execution (which is available on all plans, including Free).

For example, a property management company created a custom Skill for lease summaries. The Skill included their standard legal terminology, required disclosure language, and preferred formatting. Now, whenever a team member asks Claude to summarize a lease, the result meets the company's standards without anyone having to explain the requirements.

Organization-wide Skills

If you're on a Team or Enterprise plan, your organization's administrator can push Skills out to every user at once from the Settings admin panel. This means your entire team can access the same Skills without each person having to upload them individually. You can toggle these organizational Skills on or off in your own settings to control whether Claude uses them in your conversations.

Setting Up and Using Skills

Skills require a quick setup before they can become a natural part of how you work with Claude. This section walks you through enabling Skills, understanding your options, and getting consistent results.

Activating the Skills you need

The built-in Anthropic Skills activate automatically whenever code execution is enabled. No toggling is required.

Here's how to enable code execution on any plan, including Free:

1. **If the sidebar is hidden, display it by clicking or tapping the sidebar icon in the upper-left corner of the screen (and shown in the margin).**
2. **Click or tap your profile icon (your initials), and then click or tap Settings.**
3. **In the Settings menu, select Capabilities.**
4. **Scroll down to Code Execution and File Creation and toggle it on, as shown in Figure 6-2.**

   That's all you need for the built-in document Skills. Claude now creates Word, Excel, PowerPoint, and PDF files automatically when your request calls for them.

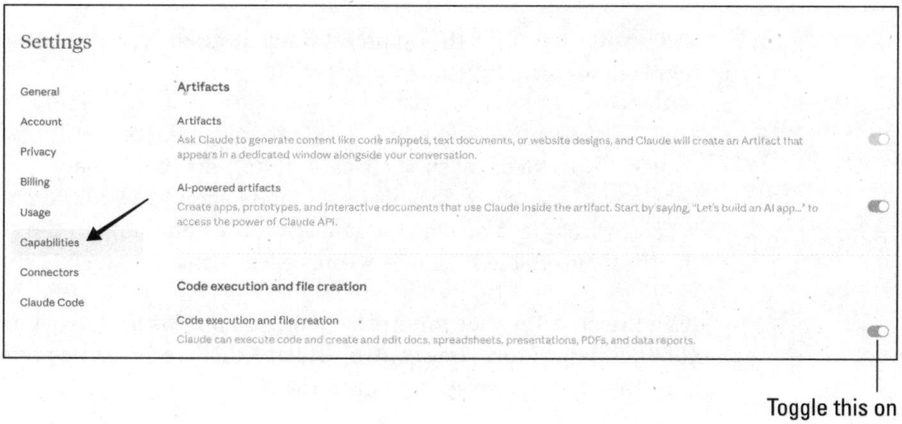

FIGURE 6-2: The Code Execution and File Creation toggle in Settings.

With any plan, including Free, you can browse and enable additional Skills through the Customize sidebar:

1. **Click Customize in the left sidebar to open the Customize panel.**
2. **Select Skills.**

   You see a list of available Skills that include both Anthropic-built example Skills and any custom Skills you've uploaded, as shown in Figure 6-3.
3. **Toggle on any Skills you want Claude to use.**

   Each Skill has a toggle switch to its right. Slide it to the right to enable the Skill; slide it left to disable it. These Skills remain available until you turn them off.

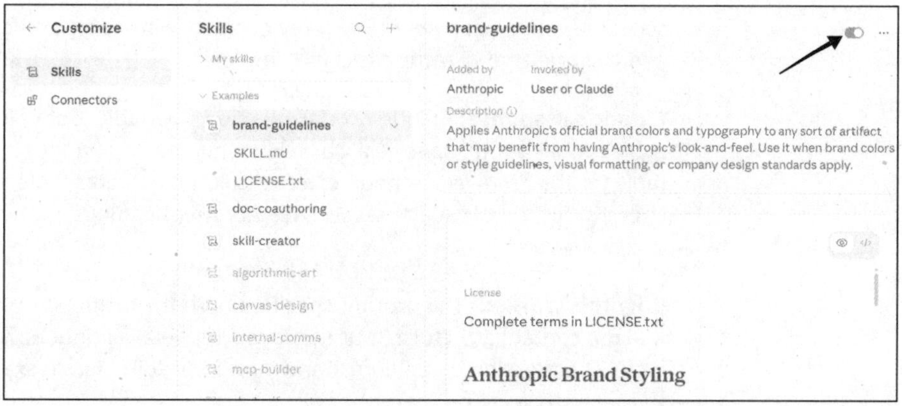

FIGURE 6-3: Toggling individual Skills on or off in the Customize sidebar.

Example Skills include applying brand guidelines, coauthoring documents, generating professional internal communications, and building interactive web components. Not every example Skill applies to every workflow, so browse the list and enable the ones that match how you work. You can always come back and toggle more on or off later.

TIP

The Code Execution and File Creation toggle is the controlling switch that enables Claude to perform tasks such as building documents and generating files in a secure workspace. (It doesn't give Claude access to your computer or your data.) When the toggle is disabled, Claude produces only text in the chat window. When the toggle is enabled, Claude creates files you can download and use.

REMEMBER

If you're on a Team or Enterprise plan and don't see Skills you expect, check with your administrator. They control which Skills are available organization-wide and may need to activate specific ones for your account.

Using Skills in conversations

Once you have Skills enabled, using them will soon feel natural. You describe what you want, mention the file type, and Claude handles the output. Here's how this works in practice:

Situation: An HR director needed onboarding materials for new employees. They had been copying and pasting text from Claude chats into Word documents and manually reformatting it, which took nearly an hour per new-hire packet.

Prompt: "Create a Word document welcoming new team members to our marketing department. Include sections for our team mission, first-week schedule with placeholder times, key contacts with name and role columns, and a checklist of IT setup tasks to complete."

Claude's response: Claude produced a downloadable .docx file with a professional layout, specifically a welcoming opening paragraph, a formatted table for the first-week schedule, a two-column contacts table, and a bulleted checklist for IT tasks. Each section used proper headings, giving the document a clean hierarchy.

Why this worked: The prompt specified both the format (Word document) and the content structure (four sections with details about how each should look). The mention of "columns" and "checklist" told Claude exactly how to format each section.

Template: "Create a [file type] for [purpose/audience]. Include sections for [section 1 with format detail], [section 2 with format detail], [section 3 with format detail], and [section 4 with format detail]."

Here are some additional prompts that can reliably trigger different Skills:

- **For spreadsheets:** A small business owner asked "Create an Excel spreadsheet tracking monthly expenses with categories for rent, utilities, supplies, and marketing. Include formulas that calculate monthly totals and a yearly summary row." Claude delivered an .xlsx file with labeled columns, working SUM formulas, and conditional formatting highlighting months where spending exceeded the average.
- **For presentations:** A team lead prompted "Build a PowerPoint presentation introducing our new product line. Include slides for product overview, three key features, target customer profile, and pricing comparison." Claude produced a .pptx file with six slides following a logical flow.
- **For PDFs:** A freelance consultant prompted "Create a PDF one-pager summarizing my consulting services. Include three service tiers with descriptions, a brief bio, and contact information at the bottom." Claude generated a clean, professional PDF.
- **For web interfaces:** A fitness studio owner prompted "Create an interactive calculator that helps users estimate their monthly membership cost based on visit frequency and class type." Claude produced the HTML, CSS, and JavaScript for a working web-based calculator that the owner could open locally or host on a website.

TIP

Did you notice a pattern in these successful prompts? Each one names the file type, describes the purpose, and lists specific sections or elements. The more structural detail you provide, the closer Claude's first output will match what you need.

Browsing and Connecting External Services

Claude connects to outside tools in two ways. The first method is using Anthropic-built Connectors for services such as Google Drive, Gmail, Google Calendar, GitHub, and Slack. These Connectors reside inside Claude, give it direct access to your data, and work the same way across every conversation.

The second way to connect to outside tools is by using a growing directory of partner-built integrations, where companies like Canva and Figma have built Claude access into their products. Claude works inside a partner Connector directly, so you can, for example, create a design in Canva or build a presentation in Gamma without leaving the conversation.

The step-by-step connection process is the same for both types; what differs is where the work happens. Anthropic-built Connectors pull data into your Claude conversation, while partner Connectors push Claude's capabilities into the partner tool.

REMEMBER

All Connectors in the Connectors Directory are available on all plans, including Free. Google Drive, Gmail, Google Calendar, GitHub, Slack, and partner Connectors such as Gamma, Canva, and Figma included.

Custom Connectors, which let you connect to services outside the directory using your own remote MCP server, are also available on all plans, but Free accounts are limited to one custom Connector at a time. Team and Enterprise plans add administrator controls so organization owners can manage which Connectors are enabled for their users.

Claude offers Connectors to services you might already use:

- **Google Drive:** Access your documents, spreadsheets, and presentations.
- **Gmail:** Search and reference your emails without leaving Claude.
- **Google Calendar:** Check your schedule and upcoming events.
- **Slack:** Search messages, catch up on channel history, and send messages to your team.
- **GitHub:** Access repositories and code for development workflows.
- **Partner-Built Connectors:** The Connectors directory includes tools built by third-party companies that have integrated with Claude. You'll find options ranging from CRM and meeting tools to specialized research databases. The directory expands regularly. Click Browse Connectors in Settings and use the Categories drop-down menu to explore what fits your workflow.

The next section walks you through connecting Claude to one of these services.

Connecting to a service

Connecting Claude to an external service takes only a few minutes. You authorize access once, and Claude can then pull from that service whenever it's relevant to your conversation. No copy and pasting required. Simply follow these steps:

1. **Click or tap the + button in the lower-left area of the chat interface.**
2. **Select Add Connectors from the menu that appears, as shown in Figure 6-4.**

   If you haven't connected any services yet, clicking Add Connectors takes you directly to the Connectors directory.

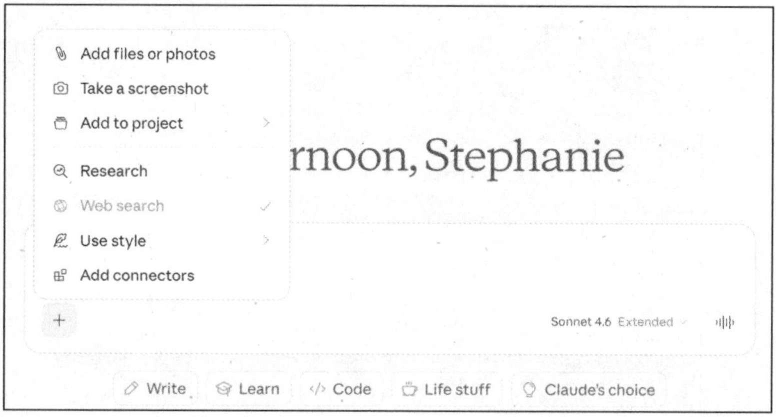

FIGURE 6-4: Click the + button in chat to reach the Connectors option.

3. **If you've already made at least one connection, select Manage Connectors.**

   You see the Connectors directory.

4. **Click or tap + to the right of the Connectors heading, and then click or tap either Browse Connectors or Add Custom Connector.**
5. **Find the Connector you want and click or tap its card to open the detail page.**
6. **Click or tap the + button on the detail page.**
7. **Sign in to the service if prompted.**
8. **Review and authorize the permissions Claude needs.**
9. **Click or tap Confirm to complete the connection.**

To explore partner-built Connectors such as Gamma, Canva, and Figma, click Browse Connectors in Step 4. The Connectors directory opens, as shown in Figure 6-5, with the Search field and the Sort, Type and Categories drop-down menus.

Above the tabs are four controls that help you narrow down what you're looking for:

- **Search box:** Searches by tool name.
- **Sort menu:** Orders results by relevance or other criteria.
- **Type menu:** Filters by connection type.
- **Categories menu:** Filters by topic area, such as productivity or developer tools.

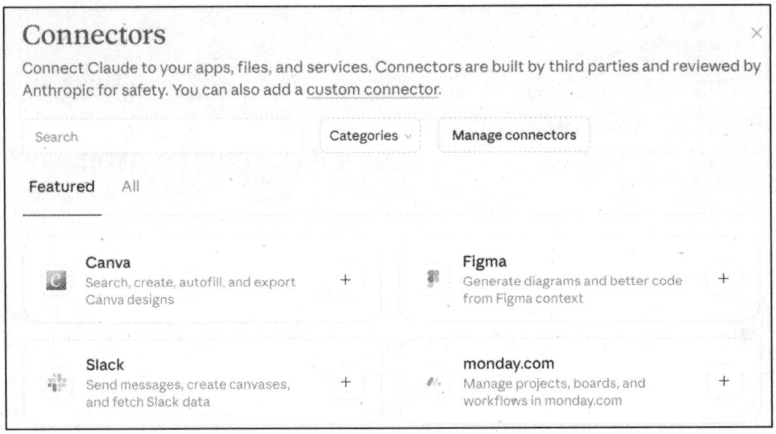

FIGURE 6-5: The Connectors directory.

When you find a Connector that fits your workflow, click its card. You'll see a detail page that lists what the Connector does, example use cases, and the permissions it needs. For example, if you click Figma, you see the detail page shown in Figure 6-6. The page provides example prompts, so you know what types of requests the Connector supports.

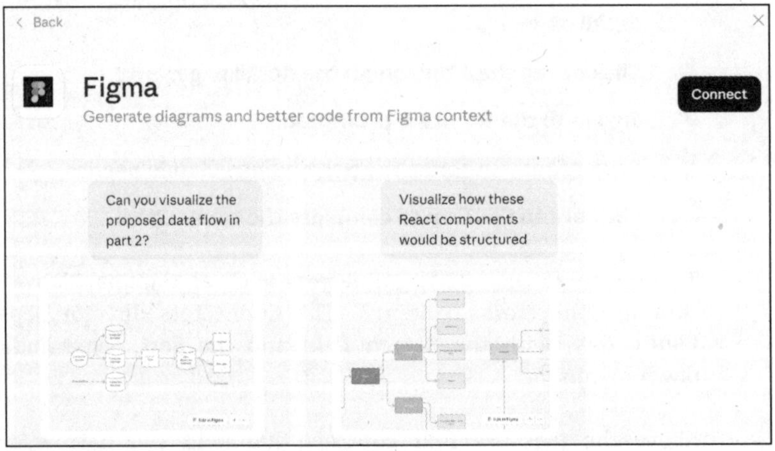

FIGURE 6-6: Each Connector's detail page spells out what you're getting, with example prompts and a Connect button.

To add a Connector to your account:

1. **Click or tap the Connector's + button.**
2. **Sign in to the service if prompted.**
3. **Authorize Claude to access specific data.**
4. **Confirm the connection.**

WARNING

When authorizing Connectors, review the permissions carefully. Grant Claude access to what it needs for your work, but don't share everything. Each Connector's detail page lists its read and write permissions. Some Connectors can take actions on your behalf (such as creating tasks or sending messages), so take an extra moment to review what you're granting before you click Confirm.

Working with a connected service

You can review and modify your active connections at any time. To manage your connected services, select Connectors from the sidebar (or click or tap the + button in chat). The screen shown in Figure 6-7 appears, listing your active connections. In this example, Figma has been connected and appears at the top of the Connectors list. You can click the Disconnect button or the three-dot menu in the upper right for additional options.

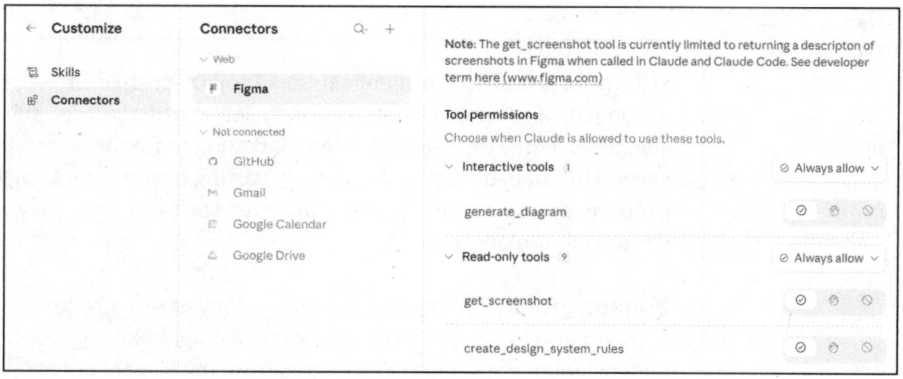

FIGURE 6-7: Your active connections.

From the Connectors screen, you have several options:

- **To disconnect a service:** Find the connected Connector and select the option to disconnect or revoke access. Claude will no longer be able to access that service.
- **To update permissions:** Open the Connector and look for the Tool Permissions section, where you can adjust what Claude can access without fully disconnecting.

REMEMBER

Connectors and Skills do different jobs. Skills teach Claude how to perform tasks (like building a formatted Word document). Connectors give Claude access to your external services (such as Google Drive files or Slack channels). Partner Skills often pair with their matching Connectors. The Skill teaches Claude how to work with a tool, and the Connector gives Claude access to that tool.

Blending Skills with Other Features

Skills produce better results when combined with Projects and Memory. (See Chapter 5 for details on setting up Projects and Memory.) Together, these three features create a workflow in which Claude understands your situation and produces output based on that understanding.

Combining Skills with Projects for better output

A Project gives Claude background knowledge about your work. Skills let Claude turn that knowledge into a polished deliverable. The combination means you skip the step of explaining your business every time you need a document. Here's a real-world case:

Situation: A real estate agent set up a Project for their brokerage that included branding guidelines, property listing descriptions, and their professional bio. Every time they needed marketing materials, they spent the first several minutes of each conversation pasting brand colors, taglines, and property details before Claude could even start working. They wanted to streamline the process.

Prompt: Inside their real estate Project, they asked "Create a PowerPoint presentation showcasing the Oak Street listing, following our brand guidelines and including the property highlights from my Project notes."

Claude's response: Claude combined Project knowledge with PowerPoint Skills to produce five slides: the brokerage's color scheme applied to headings, property photos referenced by description, key selling points drawn from the listing notes, and the agent's contact information pulled from their bio.

Why this worked: The Project stored an ongoing context that Claude could automatically reference. The agent did not paste brand guidelines or listing details into the prompt. They pointed Claude toward the relevant Project, and Claude assembled everything from the stored context.

Template: Inside a Project containing your business context, prompt "Create a [file type] for [specific item/client/event], following [reference to Project materials] and including [specific elements from your Project notes]."

You can apply the combination of a Project and a presentation Skill across many professional scenarios. A client Project paired with a document Skill create proposals, reports, and summaries that reference client-specific information stored in the Project. A team Project paired with a spreadsheet Skill build tracking documents using team data and conventions. A personal Project paired with a presentation Skill develop materials that reflect your ongoing work and preferences.

Projects provide the "what" (your background knowledge and context), and Skills give the "how" (the capability to create specific file formats). Combining them means Claude produces professional deliverables based on your situation rather than starting from a generic template.

Pairing Skills with Memory

The Memory feature enhances how the Skills feature works by carrying your preferences across conversations. When Claude remembers how you like things done, the documents it creates reflect those preferences automatically. (See Chapter 5 for details on the Memory feature.) Here's how that works in practice:

> **Situation:** A financial planner who tracked client interactions found that using Memory and Skills together saved significant setup time.
>
> **Prompt:** "Create an Excel template for tracking quarterly client reviews with columns for client name, portfolio performance, discussion topics, action items, and next review date."
>
> **Claude's response:** It produced a spreadsheet that included conditional formatting for overdue reviews (because Memory noted they valued visual organization), a separate tab for summary statistics (because Memory recorded their preference for data-driven reporting), and column widths optimized for readability.
>
> **Result:** The planner had not specified these preferences in the prompt. Memory supplied them automatically.
>
> **Why this worked:** The prompt specified the file type, the recurring task, and the specific columns needed. Memory then layered in preferences Claude had learned from previous conversations, visual organization style, and data reporting preferences without the planner having to mention them.
>
> **Template:** "Create a [file type] template for [recurring task] with columns/sections for [element 1], [element 2], [element 3], and [element 4]."

Skills, Projects, and Memory work as layers. Memory shapes Claude's general approach based on who you are. Projects provide a work context based on what you're doing. Skills determine what Claude can produce. All three inform the final deliverable.

REMEMBER

Memory works across all your conversations, while a Project's context stays within that Project. Use Memory for preferences that apply everywhere (like your preferred document formatting) and Projects for context that applies to specific work.

Taking Skills further

As you get more comfortable with Skills, you can take advantage of several advanced approaches that will increase their value. Here are several to consider:

- **Request multiple outputs at once.** A training coordinator prompted: "Create a Word document with the full training manual and a PowerPoint with the presentation version for facilitators." Claude produced both files in one response, maintaining consistency between them.
- **Revise Skill outputs.** After Claude creates a document, you can request changes without starting over. Prompt Claude to "Add a fourth column for quarterly projections" or "Move the pricing slide before the features slide," and Claude will modify the existing file. An interior designer regularly uses this approach, refining Project proposals through several rounds of edits in a single conversation.
- **Combine Skills with analysis.** You can ask Claude to analyze information and then produce a document based on that analysis. For example, a restaurant owner uploaded three months of sales data and prompted: "Review this data, identify the three most important trends, and create a presentation highlighting those trends with supporting charts." Claude analyzed the data, identified patterns, and created a PowerPoint presentation with visualizations.
- **Build reusable templates.** A project manager prompted: "Create an Excel template I can reuse for monthly status reports, with placeholder text showing what goes in each field and conditional formatting that highlights overdue items in red." Claude produced a reusable starting point rather than a one-time document.

Pay attention to what works well in your first few Skill-created documents and what needs manual adjustment. Over time, you'll develop prompts that produce output closer to your final needs, reducing the polish required after Claude delivers.

WARNING

The Skills feature produces files based on the information you provide. If your prompt contains inaccurate data or incomplete context, the document will reflect those gaps. Always review Skill output before sharing with clients or stakeholders, just as you would review any draft.

Skills improve your workflow most when you treat them as a starting point for professional documents rather than a replacement for your judgment. The time you save on formatting and structure gives you more time to focus on the content and decisions that require your expertise.

Start simple. Ask Claude for one document type you create regularly, such as a weekly report, client proposal, or meeting agenda. Once you see the quality of the first output, you'll quickly spot other documents worth automating.

2 Mastering Prompting

IN THIS PART . . .

Let a good template do the heavy lifting for you.

Learn to read Claude's responses and adjust on the fly.

Get better results every time.

IN THIS CHAPTER

» Understanding why templates save time

» Using ready-made templates for writing, learning, and analysis

» Customizing templates for your specific needs

Chapter 7 Starting with Proven Prompt Templates

A consultant spent three hours crafting the perfect prompt to help their client understand market trends. The next week, they faced a similar task for a different client and had to start from scratch again.

After the fourth time rebuilding essentially the same prompt, they realized they needed a better approach. They began saving their successful prompts as templates with customizable parts marked in brackets. Now they adapt proven patterns in minutes instead of rebuilding from square one every time.

Templates transform prompting from an art into a reliable process. This chapter gives you copy-and-paste-ready templates organized by purpose. You also discover how to customize them and build your own template library.

Understanding Why You Should Use Templates

Templates are proven patterns that consistently produce good results because they include the elements Claude and other AI tools need to respond more accurately and efficiently.

Learning why templates beat starting from scratch

Starting with a blank prompt forces you to remember every technique you've learned about being specific, providing context, and requesting the right format. Templates handle the structure so you can focus on your needs and goals.

A financial advisor used to struggle with writing client update emails. They created a template asking Claude to write updates in their voice, highlighting specific achievements and ending with clear next steps. Now they can fill in client details and get personalized emails in seconds, instead of drafting each message from the ground up.

Templates also help you avoid common mistakes. When you build prompts from scratch, you might forget to specify the audience level, omit necessary context, or request output in a format that doesn't work for your purpose.

REMEMBER

Templates remind you what matters by including slots for essential information like audience, constraints, and desired outcome.

Starting with built-in conversation starters and going beyond them

When you open a new chat in Claude, you'll see buttons below the text input box: Write, Learn, Code, Life Stuff, and Claude's Choice, as shown in Figure 7-1.

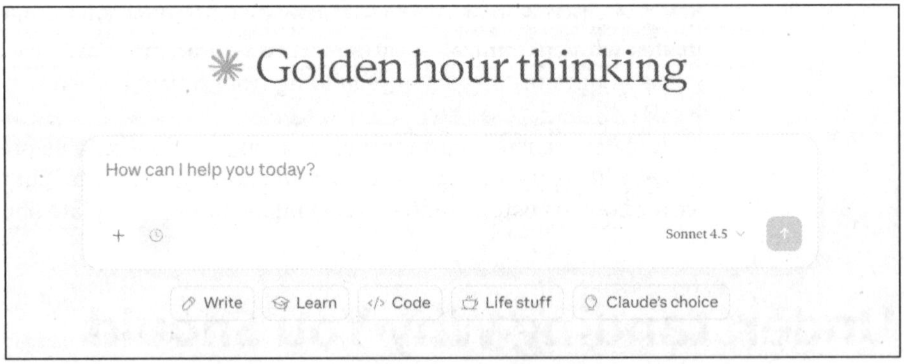

FIGURE 7-1: Claude's built-in conversation starter buttons.

TIP

If the starter buttons don't appear in your new chat, don't worry. You can just type your request directly in the text box. Claude responds just as well to direct input as to conversation starters.

Select any category to find suggested prompts. These built-in starters help you begin conversations quickly. Here's an example of using a starter:

Situation: A marketing consultant needed help writing product descriptions for a quarterly report.

First prompt: The consultant opened a new conversation with Claude, selected the Write category button, and browsed the suggested prompts. They then selected Write Product Descriptions, as shown in Figure 7-2.

Claude's response: It produced solid generic content covering standard elements — features, benefits, and use cases. The structure worked fine, but the descriptions felt applicable to any product in any industry.

Second prompt: The consultant tried again with specifics. "Write product descriptions for project management software sold to small business teams. Focus on time-saving benefits, ease of use for non-technical users, and ROI within 90 days. Our audience is small business owners who currently use spreadsheets and email to coordinate work."

Claude's response: This time, it targeted their exact situation. Instead of generic features, it highlighted visual task boards and automated reminders. Instead of vague benefits, it quantified hours saved per week and showed concrete workflow improvements.

Result: The specificity resulted in descriptions that customers could connect with.

Why this worked: The built-in conversation starters provide templates that accelerate your work. They show you what kinds of tasks Claude handles well. They demonstrate that you don't need to invent every prompt from scratch. But they also reveal why customization matters. A prompt that works for everyone works perfectly for no one.

TIP

Use the conversation starters when you're exploring what Claude can do or when you need quick inspiration. Then level up by adapting those generic templates to your context, audience, and goals. The specificity transforms an okay response into exactly what you need.

FIGURE 7-2: Prompts for the Write category button.

Building a personal pattern library

You'll find that certain types of requests come up repeatedly in your work. A project manager noticed they kept asking Claude to break down complex initiatives. They saved their best version as a template. Now, when new projects arrive, they adapt their proven pattern instead of inventing a prompt each time and wondering what they forgot to include. Your template library grows naturally as you identify patterns in your work.

TIP

Start with templates from this chapter, and then save your own successful prompts when you notice you're solving the same type of problem multiple times. Mark with brackets the parts that change, and you've created a reusable tool you can refine over time.

Customizing versus using as is

Templates work best when you adapt them to your specific situation. The brackets show you exactly what to customize. The following is an example:

Template: "Write [content type] about [topic] for [audience]."

Situation: A marketing manager needed to write content for an email campaign.

Prompt: "Write a promotional email about our new project management software for small business owners struggling with team coordination."

Why this worked: Because the manager was specific when replacing the bracketed sections, Claude's output was immediately useful with little editing.

REMEMBER

Some templates need minimal customization while others benefit from detailed adaptation. Simple tasks might need only the bracketed items filled in.

TIP

When creating a template for a complex task, add constraints, examples, or additional context beyond the basic template structure. In this way, Claude can make more precise choices instead of guessing your preferences.

The templates in this chapter are organized by purpose: writing, learning, analyzing, and planning. We start with the writing templates because they're the most commonly used and easiest to understand.

Reviewing Copy-and-Use Writing Templates

Writing templates help you create and improve written content faster. The four patterns in this section will handle most writing tasks you encounter: creating content from scratch, improving existing text, changing styles or formats, and adjusting length.

Generating content for specific audiences

The following basic template works for any writing task that requires content created from scratch:

Template: "Using [tone] write [content type] about [topic] for [audience]." Replace [content type] with what you need (email, blog post, product description, announcement), [topic] with your subject, and [audience] with who will read it. The more specific your audience description, the better Claude can match the right tone and approach.

Situation: A nonprofit director needed to create fundraising appeal letters but isn't a natural writer.

Prompt: "Write a fundraising letter about our literacy program for donors who previously contributed but haven't given in over a year."

Claude's response: It created a warm, personal letter that acknowledged their past support, shared recent program successes, and made a clear case for renewed giving. Claude's email began, "Your support two years ago helped 47 adults learn to read. Sarah, one of our students, now reads bedtime stories to her children every night."

Result: After the director customized a few details, the letter was ready for mailing.

Some other options:

- **For technical writing, add expertise level:** "Write a tutorial about setting up two-factor authentication for people who can use email but aren't technical."
- **For persuasive writing, include the goal:** "Write a proposal about implementing flexible work schedules for executives concerned about productivity."

Improving and refining existing text

When you have existing content that needs enhancement, the following template helps you specify the improvements you want:

Template: "Improve this by making it [qualities]."

Situation: A sales professional wrote a product pitch that felt flat.

Prompt: They shared it with Claude along with the prompt, "Improve this by making it more conversational, benefit-focused, and specific about ROI."

Claude's response: Claude restructured their pitch to use natural language, turned feature descriptions into customer benefits, and added concrete examples of cost savings.

Result: The revision took two minutes instead of two hours of struggling with multiple drafts.

Following are some common qualities to request:

- Concise
- Professional
- Conversational
- Persuasive
- Specific

You can combine qualities, such as "Improve this by making it more concise and more action-oriented." You can also specify what to preserve: "Improve this by making it more professional while keeping the friendly tone." Two additional options:

- **For emails:** "Improve this by making it more diplomatic and solution-focused."
- **For marketing:** "Improve this by making it more benefit-driven and less jargon-heavy."

Transforming content between different styles

Sometimes you don't need to improve the content; you need to adapt it for a different audience or purpose. The following template helps you adapt existing content for different contexts or audiences without starting over:

Template: "Transform this from [style] to [style]."

Situation: An executive assistant wrote a detailed project update for their boss. Later, they needed to share the same information with the full team.

Prompt: Instead of rewriting everything, they asked Claude to "Transform this from an executive summary to a team update email."

Claude's response: It kept the key facts but shifted the tone from a high-level overview to practical details on next steps and individual responsibilities.

Common transformations you will encounter include:

- Formal to casual (or vice versa)
- Technical to plain language
- Long-form to bullet points
- Email to presentation
- First-person to third-person
- Past tense to present tense

Here are two examples:

- **For presentation prep:** "Transform this detailed report from paragraph form to slide bullets."
- **For audience adaptation:** "Transform this technical explanation from engineer language to customer language."

Adjusting length without losing meaning

Content created or transformed often needs length adjustments to fit your constraints. The following template helps you adjust without losing key content or adding fluff:

Template: "Expand this to [length]" or "Condense this to [length]."

Situation: A consultant wrote a 500-word client email with important recommendations. Their colleague pointed out that busy clients rarely read long emails.

Prompt: "Condense this to 150 words, keeping the three main recommendations and the cost estimate."

Claude's response: It extracted the essential points and delivered a focused message that clients would read.

Here are some other ways to adjust the length:

- **For expanding, specify what to add:** "Expand this to 800 words by adding examples for each point."
- **For condensing, specify what to keep:** "Condense this to 200 words, keeping the key benefits and the call to action."
- **For percentage:** "Condense this by 50 percent" or "Expand this by 30 percent."
- **For professional writing:** "Condense this email to three short paragraphs."
- **For presentations:** "Expand this slide concept into speaker notes of about 200 words."

Exploring Copy-and-Use Learning Templates

Learning templates transform Claude into a personal tutor. These upcoming four patterns help you understand complex topics at your level, compare unfamiliar concepts, master new skills step by step, and diagnose problems in your work. Whether you're learning for work or personal growth, these templates adapt to your starting knowledge.

Getting explanations tailored to your level

Most explanations online assume that you're a complete beginner or an expert, nothing in between. You end up bored by information you already know or lost in jargon you don't understand. The solution is telling Claude where your knowledge starts:

Template: "Explain [topic] like I'm someone who [your knowledge level]."

Situation: A bookstore owner needed to understand blockchain for a customer discussion group. Technical articles lost their clarity in jargon but beginner explanations felt patronizing.

Prompt: "Explain blockchain like I'm someone who is comfortable with online banking and smartphone apps but hasn't studied computer science."

Claude's response: It used familiar analogies from their existing knowledge (shared documents, receipt tracking) and avoided technical terms they didn't need.

Result: Within five minutes, the bookstore owner understood enough to facilitate an informed discussion with their customers.

Here are some common descriptions that include knowledge level:

- "Like I'm five." Extremely simple.
- "Like I'm [profession]." Uses domain knowledge.
- "Like I'm comfortable with [related topic] but new to this."
- "Like I have [specific background]."

For specific topics, consider these:

- **For technical topics:** "Explain machine learning like I'm a marketer who understands analytics but hasn't programmed."
- **For complex processes:** "Explain how stock options work like I'm an employee receiving them for the first time."

Comparing concepts and highlighting differences

Understanding new concepts often requires seeing how they differ from similar things. When you're trying to choose between options or understand how concepts differ, most explanations give you separate descriptions of each thing, leaving you to figure out the comparison yourself. You waste time going back and forth, and you could miss the distinctions that matter most. Instead, you can ask Claude to compare them directly, focusing on the specific aspects you care about:

Template: "Compare [A] and [B], focusing on [what matters to you]."

Situation: A small business owner needed to choose between an LLC and an S Corp structure. Generic comparison articles covered many factors they didn't care about, while skipping the three that mattered to their situation.

Prompt: "Compare LLC and S Corp, focusing on tax implications, setup complexity, and ongoing compliance requirements for a single-owner service business making $150K annually."

Claude's response: It delivered the comparison they needed to make an informed decision.

Here are some other comparisons you can use:

- **For product decisions:** "Compare standing desks and desk converters, focusing on cost, space requirements, and setup difficulty."
- **For methodology decisions:** "Compare agile and waterfall project management, focusing on team size requirements, timeline flexibility, and documentation needs."
- **Add your constraints to get more relevant comparisons**: "Compare [A] and [B], focusing on [aspects] for [your situation]."

Mastering skills with step-by-step guidance

Often, online tutorials either move too fast or skip steps. You're left pausing, rewinding, or jumping around, trying to find the right pace. You can tell Claude your starting point and what you want to accomplish, and it creates a tutorial that moves at the speed you need:

Template: "Teach me [skill] step by step, assuming I [your starting knowledge level]."

Situation: A consultant needed to learn about pivot tables but feels intimidated by the feature.

Prompt: "Teach me Excel pivot tables step by step, assuming I'm comfortable with basic Excel functions but have never used its advanced features."

Claude's response: It broke the process into small steps, explained what each step accomplished, and provided practice exercises after each section.

Result: The consultant mastered pivot tables in an afternoon instead of continuing to avoid them.

Some other ways to vary the template include the following:

- **Add your level:** "Teach me [skill] step by step, assuming I'm [your level]."
- **Specify your goal:** "Teach me [skill] step by step so I can [specific goal]."
- **For software skills:** "Teach me mail merge in Word step by step so I can send personalized letters to 50 customers."
- **For practical skills:** "Teach me basic photography composition step by step, assuming I just got my first good camera."

Diagnosing problems and getting expert fixes

When you need feedback, vague comments such as "It needs work" or "Something feels off" don't help. You're left guessing what to change. The following template gets you specific, actionable feedback you can implement immediately. You tell Claude what you created and what it's for, and it tells you what's not working and how to fix it:

Template: "What's wrong with this [content], and how do I fix it for [specific purpose]?"

Situation: A job seeker kept sending resumes without getting interviews.

Prompt: They shared their resume with Claude and asked, "What's wrong with this resume, and how do I fix it for a project management position?"

Claude's response: It identified that their bullets described responsibilities instead of achievements, used passive voice, and buried their relevant experience.

Result: The job seeker spent an hour implementing the specific fixes and started getting interview requests.

The template works even better when you specify what you're using the content for:

- **Add context about intended use:** "What's wrong with this [content] and how do I fix it for [purpose]?"
- **For writing:** "What's wrong with this email and how do I fix it to sound more professional but still friendly?"
- **For presentations:** "What's wrong with this slide deck and how do I fix it for an audience of potential investors?"

Looking at Copy-and-Use Analysis Templates

Analysis templates help you extract insights from content, data, or situations. The following four patterns find what matters, highlight key points, and help you make informed decisions quickly.

Analyzing content against specific criteria

When you need to evaluate content, generic analysis wastes your time with observations you don't care about. You get paragraphs about tone and structure when all you want to know is whether specific requirements were met. If you tell Claude what criteria matter, it can focus its analysis on those factors only:

Template: "Analyze [content] for [specific criteria]."

Situation: A hiring manager received 50 applications for one position. Reading every cover letter thoroughly would take hours.

Prompt: "Analyze these cover letters for specific examples of project management experience, team leadership, and problem-solving."

Claude's response: It quickly identified the candidates who provided concrete examples versus those who made generic claims.

Result: The manager spent their time interviewing qualified candidates instead of reading vague applications.

Some other alternatives:

- **For business documents:** "Analyze this proposal for cost-benefit clarity, implementation timeline, and risk mitigation."
- **For written content:** "Analyze this article for main arguments, supporting evidence quality, and potential biases."
- **For customer feedback:** "Analyze these reviews for common complaints, feature requests, and praise patterns."

Finding insights in data and documents

When you're working with large documents or datasets, reading everything to find what you need wastes hours. You skim through pages of mostly irrelevant information, hoping you don't miss the important parts. Instead, tell Claude exactly what you're looking for, and it will extract just those insights from the larger content:

Template: "Find [specific insights] in this [data/document]."

Situation: An accountant received a 40-page financial report but only needed information about three specific cost centers.

Prompt: "Find budget variances, unusual expenses, and trend changes in this quarterly report for the marketing, IT, and facilities departments."

Claude's response: It pulled exactly the information the accountant needed for their executive summary.

Result: The task took five minutes instead of an hour of reading and note-taking.

Here are some alternatives:

- **For research:** "Find key findings, methodology limitations, and recommendations in this study."
- **For contracts:** "Find termination clauses, payment terms, and renewal conditions in this agreement."
- **For meeting notes:** "Find action items, decision points, and unresolved questions in these meeting notes."

Summarizing while highlighting what matters

Most summaries treat every point as equally important, forcing you to read the entire summary to find what matters to you. You end up with a shorter version of the same problem. You have too much information, with no clear priorities. If you tell Claude what aspects you care about most, it can create a summary that highlights those elements while still providing context:

> **Template:** "Summarize [content], highlighting [what matters to you]."
>
> **Situation:** A product manager needed to brief executives on customer feedback from multiple channels.
>
> **Prompt:** "Summarize this customer feedback, highlighting feature requests mentioned more than five times, critical bugs, and positive comments about recent changes."
>
> **Claude's response:** It created a focused summary that executives could read in two minutes while preserving the details that would drive product decisions.

Here are some other prompts to consider:

- **For articles:** "Summarize this research, highlighting practical applications for small businesses."
- **For reports:** "Summarize this market analysis, highlighting threats to our current strategy."
- **For long emails:** "Summarize this email thread, highlighting decisions made, pending questions, and my action items."

Evaluating options based on your priorities

When you're comparing options, each source emphasizes different features and benefits, making a side-by-side comparison nearly impossible. You spend hours switching between tabs, trying to remember what the first option offered while reading about the fifth. Instead, give Claude your criteria and all the possibilities, and it will evaluate everything against the same factors, showing you which choice best matches what you care about:

Template: "Evaluate [options] based on [your specific factors]."

Situation: A small business owner needed to choose an accounting software package from eight options. Each vendor site emphasizes different features, making comparison difficult.

Prompt: "Evaluate these accounting software options based on cost for businesses under 10 employees, ease of use for non-accountants, and integration with QuickBooks data."

Claude's response: It created a clear comparison showing which solutions met the requirements and which didn't.

Result: The business owner made a confident choice in 20 minutes, rather than spending days confused by vendor marketing.

Here are some other uses:

- **For vendor selection:** "Evaluate these CRM platforms based on cost, ease of implementation, and email marketing capabilities."
- **For strategy decisions:** "Evaluate these market expansion options based on required investment, time to profitability, and risk level."
- **For hiring decisions:** "Evaluate these candidates based on relevant experience, culture fit indicators, and salary expectations."

Viewing Copy-and-Use Planning Templates

Planning templates help you break down goals, organize projects, and create actionable steps. The following four patterns make planning faster and more thorough.

Building action plans that account for constraints

Most planning advice assumes you have unlimited time, budget, and resources. You get beautiful strategies that fall apart the moment they hit your real-world limitations. If you tell Claude upfront about your constraints, such as time, money, or team size, it can build a plan that works within those boundaries instead of pretending they don't exist:

Template: "Create a plan to [goal], considering [these constraints]."

Situation: A consultant wanted to build their email list but has limited time and budget.

Prompt: "Create a plan to grow my email list to 1,000 subscribers in six months, considering that I have only three hours weekly, no advertising budget, and my audience is small business owners."

Claude's response: It developed a realistic plan focused on LinkedIn content, strategic partnerships, and a simple lead magnet.

Result: The plan worked within the consultant's constraints instead of suggesting tactics that required resources they didn't have.

A *lead magnet* is free content (such as a checklist, template, or guide) that you offer in exchange for someone's email address. It attracts potential customers by giving them something valuable upfront.

Common constraints include time available, budget limits, team size, technical skills, existing resources, and deadlines. In addition, consider these:

- **For professional goals:** "Create a plan to improve my public speaking skills, considering that I work full-time and live in a small town with limited networking events."
- **For business goals:** "Create a plan to launch a new service line, considering our current team capacity and the need to maintain existing client work."

Breaking big projects into manageable steps

When you face a big project, it's easy to feel paralyzed when you can't see the path from start to finish. You know what you want to accomplish, but not what to do first, second, or third. If you describe your overall goal to Claude, it can break the work down into specific, actionable steps that you can tackle one at a time:

> **Template:** "Break down [project] into actionable steps."
>
> **Situation:** A new manager needed to implement a performance review system but doesn't know where to start.
>
> **Prompt:** "Break down creating a fair, consistent performance review process into actionable steps for a team of 12 people who have never had formal reviews."
>
> **Claude's response:** It provided a step-by-step plan starting with researching review templates, drafting criteria with team input, training managers, and scheduling review meetings. Each step was specific enough for the manager to implement.

Some additional ideas:

- **Add context for better steps:** "Break down [project] into actionable steps for [your situation]."
- **For personal projects:** "Break down getting a professional website live into actionable steps for someone with no web development experience."
- **For business projects:** "Break down implementing a customer feedback system into actionable steps for a service business with 200 clients."

Generating targeted ideas on demand

When brainstorming alone, most people quickly exhaust their first few obvious ideas and get stuck. You know you need more options, but your brain keeps circling back to the same concepts. If you tell Claude how many ideas you need and what they're for, it will generate a list of options you can choose from, adapt, or use as springboards to even better ideas:

Template: "Generate [number] ideas for [specific purpose]."

Situation: A community group wanted ideas to raise funds but keeps cycling through the same three tired ideas.

Prompt: "Generate 15 ideas for fundraising events that work for a small town with 5,000 residents and appeal to families."

Claude's response: It suggested options the group hadn't considered, including local business sponsorships, virtual events, and seasonal activities.

Result: The group chose three ideas from the list and exceeded their fund-raising goal.

TIP

Ask for more ideas than you need so you have real choices. Ten ideas give you options to evaluate. Three ideas force you to use something that might not fit.

Some other possibilities:

- **For content creation:** "Generate 20 ideas for blog posts that help small business owners understand social media marketing."
- **For business development:** "Generate 10 ideas for partnership opportunities between our bookstore and other local businesses."
- **For personal goals:** "Generate 15 ideas for side projects that use my graphic design skills and require less than five hours weekly."

Developing templates for recurring tasks

When you perform the same type of task repeatedly, such as writing weekly reports, client onboarding emails, or project kickoff documents, you waste time reinventing the structure each time. You either start from scratch or dig through old files, hoping to find a good example to copy.

If you describe the task you do regularly, Claude will create a reusable template with clear placeholders showing exactly what to customize each time:

Template: "Build a template for [recurring task]."

Situation: A sales manager sent similar proposal emails dozens of times with slight variations.

Prompt: "Build a template for proposal follow-up emails that I can customize with client name, product discussed, key benefits mentioned in our call, and next meeting date."

Claude's response: It created a template with clear bracketed sections for each variable.

Result: Now the manager sends personalized follow-ups in 60 seconds instead of 10 minutes.

Some other possibilities:

- **For communication:** "Build a template for project status updates that I can customize with project name, completed milestones, current challenges, and next week's priorities."
- **For documentation:** "Build a template for client onboarding checklists that I can customize with client industry, team size, and specific services purchased."
- **For planning:** "Build a template for weekly priorities that I can customize with current projects, urgent items, and upcoming deadlines."

Troubleshooting Template Results

Templates work consistently, but they're not magic formulas that guarantee perfect results every time. Sometimes you fill in the brackets correctly and still get responses that miss the mark. When that happens, the problem usually lies in one of three areas: your variable choices, missing context, or output specifications. Here's an example:

Situation: A project manager used the "Break down [project] into actionable steps" template for launching a new client portal.

Prompt: "Break down launching our client portal into actionable steps."

Claude's response: It provided generic steps that could apply to any software launch. The manager realized that the template didn't know anything specific about the situation.

Second prompt: "Break down launching our client portal into actionable steps for a team of three people with no developer, working with our existing WordPress site, targeting fifty clients in the first month."

Claude's response: The second response gave the manager realistic, specific steps they could follow.

The bracketed variables are where templates get their power, but vague variables produce vague results. When a template fails, check what you put in the brackets first. "Write a blog post about marketing" gives Claude almost nothing to work with. "Write a blog post about email marketing for small business owners who feel overwhelmed by automation tools" gives Claude direction. The more specific your variables, the more useful your results.

Sometimes the template itself is fine, but you need to add constraints it doesn't include:

Situation: A consultant used "Generate 15 ideas for [purpose]" and asked for client retention strategies. Claude provided 15 ideas, but many required resources that the consultant didn't have. Adding one sentence fixed everything.

Prompt: "Generate 15 ideas for client retention strategies that require no additional budget and less than two hours weekly to implement." The constraint turned theoretical suggestions into practical options.

Other times, the output format needs adjustment:

Situation: A sales professional used a writing template and got three long paragraphs when they needed five bullet points for a presentation slide. They didn't need a different template; they needed to add the output format.

Prompt: "Format the response as five concise bullet points, each under 15 words." Templates give you structure, but you control the details.

When you're disappointed by template results, don't abandon templates or try a different approach. Instead, examine:

- What you put in the brackets
- What constraints you didn't mention
- Whether you specified the output format you need

Small adjustments to these three elements usually transform weak results into what you need.

REMEMBER

The templates in this chapter handle the most common prompting tasks. Start using them immediately instead of building prompts from scratch.

TIP

As you work with these patterns, you'll discover which ones you use most often and start creating your own variations. Save your successful customizations to build a personal template library that makes working with Claude faster and more effective every day.

IN THIS CHAPTER

» Reading responses efficiently

» Using regenerate (retry) strategically

» Building productive conversations

Chapter 8

Understanding and Evaluating Claude's Responses

Getting a response from Claude is just the beginning. Knowing whether that response solves your problem, and what to do if it doesn't, makes the difference between frustration and success. Many people treat Claude like a search engine. They ask a question, get an answer, and stop. However, Claude works better as a conversation partner.

This chapter shows you how to evaluate responses, spot the difference between good answers and confident-sounding mistakes, and turn good responses into great ones. The tips in this chapter help you turn Claude from a one-time answer machine into a problem-solving tool.

Reading Claude's Responses Effectively

Claude structures responses to make information easy to find and use. Understanding these patterns helps you extract exactly what you need, whether you're scanning for a quick answer or working through detailed instructions.

Understanding how Claude formats answers

Claude adapts formatting to match what you need. Table 8-1 shows what the different Claude formats indicate.

TABLE 8-1 What Claude Formats Mean

Claude Formatting	What It Means
Bullet points	Lists of options: you choose what works for you
Numbered steps	Step-by-step instructions to follow in order
Paragraphs with section breaks	Analysis or detailed explanations
Tables	Comparisons to examine side-by-side
Bold text	Key terms and conclusions; remember this
Section breaks	Transition to a new topic
White space	Visual boundaries between separate ideas

Once you recognize these patterns, you can extract and navigate information faster.

Following code and technical instructions

When Claude provides code or technical instructions, scan the entire response before starting. Look for:

- Prerequisites mentioned upfront (for example, "requires admin permissions")
- Explanatory text before code blocks
- Comments within code
- Notes on common variations (for example, "On Windows, you'll need")
- Error-handling tips

Reading through the entire response once before starting helps you gather requirements and understand the overall process.

REMEMBER

Technical responses often include variations. "If you're using Version 2, do this instead," or "On Windows, you'll need this extra step." These notes show what's flexible and what's required, which helps when something doesn't work as expected.

Knowing When You Got a Good Answer

Not every response hits the mark perfectly. Learning to evaluate Claude's answers helps you differentiate between responses that solve your problem and ones that need refinement.

Checking for completeness and accuracy

A complete answer addresses all parts of your question. If you asked three questions, you should see three distinct answers. Missing pieces signal that you need to follow up with additional prompts.

Look for responses that address all parts of your question, match your specific situation (not generic scenarios), include concrete actionable information, acknowledge your constraints and context, and provide specific examples or steps you can implement.

REMEMBER

Look for concrete, actionable information rather than vague platitudes. "Improve your marketing" won't help much but "Create a weekly email newsletter featuring customer success stories" gives you something specific you can implement.

TIP

You have a good answer when the response directly solves your problem. If you find yourself asking "but what about . . . ." multiple times while reading, you haven't received a sufficient answer yet. Trust this instinct, which signals gaps that need filling.

Here's what happens when you start too broad:

Situation: A small business owner wanted to know how to improve customer retention.

First prompt: "How can I improve customer retention?"

Claude's response: Build stronger relationships with customers, create a loyalty program, improve your customer service, and stay in regular contact.

Second prompt: "I run an independent bookstore in Portland specializing in literary fiction and poetry. My customers are mostly 35-55, well-educated, and value community. What are three specific, actionable ways I could increase customer retention that fit my customer base and specialty?"

Claude's response:

1. Host monthly author readings featuring debut literary fiction writers — this builds community around discovery.
2. Create a "First Editions" subscription box ($30/month) with a signed debut novel, poetry chapbook, and curator notes explaining why you chose each book.
3. Start a book club with a 15 percent member discount on all purchases and quarterly special events.

Why this worked: The specificity about the person's specialty, customer demographics, and what they value meant Claude could suggest tactics that matched the situation rather than generic bookstore advice. The specificity made it immediately useful.

Template: "I [run/manage/work with] [specific type of business/situation] in [location], specializing in [specialty]. My [customers/users/audience] are mostly [demographics] who value [what matters to them]. What are [number] specific, actionable ways I could [goal] that fit my [customer base/situation] and [specialty/constraints]?"

Verifying facts and claims

Recent events or rapidly changing topics need verification. When you see dates, statistics, or current-event references, cross-check them to know whether they'll affect important decisions. (See Chapter 17 for more about accessing current information.)

TIP

Create a verification strategy based on the stakes and time sensitivity. For critical business decisions, verify key facts before acting. For casual learning or brainstorming, verification can wait or might not be necessary. You don't need to verify everything. Save your effort for what matters.

Spotting confident-sounding mistakes

Claude presents information clearly and directly, which sometimes masks uncertainty. A confidently worded response may not be accurate. Watch for answers that seem overly specific when you asked general questions, or generic responses when you provided detailed context.

Red flags include responses that:

- » Contradict themselves internally
- » Have suspiciously round numbers for specific statistics
- » Include details that seem oddly convenient for your question
- » Provide answers that give you what you want to hear without caveats
- » Jump from premise to conclusion without showing the connection
- » Contain inconsistencies across multiple responses to similar questions

If Claude gives you what you want to hear without caveats, double-check it. Real answers usually include nuance. When something feels off, trust your instinct. If an answer contradicts your understanding or seems to miss important nuances you're aware of, investigate further.

TIP

When answers seem suspiciously specific or convenient, use this template: "How did you arrive at [specific claim]? Can you explain your reasoning?" or "What assumptions are you making about [unclear aspect]?"

Understanding Claude's knowledge cutoff

As of this writing, Claude's training data has a cutoff date in early-to-mid 2025 depending on the model. Information about events or changes after that date won't appear in responses unless you provide it. The cutoff strongly affects current events, recent product releases, evolving technologies, and recent regulations. It minimally affects historical information, established concepts, and fundamental principles.

REMEMBER

To find the current cutoff at any time, simply ask Claude: "What is your knowledge cutoff date?" Claude will give you the exact date.

If your question includes *current*, *latest*, or *recent*, the cutoff probably matters. If you need current information, provide recent developments in your prompt. Copy a news article, share recent statistics, or describe new features. Alternatively, use search features available in all plans to get up-to-date details.

Using Regenerate and Revision Strategically

The regenerate (retry) icon, shown in Figure 8-1, isn't just a "try again and hope for a better answer" option. Used strategically, it becomes a powerful tool for exploring different approaches and refining responses. See Chapter 2 for details about using the regenerate (retry) icon.

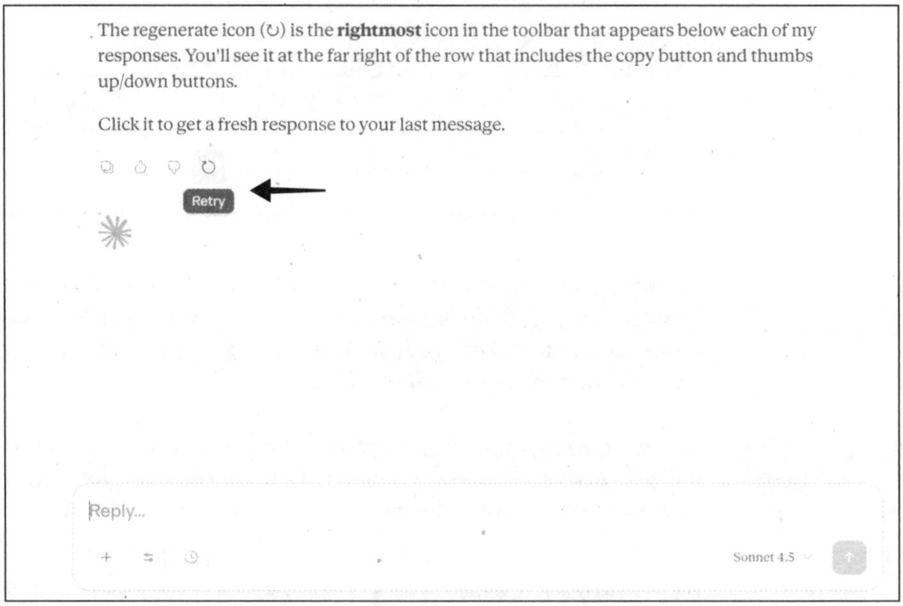

FIGURE 8-1: The regenerate icon.

Using retry effectively

Regenerate works best when Claude understands your request, but the execution falls short. Maybe the tone feels too formal when you wanted casual, or the explanation stays too high-level when you needed practical details.

Use regenerate when the tone or style is off but the content is right; you want to see alternative approaches to the same problem; you got most of what you wanted and might get closer with another try; or you want to compare different valid solutions before choosing.

REMEMBER

Don't use regenerate when three regenerations have missed what you need; rewrite your prompt instead. Claude fundamentally misunderstood what you're asking for, so add more context and clarify your request with more detail.

Regenerate shines when you want to see alternative approaches. Different regenerations might emphasize different aspects or suggest other solutions. One version might focus on quick wins while another emphasizes long-term strategy.

Here's how a single prompt can miss the mark when you're juggling multiple stakeholder needs:

Situation: A team leader needed to announce a tool change to the team. However, different people in the organization cared about various things: Some wanted efficiency, others wanted ease of use, and leadership wanted to control costs.

First prompt: "Write a professional email explaining to my team why we're changing the project management tools."

First regeneration request: Emphasize efficiency gains and time savings for team members.

Second regeneration request: Focus on collaboration benefits and easier communication.

Third regeneration request: Highlight cost savings and return on investment.

The team leader combined elements, using collaboration language from version two for the team message and adding cost information from version three when presenting to leadership.

Why this worked: The regeneration strategy let them explore different framings and then cherry-pick the strongest elements that were relevant to multiple audiences.

How to use this: Generate two or three versions of content when you need to speak to different audiences, and then combine the strongest elements rather than choosing just one version.

Asking for specific changes

Instead of regenerating and hoping, tell Claude exactly what needs to change. Specific revision requests consistently outperform regeneration for targeted improvements.

You can request the following:

- **Length adjustments:** "Make this more concise." "Expand the second section with more detail."
- **Style changes:** "Rewrite this in a friendlier tone." "Make this more formal."
- **Technical depth:** "Add more technical detail." "Simplify this for non-technical readers."
- **Structural changes:** "Reorganize with the most important point first."
- **Focus shifts:** "Focus more on practical implementation and less on theory."

Claude includes the context of what it just provided when working with these new prompts. However, you can combine specific requests with parts you want to keep. "Keep the structure but make the examples more concrete," or "Maintain the technical accuracy but explain it more simply." Hybrid requests preserve what works while fixing what doesn't.

Here's an example of how that scenario unfolds:

Situation: The team leader reviewed Claude's draft email and noticed a specific problem: It was too formal for their casual team culture.

Revision request: "This is good, but too formal for my team. Make it more conversational while keeping the key information. Also, add one concrete example of how the new tool will help with our biggest pain point: tracking who's responsible for what."

Claude's response:

"Hey team,

Quick update on the project tracking tool we're rolling out next week. I know change can be annoying, but this one's going to save us headaches.

You know how we're always asking 'who's handling the client demo?' or scrolling through endless Slack threads to figure out task ownership? This tool makes assignments visible to everyone in one place. You'll see immediately who owns what, no detective work required. The training session is on Tuesday at 2 pm. See you there!"

Why this worked: The targeted request, change in tone, and specific example delivered exactly what the team leader needed in one exchange instead of multiple regenerations. Claude kept the essential information while transforming the formality level and adding the requested concrete pain-point example.

Template: "[Keep/Change] [specific element] but [make it more/add/remove] [specific change]. Also [additional specific request]."

REMEMBER

You can stack multiple changes into a single request: "Make this shorter, more casual, and add one real-world example per section." Claude handles multiple revision criteria simultaneously.

Combining the best parts of multiple attempts

Sometimes your best answer comes from multiple responses. One regeneration nails the introduction but fumbles the conclusion. Another version has perfect examples but misses the key context. You don't have to choose one. Instead, you can combine the best elements.

For example, ask Claude to merge specific parts: "Take the introduction from your first response and combine it with the detailed examples from your second response." Point out which pieces work best: "The examples from response 2 were perfect, but I prefer the structure from response 1." This approach works especially well for complex requests where different attempts excel at other aspects.

The regenerate feature shines when you want to explore different creative approaches without starting from scratch:

Situation: A marketing manager needed website copy for a product launch. They generated three versions to explore different angles. Version 1 had the perfect headline that captured attention. Version 2 had better benefits descriptions with specific outcomes. Version 3 had the best call to action with urgency and clarity.

Regeneration request: "Combine the headline from version 1, the benefits section from version 2, and the call to action from version 3."

Why this worked: The result was stronger than any single version. Each attempt contributed its strongest element to a cohesive final piece.

Template: "Combine [specific element] from [version X], [specific element] from [version Y], and [specific element] from [version Z]."

Building Effective Multi-Turn Conversations

The real power of working with Claude emerges through conversation. Each exchange builds on previous ones, letting you refine ideas, explore variations, and dig deeper into topics.

Following up to add depth

Initial responses often provide solid foundations that need development. Your first answer might outline a strategy. Follow up to flesh out specific tactics. Ask for concrete examples. Each layer adds practical value.

Effective follow-ups reference what came before. Here are some examples:

- "In your third point about budget allocation, can you break down the percentages?"
- "Tell me more about the testing phase you mentioned."

- "How does this fit with the overall timeline?"
- "Take that marketing strategy and show me what it looks like for a small business."

These follow-ups work because they reference what came before rather than starting afresh. This specificity helps Claude build on previous responses rather than starting over. You're having a conversation, not issuing disconnected commands.

The power of layered follow-ups is that each response benefits from everything that came before. By the third or fourth exchange, Claude has a rich understanding of your context, constraints, and goals. Responses become more targeted as you add layers.

Catching and correcting misunderstandings early

When Claude misunderstands something, address it immediately. Letting misunderstandings persist means subsequent responses build on faulty assumptions. One quick correction saves multiple rounds of increasingly divergent responses.

Be specific about what's wrong. For example:

- "Actually, I'm targeting enterprise customers, not consumers."
- "I need this for internal communication, not marketing materials."
- "This project has a $5K budget, not $50K."
- "I wasn't specific enough. I need this for mobile devices specifically."

These clarifications reset Claude's understanding without requiring you to rewrite your entire request. You'll spot misunderstandings quickly when responses feel off-target or include irrelevant suggestions, such as when Claude gives you advice for beginners when you're an expert, or suggests consumer strategies when you're B2B. Trust this instinct and correct course immediately.

Sometimes you'll realize that you weren't clear in your original request. Just clarify now. "Let me add more context. This is for a nonprofit, not a commercial business," or "I wasn't specific enough. This needs to work on mobile devices specifically."

Managing context in long conversations

Long conversations accumulate helpful context. New exchanges build on this foundation without requiring you to repeat information.

However, extremely long conversations can become unwieldy. If you find yourself constantly reminding Claude of earlier details or responses start feeling generic despite extensive prior context, the conversation might have become too sprawling.

TIP

You can refresh context without starting over. Summarize key points from earlier in the conversation and restate your current focus: "To recap: we established that the target audience is young professionals, the tone should be casual, and the focus is on the mobile experience. Now I want to explore the onboarding flow specifically." This mid-conversation reset maintains useful history while refocusing attention.

Use Projects (covered in Chapter 5) for work that spans multiple conversations. Projects maintain context across sessions, so you don't lose accumulated understanding when you start a new chat. Note that Projects are available on paid plans (Pro, Max, Team, and Enterprise) and in limited form on Free (up to five Projects).

Continuing versus starting afresh

Continue the conversation when building on previous work or iterating on something specific, when exploring related questions within the same context, when refining responses with additional details or changes, or when working through a multistep process.

Start afresh when switching to a completely different topic, when conversations become too long to manage effectively, when you want to approach a problem from a different angle, or when you're testing whether your refined prompt stands on its own.

Sometimes you'll want to continue and start afresh at the same time. Copy your refined prompt from a long conversation and start a new chat with it. This approach tests whether your prompt now communicates clearly without requiring extensive back-and-forth context.

REMEMBER

Starting afresh also helps when previous responses are anchored on an approach that isn't working. Sometimes a conversation takes a path that seemed right at first but doesn't pan out. Rather than trying to redirect extensively, starting over with a better-framed initial request gets you to good results faster.

IN THIS CHAPTER

» Layering multiple instructions for complex requests

» Using ready-made powerful combinations

» Knowing when to keep prompts simple

Chapter 9
Combining Techniques for Power Results

Combining techniques isn't about cramming everything into one prompt. It's about knowing when additional elements reinforce each other or make things more confusing. Knowing what to prompt may sound like it requires years of practice, but the patterns are easy to learn. And once you see how combinations work, complex requests are no longer intimidating. You can use techniques like layering and combining:

» Layering means stacking multiple instructions, such as context, format requirements, and examples, in a single prompt.

» Combinations are sets of techniques that work especially well together, such as role plus context plus style.

I cover both approaches in this chapter.

Here's an example. A marketing director spent weeks learning individual prompting techniques. They knew how to provide context, use examples, and specify formats. But when faced with a complex project requiring all three at once, they froze. Should they include the role first or the examples? Would adding constraints make the prompt too long? Once you see the patterns, even complicated requests start to feel manageable.

In this chapter, you learn when layering techniques add value and when they just add words. You discover ready-to-use combinations that handle sophisticated requests. Most importantly, you develop judgment about when complexity helps and when simplicity wins.

Understanding Why Combining Techniques Works

Being specific produces better results than being vague. Providing context helps Claude understand your situation. Examples guide output toward what you want. After you know how to use each technique separately, it's time to learn how to combine them effectively.

Seeing how Claude handles multiple requirements

Claude processes all the elements in your prompt together, not sequentially. When you give context, ask for a format, and include an example, the AI considers all of it together and produces an answer that tries to meet every requirement. The order of your elements matters less than their clarity and compatibility.

Think of it like giving directions to a skilled assistant. If you say, "Write a formal email, keep it under 200 words, and make sure to mention the deadline," the assistant doesn't address each instruction separately. They craft one message that's formal, concise, and includes the deadline. Claude works the same way, balancing multiple requirements in a single output.

WARNING

Problems arise when requirements conflict. Asking for "comprehensive detail" and "keep it brief" in the same prompt forces Claude to guess which matters more. The best combinations work because the instructions support each other instead of pulling the response in different directions.

Knowing when layering adds real value

Not every task benefits from combining techniques. Simple questions deserve simple prompts. You wouldn't write a paragraph of context to ask what the capital of France is. The real skill is using just enough structure to match the task you're trying to accomplish.

TIP

Layering adds value when your task has multiple dimensions that need attention. Writing a client proposal might require the right tone (professional but warm), the right structure (executive summary, approach, timeline), and the right length (concise enough to read, detailed enough to convince). Each part of the task usually needs its own clear instructions.

Layering also helps when you've tried a simple approach but the results missed something. If "summarize this report" produced output that's too long, adding "in five bullet points" solves the problem. If the output is the right length but too technical, adding "for a non-expert audience" addresses that gap. Each layer solves a specific limitation.

Layering Multiple Instructions Effectively

Some tasks require multiple elements working together. The skill lies in knowing which elements to combine and in what order. When layering works, it produces results that no single technique could achieve on its own.

REMEMBER

Order matters more when you're combining different types of instructions, such as context + task + style + format. Claude processes prompts sequentially, so leading with your main goal and then layering refinements typically produces better results than scattering instructions randomly. But that said, don't overthink it. If your instructions are clear and compatible, Claude will usually figure out what you mean regardless of the order. Focus first on including the right elements, and then refine the order if the results feel off.

Adding role + task + constraints

Role-setting is one of the most misunderstood prompting techniques. You may have seen advice to start prompts with "You are an expert in", but this approach often adds words without changing results. The key distinction is between functional role-setting and decorative role-setting.

Understanding when role-setting helps

Before adding a role to your prompt, ask yourself, "Does this role change what Claude does, or am I just adding words?"

TIP

Functional role-setting changes Claude's approach. It shifts perspective, creates simulations, alters voice, or focuses analysis through a specific lens. When you ask Claude to "review this as a skeptical reader would," you get different feedback than when you ask for a general review. The role changes the output because it changes the task.

Decorative role-setting sounds impressive, but it doesn't change what the AI does. "You are a marketing expert" before a marketing question produces the same response as asking the question directly. Claude already applies relevant knowledge to your questions. Declaring expertise doesn't unlock hidden capabilities or change how Claude approaches the problem.

This fact matters because decorative roles take up space without improving the result. Worse, they can make prompts feel like magic formulas rather than clear communication.

REMEMBER

Role-setting isn't about convincing Claude to try harder. It's about genuinely changing the task you're asking Claude to perform.

Role-setting works when it:

- **Shifts perspective:** "Review this proposal as if you were a skeptical board member looking for weaknesses."
- **Creates a simulation:** "Act as an interviewer asking tough questions about my qualifications."
- **Changes the voice or approach:** "Explain this concept like a patient teacher would to a confused student."
- **Focuses the analysis through a domain lens:** "Analyze this contract the way a lawyer would, flagging liability concerns."

Note that each example asks Claude to do something differently, not just to claim expertise before doing the same thing. Here are some examples:

Situation: A product manager preparing for a senior role interview wanted to practice handling difficult questions. They started with a simple request.

First prompt: "What questions might I get asked in a senior product manager interview?"

Claude's response: It provided a helpful list of common questions with notes on what interviewers look for. But reading questions isn't the same as answering them under pressure. They needed practice, not information.

Second prompt: "Act as a hiring manager interviewing me for a senior product manager role at a B2B SaaS company. Ask me one challenging question at a time. After I answer, give me direct feedback on what worked and what I should improve. Then ask the next question. Start with a question about handling competing priorities from stakeholders."

Why this worked: The role transformed the interaction from information delivery to active practice. Claude asked probing follow-up questions, pushed back on vague answers, and provided specific coaching after each response. The manager could practice articulating their experience, handling curveballs, and building on feedback in real time. The role created a simulation rather than a summary.

Template: "Act as [role conducting specific interaction]. [What to do after each exchange]. Start with [specific starting point]."

Situation: A startup founder needs to send a funding update to investors.

Prompt: "Review this email as if you were a busy CFO who receives dozens of funding updates from investors weekly and has limited patience for vague ones." The perspective shift caught problems the founder had missed: buried key metrics, unclear asks, and too much context before the point. A generic "review this email" request wouldn't have surfaced these issues because it wouldn't have shifted the perspective.

Situation: A manager needed to explain a complex benefits change to employees without HR backgrounds.

Prompt: "Explain this policy change like a patient teacher who never makes people feel stupid for not understanding."

Claude's response: It used analogies, anticipated confusion points, and avoided jargon. The role shaped the approach, not just the content.

Here are some examples of functional role-setting templates:

- "Review this as [skeptical audience] looking for [specific concerns]."
- "Act as [role] conducting [interaction type]. [Instructions for the exchange]."

» "Explain this like [teaching style] to [audience level]."

» "Analyze this the way [professional] would, focusing on [domain concerns]."

Combining examples + style + format

When you need output that matches a specific standard, combining an example with style and format instructions gives Claude multiple reference points. Each element reinforces the others. Consider this example:

Situation: A content writer is struggling to match their company's brand voice.

First prompt: A generic "write in a professional tone" instruction produced a generic result.

Second prompt: The writer modified their prompt by including a sample paragraph from existing content, specifying "match this conversational but authoritative style," and requesting "short paragraphs with one main idea each."

Result: The three elements together produced content that fit seamlessly with existing materials.

Why this worked: The example showed what the style looked like in practice. The style instruction named the qualities to match. The format requirement ensured structural consistency. Together, they provided Claude with enough information to replicate the company's voice.

Template: "Here's an example of the style I need: [sample]. Write [content type] matching [specific style qualities]. Format as [structure requirements]."

Applying pattern + context + specific requirements

Sometimes you know what works but need to make it fit your situation. Using the pattern + context + specific requirements prompt works because you give the AI three things: a structure to follow, details about your situation, and clear instructions about what matters most. Here's an example:

Situation: A sales manager had a cold email formula that worked well in one industry, but they needed to adapt it for a different market.

Prompt: The manager shared their pattern (hook, pain point, solution, single ask), provided context about the new industry and its priorities, and specified requirements (mention regulatory concerns, keep under 100 words, end with a soft ask for a call).

Claude's response: It produced an adapted version that preserved what worked while fitting the new context.

Template: "Follow this pattern: [proven structure]. Context: [your specific situation]. Requirements: [what matters most]."

Reviewing Ready-to-Use Powerful Combinations

Why experiment when you can start with combinations that already work? A ready-made combination can handle sophisticated requests without requiring you to invent the structure yourself. Think of ready-made combinations as recipes you can customize rather than formulas you must follow exactly.

Combining role + context + style approach

Sometimes you need Claude to think like someone else, understand your situation, and communicate in a specific way, all at once. Use the role + context + style approach when you need output shaped by perspective, informed by the situation, and delivered in a particular voice. Each element handles a different dimension of the request. Here's how it works in practice:

Situation: A nonprofit director needed talking points for a difficult board meeting about budget cuts.

Prompt: The director combined a functional role ("Help me think through this as a board member would"), context (the specific budget situation and stakeholder concerns), and style ("direct and solution-focused, not defensive").

Why this worked: The combination produced talking points that anticipated tough questions and framed cuts as strategic decisions rather than failures.

Template: "[Functional role that shifts perspective]. Here's the situation: [relevant context]. I need this to be [style/tone requirements]."

Framing question type + reasoning + critique method

When the stakes are high, you want Claude to reason carefully and then poke holes in its own logic. Using the question type + reasoning + critique method helps when you need thorough analysis, not just answers. Using this prompt forces the AI to explain its thinking and then question its answer. This combination is especially useful for decisions you don't want to rush. Here's an example:

Situation: An entrepreneur evaluating a business pivot needed more than a yes-or-no recommendation.

Prompt: The entrepreneur asked Claude to "analyze whether I should pursue this new market" (question type), "walk through your reasoning step by step" (reasoning), and "then argue the opposite case to help me see what I might be missing" (critique). The structure helped them avoid talking themselves into one answer and revealed issues they hadn't considered.

Template: "[Analysis question]. Walk through your reasoning step by step. Then [critique method: argue the opposite/identify weaknesses/play devil's advocate]."

Anchoring example + template + constraint technique

The example + template + constraint technique works when you need consistent output that follows a proven pattern. It's especially useful for recurring tasks where you've already figured out what works. Consider this example:

Situation: A consultant creating client proposals found that each one took hours to write from scratch.

Prompt: The consultant provided Claude with a successful past proposal as an example, specified the template structure they needed (executive summary, approach, timeline, investment), and added constraints ("under 1,500 words, no jargon, specific deliverables in each phase").

Result: Now the consultant generates solid first drafts in minutes that follow their proven format.

Template: "Here's an example of what works: [sample]. Follow this structure: [template elements]. Constraints: [length/style/content limits]."

TIP

For complex decisions that benefit from deeper analysis, see Chapter 18 for details on extended thinking and adaptive thinking modes. Opus 4.7's adaptive thinking automatically adjusts the reasoning depth to match your task's complexity.

Knowing When to Keep It Simple

More techniques don't always mean better results. Sometimes elaborate prompts produce worse output than straightforward requests. Knowing when to stop adding is as important as knowing what to add.

Recognizing overengineering

Sometimes, it's tempting to throw every technique you've learned at a single prompt. Consider this:

Situation: A project manager wanted help writing a simple status update email.

First prompt: The manager crafts an elaborate prompt, saying, "Act as an expert business communicator. Using the BLUF (bottom line up front) methodology, combined with the principles of clear writing from The Economist style guide, create a status update that follows the situation-complication-resolution framework while maintaining a professional but approachable tone." The result was stiff and overthought.

Second prompt: The manager tried again, saying, "Help me write a quick status update for my team. Project X is on track. We finished the design phase. Next week, we start development. Any risks? Just the vendor delivery date is uncertain."

Why this worked: The simpler prompt produced a better email. The added complexity served only to introduce formality that didn't fit the situation. The manager confused the prompting technique with the quality of the prompting.

Here are signs you've overcomplicated your prompt:

- Claude's response sounds forced or unnatural.
- You spent more time on the prompt than the task warrants.
- The output focuses on following your instructions rather than solving your problem.
- Simpler follow-up prompts produce better results than your elaborate original.

Understanding when one technique is enough

Many tasks need just one technique applied well. If you need a quick summary, ask for a summary. If the result isn't quite right, add one constraint (such as "in three bullet points") rather than rebuilding the entire prompt with roles, examples, and frameworks.

REMEMBER

Prompting works best as a conversation, not as engineering. You're communicating with Claude, not programming it.

Troubleshooting when complexity hurts results

When elaborate prompts underperform, cut them back. Remove the role if it's decorative. Cut the framework references. Keep only the elements that directly address your needs. Often, what remains works better than the original. (For more strategies when prompts aren't working, see Chapter 20.)

Here's an example. A consultant spent twenty minutes crafting a detailed prompt for competitive analysis. The result was generic. They cut it back to "Here are three competitor websites. What are they doing better than we are at explaining their value proposition?" The focused question got a focused, useful answer.

Creating Reusable Workflows

When combinations work well for recurring tasks, save them as workflows to save time and maintain consistent results. Eventually, your personal collection will become one of your most valuable sources of prompts.

Building multistep processes

Some complex tasks work better as a sequence of focused prompts rather than one elaborate request. Breaking work into steps lets you review and adjust at each stage. For example, a researcher developed a three-prompt workflow for literature reviews. Here's how they broke up the prompts:

- **First prompt:** "Identify the key themes and debates in these sources."
- **Second prompt:** "For each theme, summarize the main positions and who holds them."
- **Third prompt:** "What gaps or contradictions appear across these perspectives?"

Each prompt was built on the previous output. Using the workflow instead of asking for everything at once consistently produced a better analysis.

Breaking a task into steps works best when:

- Each step needs full attention.
- You want to review the output before proceeding.
- Later steps depend on earlier results.
- The task naturally breaks into stages.

Saving successful combinations

When a prompt or workflow produces great results, save it. Replace specific details with bracketed placeholders so you can adapt the template for future use. If you're using Projects (see Chapter 5), you can store these templates there for easy access across conversations.

A sales manager saved their winning cold email prompt as "Write a cold email to [prospect type] at [company type]. Hook: [relevant pain point]. Value prop: [specific benefit]. Ask: [clear next step]. Keep it under [length]." The manager now generates effective first drafts in seconds.

TIP

Store your templates where you'll use them. Some people keep them in a document. Others use a note-taking app. The format matters less than accessibility. If your templates are hard to find, you won't use them.

Adapting workflows to new situations

Saved workflows give you a starting point, not a script you have to follow word for word. As you use them, notice what works and what needs adjustment for different contexts. A workflow designed for internal communications might need tone adjustments for client-facing work. One built for detailed analysis might need compression for executive summaries. Adapt the pattern while keeping the structure that makes it effective.

TIP

The best workflows evolve. Each time you use one, you learn something about what makes it work. Some people version their templates, keeping old versions available while testing improvements. Others refine continuously. Either approach builds a library that gets more valuable over time.

Putting It All Together

Combining techniques is about choosing what fits the task, not throwing everything you know into one prompt. Simple requests need simple prompts. Complex requests benefit from thoughtful layering. The goal isn't elaborate prompts. The goal is effective communication that gets you what you need.

TIP

Start with the simplest approach that might work. Add elements when you have a reason. Save combinations that prove effective. Over time, you stop thinking about techniques and start focusing on the problem. Prompting becomes part of how you think, not something extra you have to manage.

REMEMBER

The following principles will serve you far better than any memorized formula:

- Use role-setting only when it changes the task, not just to add authority.
- Use combinations when elements reinforce each other.
- Keep complexity in check by starting simple.
- Build a library of workflows that speed up and standardize your repeated tasks.

3

Using Claude Every Day

IN THIS PART . . .

See how much easier writing gets with Claude's help.

Pick up new skills and research anything in minutes.

Make better decisions and plan projects with confidence.

Get quick answers from any document or file.

Create content for work and life without the blank page.

See how real workflows come together from start to finish.

IN THIS CHAPTER

» Starting when you don't know what to say

» Editing and strengthening your drafts

» Crafting messages that get results

Chapter 10
Writing Everything Better and Quicker

Writing is hard. Even professional writers stare at blank screens, struggle to find the right words, and spend hours editing sentences that still don't feel quite right. The difficulty isn't a lack of ideas or intelligence. Writing challenges your brain to perform multiple complex tasks simultaneously: organizing thoughts, choosing precise words, maintaining a consistent tone, structuring arguments, and anticipating how readers will interpret your message.

REMEMBER

Claude changes the fundamental equation. Instead of facing these challenges alone, you gain a tireless partner who can help you think through structure and generate drafts. The key isn't just about learning what prompts to type.

It's learning to diagnose what kind of writing help you need at any given moment.

This chapter shows you how to think about writing with Claude's assistance. You learn to recognize whether you need help getting started, improving what you've written, crafting difficult messages, or developing long-form content. Even more importantly, you'll understand the principles behind effective collaboration.

Understanding What Kind of Writing Help You Need

Before you ask Claude for help with writing, you should take a moment to diagnose your challenge. Writers typically face four distinct types of problems, each requiring a different kind of assistance:

- **Starting:** You've been staring at a blank document for several minutes. You know what you need to write, but you can't begin. You have scattered ideas without a clear structure, or you're stuck on the first sentence. The writing feels overwhelming because you're trying to organize, write, and evaluate all at once. You need help not with writing but with structure.
- **Improving:** You've read your draft three times but still can't pinpoint what's wrong. You've written something that doesn't quite work. The information is there, but the argument feels weak or lacks clarity. You need diagnostic feedback that identifies specific issues rather than vague "make it better" guidance.
- **Determining the tone and audience:** The words are technically correct, but the effect is wrong. Your email sounds too harsh or too weak, or your explanation is too technical or too simplistic. You're struggling to match your message to your reader's needs and expectations.
- **Developing:** You're working on a longer piece of writing but can't expand your ideas without losing coherence. You have an outline but can't flesh it out, or you've written sections that don't connect smoothly. You need help thinking through how pieces build on each other.

REMEMBER

Learning to diagnose which problem you're facing saves time and produces better results. When you ask Claude for structure help on a starting issue, you get an actionable outline. When you ask for diagnostic feedback on an improvement problem, you learn exactly what to fix. The wrong diagnosis leads to generic advice that doesn't address your challenge.

Beating Blank Page Syndrome

The blank page problem isn't about pages. It's about the feeling that you need to create something perfect from nothing. Your brain freezes because it's trying to generate ideas, organize them, choose words, and evaluate quality all at once.

TIP

Understanding why a blank page paralyzes you will help you break free from the paralysis. Your working memory can juggle only a limited number of tasks. When you try to brainstorm, organize, write, and edit simultaneously, you overload your cognitive capacity. Nothing feels good enough because you're evaluating drafts before they exist. You reject ideas before you explore them.

The solution is to work sequentially: structure first, then draft, then refine, and then polish. Each stage requires a different type of thinking, and trying to do them together leads only to frustration. Starting messy isn't a character flaw; it's how effective writing works. Your outline exists to give you direction. Your first draft exists to give you something to improve. Neither needs to be good. Both need to be done.

REMEMBER

Claude helps by separating these tasks. You can start with messy ideas and use Claude to help organize them. You can create a rough structure and use Claude to develop it. You don't need to produce good writing immediately. You need to make something you can work with.

Getting started when you don't know how to start

Are you having trouble getting started? Usually, the problem is that you're trying to begin with polished prose. Here's an example:

Situation: A consultant needed to write a proposal but couldn't get past the first sentence. Every attempt felt wrong. Then they recognized the real problem: they were trying to write and edit at the same time.

Prompt: "I need to write a consulting proposal for a retail client who wants to improve their customer retention. I have three main ideas: loyalty program redesign, staff training improvements, and customer feedback systems. Help me create a basic outline that shows how these ideas connect and the order in which I should present them."

Claude's response: Claude returned a logical flow for the proposal:

Foundation: Staff training and engagement

Current state assessment of customer service skills

The proposed training program focused on relationship building

Expected timeline and team involvement

Program enhancement: Loyalty system redesign

How trained staff can maximize loyalty program effectiveness

Specific improvements to the current program

Integration with point-of-sale systems

Feedback loop: Customer feedback systems

Using trained staff to encourage feedback participation

Connecting feedback to loyalty program improvements

Measuring retention improvements over time

This order worked because staff training creates the foundation that makes both the loyalty program and feedback systems more effective.

Result: The consultant could immediately see the logical flow. The outline revealed connections they hadn't articulated: trained staff would make the loyalty program more personal and the feedback system more effective. They could write one section at a time instead of staring at a blank space.

Why this worked: They asked for structure help, not writing help. The outline gave them a clear path forward with natural transitions already visible.

Template: "I need to write [type of document] for [audience] about [topic]. I have these main ideas: [list your ideas]. Help me create a basic outline that shows how these ideas connect and the order in which I should present them."

Creating outlines and first drafts quickly

Once you have a structure, getting words on the page becomes easier. You're not creating from nothing — you're expanding an outline. Consider this example:

Situation: A product manager needed to write a feature specification but kept getting stuck trying to write a perfect first draft.

Prompt: "Based on this outline for a user authentication feature, write a rough first draft of the technical requirements section. Don't worry about being polished or complete. I just need something to react to and improve."

Claude's response: Claude generated a draft that wasn't perfect but gave the manager something concrete to work with.

Result: The manager spent twenty minutes editing and refining rather than two hours staring at a blank page. The rough draft broke through their perfectionism.

Making Your Writing Stronger

Knowing something needs improvement is different from knowing how to improve it. You might sense that a paragraph feels awkward or an argument lacks punch, but identifying the specific problem requires looking at it from a different perspective. Claude excels at this diagnostic work.

Understanding the three levels of editing helps you ask for the right kind of help:

- ***Structural editing*** *addresses how ideas are organized and whether your logic flows clearly.*
- ***Clarity editing*** *focuses on whether readers will understand your sentences and whether you've adequately explained your concepts.*
- ***Polish editing*** *catches grammar issues, improves word choice, and refines tone.*

REMEMBER

You can't evaluate structure while wrestling with sentence-level problems. You can't polish prose when the underlying argument needs rebuilding. Working in passes — first structure, then clarity, then polish — produces better results with less effort.

Claude can help at each level, but you need to specify which level you're working on. "Make this better" gives Claude nothing useful. "Tell me where my argument has gaps," or "Point out where I'm using jargon without explanation," or "Suggest more precise word choices" gives Claude clear direction about which editing level you need.

The key is to be specific about the kind of improvement you need. Diagnostic feedback beats complete rewrites because you learn what to fix and why. You maintain your voice while solving a specific problem.

TIP

Here's a frustrating truth about editing your own work: the better you know what you meant to say, the harder it is to see the difference between that and what you wrote. Psychologists call this issue the *curse of knowledge*. Your brain fills in gaps, smooths awkward phrasing, and reads the brilliant version that exists in your head rather than the muddled version on the screen. This process isn't a character flaw. It's how memory works. When you reread something you wrote an hour ago, you're not really reading it afresh. You're partially remembering it, and memory is generous with its edits.

Professional writers know the standard fix: put the draft in a drawer for a few days, and then return with fresher eyes. But who has days? You need to send that proposal by tomorrow morning.

Claude reads exactly what you wrote, with zero memory of what you intended. When Claude summarizes your argument back to you and the summary sounds wrong, that's diagnostic information. The problem isn't Claude's reading comprehension. The problem is the gap between your intention and your execution.

REMEMBER

Claude doesn't catch everything or replace a careful human review. But Claude can spot the gaps your brain automatically papers over, giving you the "fresh eyes" effect without the waiting period.

Editing with a tireless partner

The best editing comes from getting distance from your own writing. After you've worked on something for hours, you stop seeing problems. Claude provides a new perspective without the delay of waiting for a colleague to review. Here's an example:

Situation: A team lead drafted a project retrospective but felt it was too defensive in some places and too vague in others.

Prompt: "Review this retrospective and tell me where I'm being defensive or vague instead of constructive and specific. Point out specific sentences."

Claude's response: Claude identified three defensive passages and five vague claims, explaining why each felt that way and suggesting more constructive alternatives.

Result: The team lead revised based on this feedback, maintaining their voice while addressing tone issues.

Strengthening arguments and clarity

Weak arguments often lack evidence, exhibit unclear logic, or fail to address counterarguments. Here's an example:

Situation: A consultant wrote a recommendation that their client rejected as unconvincing.

Prompt: "Analyze this recommendation and tell me where the argument feels weak or where I haven't supported my claims with evidence."

The text of their recommendation stated: "Implementing a customer relationship management system will improve your sales team's effectiveness and increase customer satisfaction. The investment will pay for itself within 18 months through improved efficiency."

Claude's response: "Your argument has three weak points:

- *Missing evidence for 'will improve effectiveness':* Add concrete examples of current problems: Are sales reps duplicating efforts? Losing track of follow-ups? Unable to see customer history?
- *Unexplained connection to customer satisfaction:* How does a CRM (an internal tool) improve what customers experience? Explain the chain: CRM gives reps customer history, they personalize interactions, and customers feel understood.
- *Unsupported ROI claim:* The 18-month payback needs justification. What efficiency gains? Show your calculation."

Claude added: "You also haven't addressed the question, 'Why not improve our current system instead of implementing something new?'"

Result: The consultant revised the text to add specific current system failures, explained how better information improves the customer experience, showed the ROI calculation, and compared improving the current system with implementing a modern CRM. The strengthened argument addressed the client's decision-making process.

Why this worked: Claude diagnosed the specific gaps rather than just saying "add more detail." The consultant knew exactly what evidence to add and where.

Template: "Analyze this [content type] and tell me where the argument feels weak or where I haven't supported my claims with evidence."

Fixing grammar, style, and tone issues

Grammar and style problems often hide in plain sight when you've been staring at your writing too long. Consider this example:

Situation: A marketing director drafted a campaign email but sensed something felt off. The sentences seemed correct individually, but the overall flow felt choppy.

Prompt: "Review this email for flow and readability. Point out where transitions feel abrupt, where sentences could be combined for better rhythm, and where I'm using passive voice unnecessarily."

Claude's response: "I notice four issues affecting flow:

- *Repetitive sentence openings:* Four consecutive sentences start with 'We,' which creates a monotonous rhythm. Consider varying your openings: start one with the benefit, another with a time marker, and another with the customer action.
- *Passive construction weakening impact:* 'Customer feedback was analyzed by our team,' buries who's acting. Flip it: 'Our team analyzed customer feedback and discovered three patterns.'
- *Abrupt transition:* Paragraph 2 jumps from the problem to the solution without connecting them. Add one sentence explaining why this solution addresses that problem.
- *Vague action statement:* 'Improvements will be implemented' doesn't tell readers what's happening or when it will happen. Be specific: 'We're implementing these improvements starting next week.'"

Result: The specific diagnosis showed the director exactly what to fix. They didn't need a complete rewrite. They needed to spot the patterns that made their writing feel stiff.

Why this worked: The director asked for specific style issues rather than asking Claude to rewrite everything. They maintained their voice while fixing the technical problems.

Template: "Review this [content type] for [specific issue: flow/clarity/conciseness]. Point out where [specific problems you suspect] and suggest more [desired quality] alternatives."

Some writing problems are straightforward. You need something shortened, expanded, or adjusted for tone. These templates handle common situations:

- **Make it concise.** "Reduce this to [length] while keeping all the key points."
- **Add detail.** "Expand this paragraph to include [specific type of detail]."
- **Adjust the formality.** "Rewrite this to be more [formal/casual] while maintaining [what to keep]."
- **Simplify.** "Rewrite this assuming the reader has no background in [topic]."

Use these templates when you know exactly what change is needed.

Writing Emails and Messages That Work

Email writing reveals a fundamental truth: the goal is not to express yourself clearly but to make the reader's response easy and obvious. Every email should make one thing clear: what happens next.

Understanding what makes email communication different helps you write more effective messages. Email lacks the feedback loops of conversation. You can't gauge understanding from facial expressions, nor can you adjust your message when confusion arises.

REMEMBER

The reader controls when and how carefully they read your message. They might skim it between meetings or read it while distracted. Your email might compete with dozens of others for attention and action.

This issue creates the clarity-brevity-action triangle. Your message needs to be:

- Clear enough that a distracted reader understands it.
- Brief enough that a busy reader finishes it.
- Action-oriented enough that an overwhelmed reader knows what to do next.

Achieving all three requires thinking more about your reader's needs than about your need to explain.

Crafting professional emails quickly

Professional emails become much easier to write when you think in terms of who is reading, what they need to know, and what you want them to do next. Here's an example:

Situation: A project coordinator needed to email four stakeholders about a timeline delay.

Prompt: "I need to inform people that our product launch is delayed two weeks. Write four versions: one for my manager (needs impact and mitigation plan), one for the client (needs reassurance and clear next steps), one for the development team (need to understand why and what changed), and one for marketing (need to know how this affects their campaign timeline)."

Claude's response: Claude generated four emails:

To the manager: "The launch date is moving from March 15 to March 29 due to critical bugs found in user testing. Impact: we'll miss the Q1 revenue target by approximately $200K but stay on track for Q2 goals. Mitigation: The development team is prioritizing the fixes. We're using the extra time to strengthen go-to-market messaging and to add two enterprise features that were cut from the original scope."

To the client: "I'm writing to let you know we're adjusting the launch timeline by two weeks to ensure that everything meets our quality standards. Your new launch date is March 29. What this means for you: you'll have access to two additional enterprise features we originally planned for a later release. Your dedicated support team will be in touch this week to update your internal rollout plan."

To the development team: "We're moving the launch to March 29 based on the critical issues found in last week's testing (login failures on mobile, payment processing errors, data sync bug). The additional two weeks give us time to fix these thoroughly rather than rushing patches. Priority order: payment processing first (blocks revenue), then login (blocks adoption), then data sync (affects enterprise customers)."

To marketing: "The product launch is moving to March 29 (from March 15). This affects your campaign timeline: social media posts push to March 29; email campaign to March 28; pause scheduled paid ads; and resume on March 27. Silver lining: we can now promote two enterprise features that weren't in the original messaging. Updated product brief coming tomorrow."

Result: Each email addressed the same fact but emphasized different aspects based on what each audience needed to know and do. The project coordinator edited each version to add details, but the framework showed them how to tailor information effectively.

Why this worked: The coordinator specified what each audience needed rather than asking for a generic announcement.

Template: "Write an email to [recipient type] about [topic]. They need to know [key information]. The tone should be [descriptor]. Make it clear that [desired action or next step]."

Getting the tone right for the situation

Tone is less about word choice and more about how the message feels to the reader, given your relationship, the stakes, and the context. Consider this:

Situation: An account manager was frustrated with a client requesting changes outside the project scope. Their draft was professional but cold. This needed to change.

Prompt: "Rewrite this to be firmer about our boundaries while staying warm and collaborative. I need to say no to the scope creep without damaging the relationship."

Claude's response: Claude reframed boundary-setting as a partnership: "I want to make sure we're setting you up for success with these new requests. Looking at our current contract, these items would be a great fit for either a brief timeline extension to fold them into the current project or a separate phase 2 project we could start right after this one wraps. Which approach works better for your needs?"

Why this worked: The revision made the boundary clear while giving the client agency. Instead of saying no, it reframed the conversation around how to say yes effectively.

Template: "Rewrite this to be [tone adjustment] while maintaining [what to preserve]. I need to [specific goal] without [unwanted consequence]."

Handling difficult communications diplomatically

Some messages require extra care, such as giving critical feedback, declining requests, or addressing problems.

> **Situation:** A manager needed to tell a team member that their work wasn't meeting expectations.
>
> **Prompt:** "Help me write feedback that's direct about the performance issues but encouraging about the person's potential. The problems are: missing deadlines, incomplete deliverables, and not asking for help when stuck. I want them to understand this is serious without crushing their confidence."
>
> **Claude's response:** Claude drafted feedback that opened with specific examples of the problems, explained why they mattered to the team, outlined clear expectations going forward, and ended by affirming the person's value and offering support.
>
> **Result:** The structure showed the manager how to be direct and kind at the same time.
>
> **Why this worked:** The manager specified what needed to be said and what feeling needed to be preserved.

Creating Long-Form Content

Everything you've practiced with shorter pieces applies also to long-form writing, but the stakes and complexity increase. Long-form writing presents a different challenge. You're developing an argument or a narrative that should build across multiple sections, maintain the reader's interest through transitions, and arrive at a satisfying conclusion. The length itself becomes an obstacle because your brain struggles to hold all the pieces simultaneously.

Understanding the stages of long-form writing prevents you from getting overwhelmed. They are as follows:

- **Structure stage:** Establishes your framework — the main points you'll make and in what order

» **Development stage:** Expands each point with evidence, examples, and explanation

» **Connection stage:** Builds transitions and ensures that ideas flow logically

» **Polish stage:** Refines individual sentences and paragraphs for clarity and impact

TIP

Most writers try to do all four stages at once. They try to organize while writing, edit while drafting, and polish while figuring out structure. This approach guarantees frustration. Your brain can't simultaneously make high-level organizational decisions and low-level word choice decisions effectively.

Working in stages produces better results with less effort. When you focus solely on structure, you can clearly see patterns and connections. When you focus on development, you can expand ideas without worrying about perfect phrasing. When you focus on connections, you can smooth transitions without restructuring entire sections. When you focus on polish, you can refine language without questioning your overall approach.

REMEMBER

Claude helps you through each stage. You can develop the structure, expand each section, refine the flow, and polish the details. The key principle is to tackle one level of the writing problem at a time. Don't try to outline, draft, and edit simultaneously.

Structuring articles, reports, and documents

Longer documents stop feeling overwhelming when you treat structure as a design problem. Consider how to arrange information so readers can follow your thinking without getting lost. Here's an example:

Situation: A researcher needed to write a white paper on cybersecurity comparing three data security approaches.

First prompt: "I need to compare three approaches across four criteria. Should I organize this by approach (describe each completely) or by criteria (compare all three for each criterion)? What are the advantages of each structure?"

Claude's response: Claude explained that organizing by approach works when approaches are fundamentally different and readers need to understand each as a complete system. Organizing by criteria works when approaches vary and readers need to make decisions. For security options where readers are decision-makers evaluating tradeoffs, a criteria-based organization made more sense.

Second prompt: The researcher then asked for an outline using a criteria-based organization.

Claude's response: Claude generated a criteria-based outline organized around the four evaluation dimensions, with all three approaches compared side by side in each section.

Result: The outline revealed that the researcher needed to add a section on migration complexity and that compliance should be the deciding factor. Thinking about structure before writing saved them from organizing ten pages incorrectly.

Template: "I need to [document goal] covering [main topics]. Should I organize by [option A] or [option B]? What are the advantages of each structure?"

Maintaining consistency across sections

Long documents suffer when sections feel disconnected. Perhaps you wrote each part at a different time and varied the tone or level of detail. Here's an example:

Situation: A technical writer needed to create documentation for their staff.

Prompt: They asked, "Review these five sections for consistency in tone, terminology, and level of detail. Point out where sections feel mismatched."

Claude's response: Claude identified that the first two sections assumed expert knowledge, while the last three explained basics, creating a confusing reading experience. It noted terminology inconsistencies: *user* in some sections, *customer* in others, and *account holder* in a third.

Result: The feedback helped the writer revise to maintain a consistent voice and clarity throughout.

Why this worked: The writer asked specifically about consistency, rather than general improvement.

Developing ideas into complete pieces

Moving from outline to finished piece requires expanding each point without losing the thread. The expansion process works best when you understand what role each section plays in your larger argument.

Situation: A business analyst needed to develop a 20-page report for their manager.

First prompt: "I have this outline for my market analysis section. For each of these five points, tell me: What question is this point answering for the reader? What evidence or examples would make this point convincing? What objections might readers have?"

Claude's response: Claude clarified that two points answered the same question from different angles, so they should be combined. Another point needed to be split because it was answering two other questions.

Result: The analysis prevented the analyst from writing five disconnected sections and helped them see how each piece contributed to the overall argument. The analyst then expanded the sections strategically. For complex points, they asked "Develop this point about market segmentation into four paragraphs showing how consumer behavior differs across segments." For straightforward points, they wrote "Give me three concrete examples of companies succeeding with this approach." The varying levels of expansion kept important ideas prominent while keeping supporting points concise.

Why this worked: The analyst thought about information architecture before writing. They understood what readers needed from each section, which made expansion purposeful rather than just adding words.

Template: "I have this outline for [document section]. For each point, tell me: What question is it answering? What evidence makes it convincing? What objections might readers have?"

TIP

Writing with Claude transforms the struggle of facing a blank page into a collaborative process of building something piece by piece. You still need to think, make decisions, and apply judgment. But you'll spend less time stuck and more time creating. The question shifts from "How do I start?" to "What kind of help do I need right now?"

Once you can diagnose your writing challenges accurately — whether you're stuck on structure, tone, clarity, or development — you'll find Claude ready to help you move forward. The blank page stops being intimidating when you realize you're not writing alone.

IN THIS CHAPTER

» Mastering new skills with personalized guidance

» Speeding up research time

» Managing information overload effectively

Chapter 11

Learning Anything Faster

Learning something new can be frustrating. You read explanations that assume you already know things you don't. You watch tutorials that move too fast, and you wonder if you're missing something obvious. The problem isn't you. Most teaching materials don't work for everyone.

Claude flips this around. Instead of you adapting to whatever explanation you find, the explanation adapts to you. Need it to be simpler? Ask. Want more depth? Ask. This chapter shows you how to learn faster with a patient tutor who never gets tired of your questions.

TIP

Traditional learning forces you to match the teacher's pace and style. You either keep up or get left behind. With Claude, you can:

- Set your own pace
- Choose the complexity level
- Decide what examples work for you

You ask questions until you understand, without worrying about looking stupid or slowing anyone down. This changes everything about how fast you can learn.

Understanding Complex Topics Your Way

Complex topics feel impossible because explanations assume you know things you don't. They use words you haven't learned. They skip steps that aren't obvious.

REMEMBER

The usual approach of reading a book, taking a course, or watching a video forces you to learn the way someone else teaches. Claude does the opposite: it teaches the way you learn.

This section shows you three key strategies for understanding complex topics. They are breaking confusing concepts into simple pieces, getting explanations adjusted to your level, and asking questions without fear of judgment.

Breaking down confusing concepts

You're reading about something and suddenly you're lost. The writer assumes knowledge you don't have. Learning stops, not because you can't understand but because the explanation doesn't match where you're starting from. Strategies that work best for getting clear explanations include the following:

- **Stop when something isn't clear and admitting when you don't know a term.** Don't wait and hope it makes sense later. Ask, "What does that word mean?" right away.
- **Ask "why" until the answer clicks.** Each "why" usually reveals another layer.
- **Ask Claude to back up and explain the basics first.** If you're missing foundational concepts, make sure to address those before moving forward.

The secret to understanding technical topics isn't memorizing jargon, it's connecting new concepts to knowledge you already have. Here's an example.

Situation: A small business owner needed to understand blockchain for a supplier relationship. Technical articles left them confused with terms like *distributed ledger* and *consensus mechanism.*

Prompt: "I'm trying to understand blockchain for a business decision. I'm comfortable with databases and cloud storage, but I've never studied computer science. Explain blockchain, focusing on why businesses use it and what makes it different from regular databases."

Claude's response: "Think of a regular database like a filing cabinet in your office. You control who opens it and what changes are made. Blockchain is more like a shared ledger that everyone in a business network can see, but no one person controls. When someone adds a transaction, everyone's copy updates automatically, and the history can't be changed. Businesses use this when they need to verify transactions with partners without trusting a single company to keep the records."

Why this worked: They specified their existing knowledge (databases and the cloud) and their actual need (a business decision, not technical mastery). Claude focused on the business value rather than the technical mechanics.

Template: "I'm trying to understand [complex topic] for [your specific purpose]. I'm comfortable with [related things you know], but I've never studied [technical field]. Explain [topic], focusing on [what matters to you] and what makes it different from [familiar comparison]."

TIP

Think of this exchange like having a conversation with a knowledgeable colleague who explains things in different ways until you understand. You're not reading a textbook that's locked into one explanation. You're co-creating the explanation that works for your brain.

The breakthrough moment comes when you realize you're in control. You're not failing to understand a concept; you're finding the right way to explain it. Sometimes you need a visual analogy, a step-by-step breakdown, or an understanding of the history. Claude adapts until you understand.

Getting explanations at your level

You can explain the same topic to a 10-year-old or a PhD student. Most explanations aim for a middle ground. Claude adjusts to exactly your level because you tell it where you're starting. Here are three ways to set the right level:

- **Use "explain like I'm . . ." to calibrate the complexity.** "Explain like I'm 12" gets you a simple explanation. For something more complex, try "Explain like I'm a manager who needs business impact, not technical details."
- **Adjust the level mid-conversation.** Say "I get that part, go deeper" or "That's over my head, make it simpler."
- **Match the explanation to your goal.** "Explain for practical use" gets different information than "Explain so I can discuss this in a meeting."

Learning new technology becomes manageable when explanations build on tools you already use every day. Consider this example.

Situation: A teacher switching to remote learning needed to understand video conferencing.

First prompt: "Explain Zoom like I'm comfortable with email and PowerPoint, but I've never done video calls. I need to run class meetings with 25 students."

Claude's response: "Zoom works like a phone call you can see. You send a meeting link (like forwarding an email) and everyone clicks it to join. Once in the meeting, you see everyone's faces in boxes (like slides in PowerPoint slide sorter view). You control who can talk using the Mute button. Think of it like having a classroom where you can politely silence disruptions. Screen sharing lets you show your PowerPoint or other materials, exactly like projecting in a classroom."

The explanation matched her existing skills. She understood every part.

Second prompt: "Now explain the security settings, like I need to protect my students from uninvited guests."

Claude's response: "Three settings protect your classroom. First, the Waiting Room makes people wait in a virtual hallway until you let them in (like students waiting outside your locked classroom). Second, meeting passwords work exactly like email passwords. Third, turn off screen sharing for students so only you can share. This prevents students from displaying inappropriate content."

Why this worked: The specifics of the person's comfort level with email and PowerPoint, along with their need to protect students, meant Claude focused on exactly what they needed to know. The progression from basics to security let them build confidence before tackling complex features.

Template this: "Explain [topic] like I'm comfortable with [familiar technology/skill], but I've never [specific thing you need to learn]. I need to [your specific goal]. Now explain [advanced feature] like I need to [your specific goal]."

TIP

Different contexts require different levels of understanding. If you're making a business decision, you need practical implications, not theoretical depth. If you're preparing for a technical interview, you need precise definitions. Tell Claude your context, and you get the right level automatically.

Learning without fear

The biggest barrier to learning is often the fear of looking stupid. In meetings or classrooms, you hesitate to ask basic questions. Everyone but you seems to understand, so you stay confused.

Claude eliminates that fear. You can ask anything without judgment. Create a private conversation just for beginner questions. Build your foundation privately, and then apply it publicly with confidence.

Here are some ways to use Claude without judgment:

- **Ask basic questions privately that you won't ask publicly.** Build your vocabulary in private conversations.
- **Check if you understood correctly.** Say, "So if I'm understanding right, you're saying [your interpretation]. Is that correct?"
- **Challenge explanations that don't make sense.** If something seems inconsistent, ask about it.
- **Request the same thing explained multiple ways.** Ask, "Can you explain that using a different example?" Different angles help concepts click.

Sometimes the most valuable learning happens when you can ask questions without worrying about looking uninformed. Consider this example.

Situation: A consultant preparing for a client meeting wanted to ask Claude questions they wouldn't ask colleagues.

Prompt: "Everyone keeps saying 'API' (application programming interface) in meetings. I know it connects to software in some way, but I don't really understand what that means. Can you explain it like I'm tech-comfortable but not a programmer?"

Claude's response: "An API is like a restaurant menu. The kitchen (one piece of software) can make many dishes, but customers (another piece of software) only see the menu, which lists what they can order. When you order 'get customer data' from the menu, you don't need to know how the kitchen finds that data. You get the result. Companies share APIs so their software can talk to other companies' software without sharing how everything works internally."

Why this worked: The consultant was honest about exactly where their understanding broke down, "I know it connects to software in some way, but I don't really understand what that means." Specifying "tech-comfortable but not a programmer" gave Claude the right baseline to avoid both vague answers and overly technical ones. The admission of social pressure ("everyone keeps saying") made it safe to ask what they couldn't ask colleagues.

Template: "I keep hearing [term] and I know it [what you think you know], but I don't really understand [what confuses you]. Explain it like I'm [your actual level]."

This private conversation enabled the person to expand their vocabulary without risking appearing uninformed in the actual meeting.

Mastering New Skills Step by Step

Understanding something isn't the same as being able to do it. Gaining a skill requires practice, feedback, and repetition. Traditional learning gives you instructions, and then leaves you alone to figure it out. Claude is with you when you practice, creates custom exercises, and gives feedback on every attempt.

This section shows you how to move from understanding to competence. You learn how to get tutorials tailored to your situation, practice with exercises designed for your level, and receive feedback that improves your work.

Following personalized tutorials

Generic tutorials teach everyone the same way at the same speed. They work great if you learn that exact way. For everyone else, they're too fast in some parts and too slow in others.

Claude creates tutorials just for you. Tell Claude what you want to learn, what you already know, and what you'll use the information for. Claude builds a tutorial based on your situation. This approach means that:

- **Examples match your real work.** A teacher gets examples about grades. A marketer gets examples of campaigns. You learn with real situations, not fake ones.
- **The pace adjusts to you.** Say, "This makes sense, so let's speed up" or "I need to slow down here."
- **The teaching style matches how you learn.** Some people need the big picture first. Others want to start small and build up.
- **You can stop and ask questions anytime.** The tutorial becomes a conversation, not a one-way lecture.

Practicing with custom examples

Reading about a skill doesn't mean you can do it. You need practice. But finding good practice problems can be difficult. If a problem is too easy, you learn nothing; too hard, and you give up. Claude bases practice problems on your progress.

Practice builds real skills when it mirrors the messy situations you'll actually face, not idealized textbook scenarios. Here's an example.

Situation: A project manager needed to write better meeting agendas, but generic templates were not helpful.

Prompt: "I run project meetings with 8 to 12 people, usually stakeholders with competing priorities. I need to practice writing agendas that keep everyone focused and productive. Create realistic practice scenarios."

Claude's response: Claude created three practice scenarios, "Create an agenda for a project kickoff where marketing wants fast delivery and engineering needs more planning time," "Write an agenda for reviewing a delayed project where the team is defensive about setbacks," and "Draft an agenda for a budget meeting where three departments are competing for the same funding pool."

Why this worked: Each scenario matched situations the person actually faced. They practiced, got feedback, refined their approach, and tried again. The realistic scenarios meant they built skills they'd use immediately. Generic practice problems teach you to solve generic problems. Customized practice prepares you for your actual work.

Template: "I [describe your work situation and constraints]. I need to practice [specific skill] that [your success criteria]. Create practice scenarios where [realistic complications you face]."

Getting feedback on your attempts

One of the most valuable parts of learning with Claude is getting immediate, specific feedback. You write, solve, or create something, and then ask: "How did I do? What could be better?" Claude evaluates your work and tells you how to improve.

Claude provides specific feedback, not generic praise. Instead of "good job," Claude said, "Your opening clearly states the main point. Your second paragraph jumps to a new idea without connecting it. Add a transition sentence." Instead of "needs work," Claude says, "This will work, but it's inefficient. Filter the data before processing to make it faster."

Template: "I created [what you made] for [your audience/purpose]. Evaluate it for [specific criteria that matter to you]. Point out the weakest parts and explain exactly how to strengthen them."

Here's how to use feedback strategically:

- **For learning:** Focus on understanding why something works or doesn't work.
- **For improvement:** Ask for specific suggestions on how to make it better.
- **For validation:** Check if you're on the right track before investing more time.
- **For alternatives:** Ask "What's a different way to approach this?"

Claude matches feedback to your level. For beginners, Claude focuses on fundamentals to get the basics right first. For experienced learners, Claude provides subtle improvements in style. Tell Claude your level so that the feedback matches.

Conducting Superfast Research

Research used to mean opening multiple browser tabs, reading many articles, taking notes, and then trying to make sense of it all. With Claude's web search — available to all users — you can significantly compress this timeline. Claude searches multiple sources, makes sense of the findings, and gives you a clear understanding, all in one conversation. (For more about using web search, see Chapter 17.)

Gathering information from multiple sources

Traditional research can be exhausting. You read article after article, trying to figure out what they agree on, where they disagree, and what it all means. The process takes hours.

With web search, you can ask Claude to research a topic. Claude searches multiple sources and gives you a clear summary with different viewpoints. The real time-saver is the summary. Instead of reading several articles yourself and piecing together the big picture, Claude does the work for you.

What makes research with Claude faster? You can:

- **Direct the research to your specific questions.** Focus on what you need to know.
- **Get a synthesized understanding, not just raw information.** Claude connects the dots.
- **Control how deep you go.** Claude cites sources in case you want to read more.
- **Verify information you've heard.** Separate facts from rumors.

Here's how Claude research plays out when you need to get up to speed on an unfamiliar industry fast:

Situation: A consultant needed to quickly understand an industry they'd never worked in.

Prompt: They asked Claude to research commercial real estate trends since 2020 and how remote work was affecting it.

Claude's response: Claude searched current sources, identified major trends, and explained how they connected.

Result: In minutes, the person got a comprehensive briefing that would have taken hours of reading.

Template: "Research [topic] since [timeframe], focusing on [specific aspect relevant to your needs]. I need to [what you'll do with this information]."

REMEMBER

You can layer research requests to go deeper. Start with "Give me an overview," then ask "Now dig deeper into the most important trend," and then "Find specific examples of companies doing this successfully." Each question builds on the last, taking you from a broad understanding to specific details.

This layered approach mirrors how experts research topics. They start broadly to understand the landscape, identify what's important, and then drill down into specifics. With traditional research, each layer requires another round of searching, reading, and synthesizing. With Claude, each layer is just another question in the same conversation.

Synthesizing key insights quickly

Raw information isn't understandable. You can collect facts all day and still not see patterns or know what to do with them. Synthesis (connecting the dots) is where real understanding happens.

After gathering the information, ask Claude to synthesize it. Claude doesn't just repeat information; it extracts meaning, identifies patterns, and highlights what matters for your situation.

The following types of synthesis will help you understand faster:

- Ask Claude to identify where experts agree and where they disagree.
- Request pattern analysis across different approaches.
- Extract situation-specific takeaways rather than comprehensive coverage.
- Flag potential risks before they become problems.
- Surface gaps in the information you've gathered.

You can ask for a synthesis at different levels, such as "Give me the key takeaways" for high-level understanding and "What are the specific steps I need to take?" for action items. Match the synthesis to what you need.

TIP

After Claude synthesizes information, ask one more question: "What's the one thing I should remember from all this?" This question forces the synthesis down to its core, which is the single most important insight you can act on immediately.

Staying current with web search

What was true last year might not be true now. Staying current used to mean constantly reading the news and hoping you didn't miss important changes. With web search, you can quickly catch up on what's new.

Ask Claude to update you on recent developments. Claude searches current sources and summarizes what's changed. For example, a marketer preparing a campaign asked what's trending on social media in health and wellness. Claude researched current trends and popular topics, giving the person insights that month-old articles couldn't provide.

Here are several ways to stay current with Claude's web search:

- **Get updates on recent developments.** "What's new in this field in the last six months?"
- **Check if advice is still current.** "Is this approach still considered best practice?"
- **Track changes over time.** "How has the approach to this evolved in the last year?"
- **Get timely briefings.** "What significant developments happened this week?"

TIP

A financial advisor stayed current without spending hours reading the news. They'd ask Claude about significant market movements, regulatory changes, and analyst opinions on their focus sectors. This daily briefing kept them informed without drowning in information.

The combination of Claude's knowledge and current web search is powerful. Claude knows the fundamentals, and then adds current information on top. You get both deep understanding and up-to-date details.

Managing Information Overload

Having too much information is as bad as having too little. You receive long reports, dense articles, and complex documents. They all demand attention. Reading everything thoroughly isn't realistic, but skimming risks missing important details. Claude processes documents for you, extracts what you need, and organizes information to support decisions rather than just add to the pile.

This section shows you three powerful techniques for managing information: summarizing dense documents, extracting specific information from long content, and organizing information to support decision-making.

Summarizing dense documents instantly

Suppose that you receive a 50-page report. You need to understand it, but you don't have time to read every word. Turning dense documents into clear summaries is one of Claude's most practical capabilities.

Upload the document and ask Claude to summarize it. Claude reads the entire document and gives you a concise summary that captures the essential information. You can then customize the summary to your needs.

REMEMBER

Document uploads are available on all Claude plans, including Free (up to 20 files, 30MB each).

Consider these ways to get the summary you need:

- **Focus on what matters to you.** "Summarize with a focus on financial implications" or "Summarize from an operational perspective."
- **Control the level of detail.** "Give me a one-paragraph overview" or "Give me a detailed summary with all the major points."
- **Understand document structure.** "Summarize each section separately."
- **Find actionable items.** "Focus on what I need to do next."
- **Ask follow-up questions about the document.** "What does section 4 say about costs?" or "Does this address the concerns from the previous proposal?" Because Claude has read the entire document, it can answer without you having to search through the document.

Extracting what matters from long content

Sometimes you don't need a summary; you need specific information buried in a long document. Ask Claude to extract what you need. Claude can extract many types of information:

- » **Action items and decisions:** "What are all the action items in this meeting transcript?"
- » **Dates and deadlines:** "Extract all the dates and deadlines mentioned."
- » **Requirements and specifications:** "What requirements does this contract specify?"
- » **Research and evidence:** "List all the research studies cited and their conclusions."

Ask Claude to analyze what it extracts. "Which action items are assigned to my team?" or "Are any deadlines in conflict?" This goes beyond simple extraction to basic analysis. A project manager used this constantly: "Extract all new requirements from this email chain" or "What decisions were made in this meeting?" This saved hours of reading and ensured that they didn't miss details buried in long communications.

Organizing information for decision-making

Information overload isn't just about volume; it's about not knowing what to do with what you have. You've collected facts, opinions, and recommendations, but you need to organize them to help you decide, not just know more.

Claude structures information for decision-making. Take everything you've gathered and ask Claude to organize it. Claude structures the information to make comparison easy. Consider the ways Claude helps organize information for decisions:

- » **Create decision matrices.** "Organize these three options comparing cost, implementation time, and risk."
- » **Identify what's missing.** "What questions do I still need to answer before deciding?"
- » **Prioritize factors.** "Which factors should weigh most heavily in this decision?"
- » **Test your thinking.** "I'm leaning toward option B because of X and Y. What am I not considering?"

When everything feels important, ask Claude to help you focus. "What's the most critical information here?" or "What am I probably underweighting?" This helps you focus on what matters instead of treating all information equally.

TIP

You're still in charge of the decision. Think of Claude as your information gatherer, not your decision-maker. Claude just makes sure you're looking at the right information, organized in the right way, with nothing important overlooked.

IN THIS CHAPTER

» Making faster, better decisions with confidence

» Planning complex projects systematically

» Exploring options without getting overwhelmed

Chapter 12
Solving Problems and Making Decisions

You face problems and decisions every day. Some are small, forcing you to choose an approach. Others are big, making you wonder whether you should go after this opportunity or that one. The challenge isn't just finding answers; it's figuring out the right questions to ask, seeing options you haven't considered, and feeling confident in your choices.

This chapter shows you how Claude transforms problem-solving and decision-making from stressful struggles into focused, productive conversations. You learn specific techniques for getting unstuck, making better decisions faster, and planning projects that work.

Getting Unstuck

Feeling stuck is frustrating. You know there's a solution somewhere, but you keep cycling through the same few ideas that don't quite work. Claude excels at breaking this pattern by helping you find solutions you couldn't see on your own, systematically explore options, and test ideas before committing.

Getting stuck usually isn't a knowledge problem. It's a perspective problem. You've been staring at the same situation from the same angle for so long that alternatives become invisible. Claude's value here isn't superior knowledge. It's a fresh perspective with no attachment to your previous thinking. Claude asks the obvious questions you stopped asking yourself.

Finding new solutions

You keep cycling through ideas, but none feel right. This is when Claude is especially useful — not because it knows your situation better than you do, but because it can break you out of that mental rut.

Start by describing your problem as if explaining it to a colleague.

Don't overthink the structure; get the circumstances out:

Situation: A customer support manager was drowning. Their team couldn't keep up with ticket volume, but hiring wasn't in the budget.

Prompt: "I manage customer support for a software company. Our response time has doubled in the past quarter, but I can't hire more people. My team of five handles about 200 tickets daily. What am I missing?"

Claude's response: Claude began by asking what types of tickets took the longest, whether the manager had analyzed patterns in when tickets arrived, and what percentage were repeat questions. Through this back-and-forth, the manager discovered that 40 percent of tickets asked the same five questions. This was something they knew instinctively but hadn't quantified. Claude suggested the following:

- Creating a searchable FAQ addressing the top 20 questions
- Adding contextual help pop-ups in the product
- Building template responses for common issues

Result: This wasn't an unexpected response, but the support manager was so focused on "we need more people" that they couldn't see other paths forward. The manager built the FAQ in a week. Within a month, ticket volume dropped by 35 percent without adding a single new hire.

TIP

When you're stuck, don't ask, "What should I do?" Instead, start with "Here's my situation" and let Claude ask you questions. The questions often reveal what you haven't considered. The customer support manager asked, "What am I missing?" This shifts Claude from answerer to thought-partner. When you're stuck, that question breaks the pattern. (See Chapter 8 for more on building effective back-and-forth conversations.)

Exploring options systematically

Your brain naturally gravitates toward familiar solutions. When faced with a problem, you probably think of two or three approaches quickly, and then stop. Claude helps you push past that initial list.

Making a decision is harder when all the options look reasonable and choosing the wrong one could cost thousands of dollars and months of frustration:

Situation: A consultant needed to help a client choose between three software vendors. All seemed viable, with subtle differences.

Prompt: "I'm advising a midsize manufacturer on choosing between three CRM vendors. They need to scale quickly but have limited IT support. Vendor A costs $50K/year with extensive features. Vendor B costs $30K with fewer features but better support. Vendor C costs $20K and is cloud-native. Help me build a decision framework."

Claude's response: Claude didn't just pick one. Before Claude made a choice, it asked the consultant about growth projections, current technical debt, and risk tolerance. Claude used their answers to build a framework weighting each factor — scalability, IT support, total cost of ownership, and implementation:

- » Scalability (weight: 30 percent) is critical given growth plans
- » IT support requirements (weight: 25 percent) are a major constraint
- » Total cost of ownership (weight: 25 percent), not just license fees
- » Implementation timeline (weight: 20 percent) needed within 90 days

Result: The client chose the middle-priced option, but more importantly, they understood why it fit their specific situation rather than being swayed by a sales pitch.

Template: "Help me brainstorm [number] different approaches to [goal], ranging from conventional to creative. For each, tell me the required resources and the results I might expect."

The real skill isn't generating more options. It's generating different types of options. Most people brainstorm variations on the same theme. Push yourself to explore categories. For example:

- What approaches are conventional?
- What ideas are creative or unconventional?
- What are the high-risk, high-reward possibilities?
- What could I do with half the budget?

This forces you to consider solutions from multiple categories.

Testing ideas before committing

The best way to evaluate an idea is to test it in a limited, low-risk way before committing fully. Claude helps you design these small experiments.

The worst business mistakes happen when you build something expensive that no one wants to buy:

Situation: A software company founder wondered whether customers would be willing to pay more for premium support.

Prompt: "We're considering adding a premium support tier at $200/month in addition to our $50/month base plan. Without rebuilding our entire support infrastructure, how can I test whether customers would pay for this?"

Claude's response: Claude suggested a 90-day pilot:

- Offer the premium tier to 10 percent of the customer base.
- Define "premium" as a priority queue and a 4-hour response guarantee.
- Track uptake rate, support costs, and customer satisfaction.
- Survey customers who declined to understand objections.

Result: The pilot showed 15 percent uptake, enough to justify the full rollout. The company refined the offering based on feedback before launching it to everyone.

Template: "I'm considering [major change]. How can I test whether [key assumption] without [major commitment you want to avoid]?"

Choosing the right approach

How do you know which technique fits your situation? Here's a quick guide:

- **If you don't know what's wrong:** Start with "what am I missing?" questions. Let Claude probe your assumptions.
- **If you know the problem but need options:** Use systematic exploration. Ask for different types of solutions, not just more of the same.
- **If you have an idea but aren't sure it'll work:** Design a small test. Find the cheapest way to validate your key assumption.

TIP

You're using Claude to discover what you can't see on your own, such as blind spots, unexplored options, or untested assumptions.

A startup founder learned this the hard way. They asked Claude to help them brainstorm marketing channels, generating dozens of options. But the real problem wasn't a lack of options. It was that they didn't know why the current approach wasn't working. They'd picked the wrong technique.

They backed up and asked, "What am I missing about why our content isn't converting?" Claude's questions revealed that they had targeted the wrong audience. All those marketing channel options were useless until they fixed the underlying problem.

Making Better Decisions Faster

Every decision involves trade-offs, and rushing through analysis often means missing important factors. Claude helps you make better decisions faster by systematically weighing options and providing an objective perspective.

TIP

Most people make decisions by gut feeling, and then rationalize them afterward. Claude helps you reverse that process. It helps you examine your options systematically first, and then trust your gut with full information. The goal is not to eliminate intuition but to inform it.

Weighing pros and cons objectively

Making a pros and cons list seems simple, but most people do it poorly, listing surface-level factors without thinking about weight or likelihood. Claude helps you create decision frameworks that clarify choices.

The hardest business decisions are not between good and bad options but between two different versions of success:

Situation: A marketing consultant had to decide whether to increase their business.

Prompt: "I'm deciding whether to expand my consulting practice by hiring two employees or to stay solo and turn down work I can't handle. I value flexibility but also want to grow. Help me think through this."

Claude's response: Claude organized the analysis into categories:

- **Financial:** Initial hiring costs versus revenue potential.
- **Time:** Gains (leverage) versus losses (management overhead).
- **Risk:** What could go wrong, and how bad would it be?
- **Personal:** Which aligns with how you want to work?

Then Claude asked a clarifying question: "Which matters more, maximizing income or maximizing flexibility? If you could only have one, which would you choose?" That question clarified that flexibility was the consultant's core priority.

Result: The decision became obvious: stay solo and be selective. The value wasn't in the framework itself. It was in the question that revealed their true priority. Often, the best decisions come not from more analysis, but from the right question at the right time.

Template: "I'm deciding between [Option A] and [Option B]. My priorities are [list two to three things that matter most]. Help me create a decision framework that weighs these factors."

Analyzing trade-offs clearly

Every decision involves trade-offs. You gain something but give up something else. Claude helps you see these clearly so you can choose with eyes wide open.

The biggest career gambles are not about taking risks but about choosing which risks to take:

Situation: A product manager was offered a role at a startup: a higher title, an equity stake, and the chance to build from scratch. But the change meant leaving stability, taking a pay cut, and accepting higher risk.

Prompt: "Map the trade-offs of leaving my corporate PM role for a startup. Current salary $150K, stable. Startup offers $120K plus 0.5 percent equity. What am I really trading?"

Claude's response: Claude mapped four categories:

- **What you gain:** Ownership, title, building something new
- **What you give up:** $30K/year, stability, established relationships
- **What stays the same:** Your skills, reputation, career direction
- **What becomes uncertain:** Work-life balance, management style, whether equity will be worth anything

Result: The key insight came when Claude asked: "At what point in your career and life are you? Can you afford this risk right now?" The manager realized that in five years, with a mortgage and possibly family obligations, they couldn't take this risk. But right now, they could. They said yes.

Templates: "If I [decision], what am I trading? Map the gains, losses, constants, and uncertainties."

"What would I need to believe for [Option A] to be the right choice? What about [Option B]?"

"If I make this decision and it turns out badly, what's the most likely reason?"

"What would a skeptic say about my reasoning here?"

Getting a second opinion instantly

Sometimes you've already decided, but you want to make sure you haven't missed something obvious. Claude acts as a sounding board, probing your assumptions.

Turning down good money feels wrong, but defaulting on work you can't deliver will feel worse:

Situation: A freelance designer was offered a rush project at a premium rate but feels overwhelmed by the current workload.

Prompt: "I'm leaning toward declining a $5,000 rush project because I'm already at capacity with three other clients. The deadline is in two weeks. Talk me through my reasoning. Am I making the right call?"

Claude's response: "What's your actual capacity? Could you reshuffle any current work? Is $5,000 worth the stress? What relationships might declining affect?"

Result: Through the conversation, the designer realized that they could postpone one internal project with flexible timing, making room for the lucrative rush work. Without the second opinion, they would have declined automatically.

Template: "I've decided to [your decision] because [your reasoning]. Probe my assumptions, what might I be missing?"

Use Claude to check for cognitive biases: Am I anchoring on the first option I heard? Overweighting recent information? Letting sunk costs influence my choice?

WARNING

Don't ask Claude to decide for you. Prompts like "Should I take this job?" or "Which option is best?" won't work. Claude doesn't know your values, risk tolerance, or life circumstances well enough to make decisions for you. Instead, ask Claude to help you think: "Help me see the trade-offs" or "What am I not considering?" You decide. Claude helps you see clearly.

Watch out for the common trap of using Claude to avoid making a decision. If you've mapped trade-offs three different ways, explored every option, probed your assumptions twice, and still can't commit, the problem isn't information. It's avoidance.

Planning Projects and Workflows

Big goals feel overwhelming because you're looking at the entire mountain instead of the path up it. Complex projects fail most often in planning. Not because the goal is impossible, but because the plan doesn't account for reality.

Breaking big goals into manageable steps

Claude helps you break any large goal into specific, actionable steps you can schedule and complete.

The hardest part of self-publishing isn't writing the book — it's knowing what to do when you've finished writing:

Situation: A writer wanted to self-publish their first novel but feels completely lost.

Prompt: "I want to independently publish my 80,000-word novel. I've finished the first draft but have no idea what comes next. Break this down for me."

Claude's response: Claude identified the major phases and dependencies:

- Revision and beta readers (4 to 6 weeks)

- Professional editing can't be formatted until revisions are done (3 to 4 weeks)
- Cover design needs professional editing before marketing (2 to 3 weeks, can overlap with editing)
- Formatting for platforms (1 week)
- Platform setup and launch strategy (2 weeks)

Result: The scary goal of "publish a book" became a project plan that the writer could execute step by step.

Template: "I want to [big goal] but don't know where to start. Break this into phases with dependencies. What has to happen before what?"

REMEMBER

A good test for any step is asking yourself, "Can I start it right now with the resources I currently have?" If not, break the step down further.

Creating realistic timelines and milestones

Most project plans fall apart when it comes to making timelines and milestones that are realistic. People underestimate time, ignore dependencies, and don't account for reality.

The fastest way to miss a deadline is to plan that everything will go perfectly:

Situation: A product manager was planning a feature release. Their initial timeline had everything completed in six weeks: design, development, QA, documentation, and training.

Prompt: "Here's my feature release plan for the next 6 weeks. Tell me where I'm being unrealistic."

Claude's response: Claude walked through the dependencies. Developers can't start until the design is finalized. QA can't test until development is done. Documentation needs the nearly final product. Claude also suggested buffer rules:

» External approvals: Add 50 percent more time.
» Coordination among multiple people: Add 30 percent.
» Anything you're doing for the first time: Double your estimate.

Result: When the product manager mapped the sequential nature, they realized the project required 12 weeks, not 6. They caught this before promising stakeholders an impossible deadline.

Template: "Here's my project plan with [timeline]. What depends on what? Where am I likely underestimating?"

TIP

These buffer rules might feel pessimistic, but they help you explore possibilities. Projects rarely finish early but frequently run late. Building in buffers doesn't slow you down. It keeps you from making promises you can't keep.

Anticipating obstacles and solutions

No plan survives contact with reality without needing changes. The question isn't whether you'll encounter obstacles, but whether you've thought about how to handle them.

The question isn't whether your renovation will hit problems — it's whether you'll have enough money left when it does:

Situation: A small business owner was planning to renovate their store.

Prompt: "Here's my renovation timeline and $40,000 budget. What problems should I prepare for?"

Claude's response: Claude identified risks with contingencies: contractors running behind (build in a 2-week buffer), costs exceeding estimates (set aside a 20 percent contingency, which equals $8,000), structural surprises (get an inspection before finalizing the budget), lost sales during construction (plan a "pardon our dust" sale).

Result: The small business owner wasn't financially strapped when outdated electrical wiring was found because they budgeted for unexpected issues.

TIP

After creating any project plan, ask Claude: "What's the one thing most likely to derail this plan?" Focus your contingency planning on the biggest risk first.

Here are some other templates for risk planning:

- "Here's my plan. What could go wrong at each stage?"
- "If [preferred approach] doesn't work, what's my Plan B?"
- "What's the one thing most likely to derail this?"

REMEMBER

The techniques in this chapter externalize your thinking. When problems and decisions stay in your head, you cycle through the same limited options. When you explain them to Claude, you're forced to think through assumptions and consider perspectives you'd otherwise miss. The goal isn't to have Claude decide for you; it's to have Claude help you think more clearly so you can choose with confidence.

TIP

For more on structuring complex requests, see Chapter 9. For handling data that informs your decisions, see Chapter 13.

IN THIS CHAPTER

- » Getting quick answers from uploaded documents
- » Creating formulas and automating spreadsheet tasks without coding
- » Working with PDFs, images, and different file formats

Chapter 13
Handling Data and Documents

Your manager sends a spreadsheet with six months of sales data at 4:30 pm on Friday. They ask, "What's driving the downturn in the Midwest region?" You could spend an hour building pivot tables in Excel and charts to find patterns, or you could upload the documents and ask Claude. If you upload the files, you can get an answer in seconds. That's the difference that Claude offers. You can

- » Upload documents and get instant answers to specific questions.
- » Analyze spreadsheets to identify patterns without manually creating charts.
- » Create formulas by describing what you need in plain English.
- » Compare multiple reports and see where they agree or conflict.
- » Extract text from images and understand charts without manual interpretation.

These aren't convenience features. They're the difference between spending your day extracting information or spending minutes making a decision. Claude handles the document processing. You handle the thinking.

Claude handles files in two different ways:

- **Upload and analyze (all plans, including Free):** Upload existing files (PDF, Word, Excel, CSV, images, text, and rich text format) and ask Claude questions about them. Claude reads, summarizes, and extracts information.
- **Create files (paid plans only):** Have Claude generate Excel spreadsheets with formulas, PowerPoint presentations, Word documents, or PDFs.

This chapter covers both capabilities.

REMEMBER

Document upload and analysis features are available on all Claude plans, including Free. Free plan users have more limited daily usage quotas (and lower priority during peak times compared to paid subscribers). Creating files (Excel, PowerPoint, Word, PDF) requires a paid plan.

Getting Instant Answers from Documents

You receive a 50-page contract from your client, and they ask you about the termination clause. You upload the document to Claude, type your question, and get your answer in seconds. Requesting specific information works for any document you need to understand quickly, such as contracts, reports, proposals, research papers, grant applications, and policy documents. Claude reads the document so you can focus on decision-making.

Uploading and asking questions

Uploading and asking questions is straightforward. The more precise your question, the more useful the response. Here's how uploading a document to ask questions about it works in practice:

Situation: A financial consultant received a 45-page vendor contract two hours before a client meeting. The client wanted to know about payment terms, late penalties, and any early payment incentives. Reading the entire contract carefully would take at least an hour. Instead, the consultant uploaded the contract and prompts Claude.

Prompt: "What are the payment terms, including due dates, late penalties, and any early payment discounts?"

Claude's response: It identified the key information scattered across sections of the contract:

- Payment terms: Net 30 from invoice date (not delivery date)
- Late penalty: 1.5 percent monthly interest on overdue balances
- Early payment discount: 2 percent if paid within 10 days
- Invoice date definition: Date invoice is sent, not date of service delivery

Result: The consultant copied these points into their meeting notes and walked into the client meeting prepared. The specificity of the question made Claude's response immediately actionable. Asking "What are the payment terms?" alone might have resulted in a vaguer answer. Adding "including due dates, late penalties, and early payment discounts" told Claude exactly what information mattered.

Why this worked: The question specified the document type (vendor contract), named the exact information needed, and used precise terms (late penalties, early payment discounts). Claude knew where to look and what to extract.

Template: "What are the [specific terms you need], including [detail 1], [detail 2], and [additional relevant information]?"

Finding specific information fast

Sometimes you need to pull multiple pieces of information from a long document. Manually searching through page after page wastes time and risks missing important details. Here's an example:

Situation: A nonprofit grant writer received a 60-page request for proposals (RFP) for a community development grant. They needed to extract eligibility requirements, submission deadlines, and required supporting documents. These details appeared throughout the RFP with no clear summary section.

Prompt: "This is the RFP for the Community Development Grant. Pull out all eligibility requirements, submission deadlines, and required supporting documents."

Claude's response: It created a structured response that included all the details of the requested items.

Result: The grant writer used this extraction as their submission checklist. They verified each item against the original RFP to ensure accuracy, and then began gathering documents. What would have taken 90 minutes of careful reading and note-taking took 10 minutes.

Why this worked: The prompt asked for structured extraction of specific categories. Claude organized scattered information from the 60-page document into clear sections. The writer didn't have to hunt through narrative text for buried requirements.

Template: "This is the [document type] for [project/purpose]. Pull out all [requirement category 1], [requirement category 2], and [requirement category 3]."

Comparing multiple documents

When you need to compare several documents, Claude can identify patterns, agreements, and contradictions. This feature works especially well when different sources provide conflicting information or when you need to synthesize multiple perspectives. See how this plays out:

Situation: A product manager received three competitive analysis reports about AI assistants from different research firms. Each report was 30 to 40 pages. Reading all three carefully would consume an entire afternoon, and extracting key comparisons would require detailed notes. Instead, the manager uploaded all three reports and prompted Claude.

Prompt: "What do all three reports agree on? Where do they disagree? What are the key differences in their conclusions?"

Claude's response: It synthesized the reports. Agreement across all three reports:

- AI assistant market will grow 40–50 percent annually through 2028.
- Enterprise adoption is significantly ahead of consumer adoption.

Key disagreements:

- Report A predicts market consolidation to 3 to 4 major players by 2027.
- Report B expects 10+ viable competitors with differentiated positioning.

Methodology differences:

- Report A is a survey of 200 enterprise IT decision-makers.
- Report B analyzed public company financial disclosures and product announcements.

Result: The product manager spotted that growth projections matched, but market predictions differed depending on the research method. That insight shaped their conversation.

Why this worked: The prompt asked for synthesis, not summary. Instead of describing each report separately, Claude compared perspectives and identified patterns. The product manager got strategic insight, not just data extraction.

Template: "What do all [number] [documents/reports/sources] agree on? Where do they disagree? What are the key differences in their [conclusions/recommendations/findings]?"

Analyzing Data without Being a Data Scientist

You don't need to be a data scientist to understand your data. You need to be able to spot patterns, explain what the numbers show, and translate findings into plain language. Claude reads your data and tells you what it means without requiring you to understand regression analysis or pivot tables.

Understanding patterns in your data

Numbers alone don't tell you much. The meaning appears when you see how the numbers are related, how they change over time, and where the outliers are. Claude finds these patterns, so you don't have to manually chart every combination.

See how this works:

Situation: A small business owner tracked website traffic for six months but couldn't figure out why the website performed significantly better some weeks rather than others. The spreadsheet had 180 rows of daily data showing visits, page views, and conversion rates. The owner assumed that there were seasonal patterns but couldn't prove it.

Prompt: "Look at this traffic data and tell me what patterns you see. Why is performance better in some weeks? Are there any days of the week or times of the month that consistently show higher traffic?"

Claude's response: It identified patterns the owner hadn't considered:

- *Strong weekly pattern:* Traffic peaks on Tuesdays and Wednesdays (averaging 40 percent higher than weekends).
- *Monthly cycle:* The first and third weeks of each month show 25 percent higher traffic than the second and fourth weeks.
- *Outlier weeks:* Three weeks showed exceptional performance, and all followed an email campaign sent on Monday mornings.

Result: The owner immediately adjusted their content publishing schedule to Tuesday mornings and aligned email campaigns with the first and third weeks of the month. Traffic increased over the next quarter simply by timing content release differently.

Why this worked: The question asked Claude to identify patterns rather than report numbers. It looked for weekly cycles, monthly trends, and outliers that explained performance variance.

Template: "Look at this [type of data] and tell me what patterns you see. Why do [some periods/items/categories] perform better? Are there any [time periods/categories/segments] that consistently show [higher/lower] [metric]?"

Creating summaries and insights

Raw data can be overwhelming. You have hundreds of rows showing transactions, customer behaviors, or metrics. You need to communicate what matters to people who won't read spreadsheets. Claude transforms data into narratives that will make sense to your audience. Here's an example:

Situation: A nonprofit program director needed to report on participant outcomes from a job training program. The data included attendance records, skill assessments, job placements, and six-month follow-up surveys for 85 participants. The board wanted a concise summary showing program effectiveness, not detailed tables.

Prompt: "Create a summary of this program data that shows the effectiveness of our training. Focus on completion rates, skill improvement, job placement, and retention. Make it clear enough for board members who haven't seen the detailed data."

Claude's response:

- *Program completion:* 72 of 85 participants completed training (85 percent).
- *Skill improvement:* Participants averaged a 3.2-point increase on skill assessments (scale of 1–0).
- *Job placement:* 61 completers secured employment within 90 days (85 percent placement rate).
- *Six-month retention:* 52 of 61 placed participants remained employed (85 percent retention).
- *Program effectiveness:* 61 percent of all enrollees secured and retained employment for six months.

Result: The director included this summary in their board presentation. The progression from enrollment through retention told the story of the program's effect without requiring the board to interpret the raw numbers.

Why this worked: The prompt specified both the metrics that mattered (completion, improvement, placement, retention) and the audience (board members needing clarity without detail). Claude structured information to show progression and ultimate effect.

Template: "Create a summary of this [data type] that shows [specific outcomes]. Focus on [key metrics]. Make it clear for [audience] who [their level of familiarity with the data]."

Getting explanations of what the numbers mean

Sometimes you understand the numbers but not their implications. You see that metric X increased while metric Y decreased, but you're not sure what that combination means for your business, project, or decision. Claude can connect the dots:

Situation: A product team analyzed user engagement metrics and found something confusing. Daily active users increased by 15 percent, while average session duration decreased by 22 percent. They couldn't determine if this represented success or a problem. More users seemed positive, but shorter sessions seemed negative.

Prompt: "I'm seeing daily active users up 15 percent, but session duration down 22 percent. What does this combination of metrics typically indicate? Is this good or bad for a productivity app?"

Claude's response: "For a productivity app, this pattern typically indicates users are achieving their goals faster. Increased daily users show the app is becoming essential to more people's workflows. Decreased session duration suggests the app is getting more efficient at helping users complete tasks quickly."

Result: The team stopped worrying about session duration and focused on supporting the growth in daily users. They recognized that they'd built a tool that people used frequently because it saved them time, not because it kept them engaged longer. This shifted their product strategy from increasing engagement time to reducing friction.

Why this worked: The question provided context (a productivity app) and asked for an interpretation rather than just a description. Claude explained what the metric combination typically means and why it matters in this specific context.

Template: "I'm seeing [metric A] do [X] while [metric B] does [Y]. What does this combination typically indicate? Is this [positive/negative/neutral] for [type of product/service/organization]?"

TIP

Upload your data and ask questions as they occur to you. You don't need to formulate the perfect question upfront. Start with "What stands out in this data?" and follow up based on what Claude identifies. The conversation will naturally lead you toward insights.

Getting Help with Spreadsheets and Automation

Spreadsheets may intimidate you. You know what you want to calculate, track, or analyze, but translating that into formulas and functions feels like learning a foreign language. Claude bridges this gap. You describe what you need in plain language, and Claude handles the technical implementation.

TECHNICAL STUFF

Creating Excel files requires enabling code execution and file creation (available for Pro, Max, Team, and Enterprise plans). See Chapter 6 for instructions on enabling this feature. However, all plans, including the Free plan, enable you to upload existing Excel files to read and analyze. CSV files can also be uploaded to all plans for reading and analysis. (A CSV file is a simple text file that stores data in a table format. Each line represents a row, and commas separate the values in each column.)

Creating formulas for your spreadsheets

If you have an existing spreadsheet, you can upload it to Claude on any plan and ask for help with formulas. If you want Claude to create a spreadsheet with formulas from scratch, you'll need a paid plan with code execution enabled.

If you need to track customer lifetime value, calculate weighted averages, or sum values that meet specific criteria, the logic makes sense in your head, but Excel's syntax doesn't. See this in action:

Situation: A bookstore owner tracked monthly sales in a spreadsheet. They wanted to know which months hit their $15,000 sales goal but didn't know how to write a formula to check.

Prompt: "I need a formula that says 'Goal Met' if sales in column B are $15,000 or more, and 'Below Goal' if they're less. Put the result in column C."

Claude's response: It provided this formula:

```
=IF(B2>=15000, "Goal Met", "Below Goal")
```

Result: The owner typed the formula into cell C2, and then used AutoFill by dragging the small green square at the bottom-right corner of C2 down through C5 to copy it to the remaining rows. Because the formula uses a relative reference, Excel automatically adjusted the row number in each cell, so C3 checked B3, C4 checked B4, and C5 checked B5. Now, every month, the owner can automatically see whether they hit their goal, as shown in Figure 13-1.

Why this worked: The prompt specified exactly what to check ($15,000), what to display (Goal Met or Below Goal), and where to put it (column C).

Template: "I need a formula that says '[result 1]' if [column] is [condition], and '[result 2]' if not. Put the result in column [X]."

	A	B	C
1	Month	Sales	Status
2	January	$12,500	Below Goal
3	February	$18,200	Goal Met
4	March	$14,000	Goal Met
5	April	$16,500	Goal Met
6			
7			
8			
9			
10			

FIGURE 13-1: The formula Claude produced is entered into the spreadsheet.

Automating repetitive work without coding

Suppose that you perform the same spreadsheet tasks repeatedly: formatting new data, creating monthly reports, and generating summary tables. Each iteration takes 20 minutes of clicking and copying. You think automation could help, but you don't know how to program macros or scripts. Consider how this enfolds:

Situation: A financial analyst received monthly expense reports from 12 departments. Each report arrived as a comma-separated values (CSV) file with an identical structure but inconsistent formatting. Each month, the analyst spends 30 minutes on each of the 12 files, applying formatting, adding totals, and creating summary charts.

Prompt: "I receive 12 CSV files monthly with expense data. Each has columns for Date, Category, Amount, and Department. I need to convert dates to MM/DD/YYYY format, add currency formatting to amounts, sum totals by category, and create a bar chart showing category totals. Create an Excel file with formulas and formatting that I can paste the data into."

REMEMBER

This example requires code execution and file creation enabled, which are available on paid plans.

Claude's response: It created a spreadsheet template with all the requested formatting.

Result: The analyst then pasted each department's raw data into the template. Formatting, calculations, and charts updated automatically. What took 30 minutes per file now takes 2 minutes. Monthly processing time dropped from 6 hours to 25 minutes.

Why this worked: The prompt described the repetitive task completely (input format, desired transformations, output requirements). Claude provided a ready-made template that eliminated manual work rather than just explaining how to do it manually.

Template: "I receive [data type] [frequency] with [structure]. I need to: [transformation 1], [transformation 2], [transformation 3]. Create an [Excel/spreadsheet] file with formulas and formatting that I can [paste/import] the data into."

Understanding what Claude provides

When Claude creates formulas or spreadsheet solutions, you get working implementations, not just advice. If you're working with an existing file you've uploaded, Claude provides formulas you can copy into your spreadsheet on any plan. If you're asking Claude to create a file, that requires a paid plan with code execution enabled.

Claude provides not only the formulas but also an explanation of them and where to place them.

This approach lets you use solutions immediately without having to translate instructions into action, saving you a lot of time.

Making simple adjustments when needed

Claude's formulas usually work right away, but sometimes you need a quick tweak. Something might be off, or you spot an issue after testing. You don't need spreadsheet expertise; just tell Claude what to change. For example:

> **Situation:** A project manager has a formula that flags projects as "At Risk" too early. Projects with 60 percent done and 30 days left didn't need urgent attention but were flagged anyway.
>
> **Prompt:** "This formula marks projects 'At Risk' when they're less than 70 percent complete and have fewer than 45 days left. Change it to fewer than 30 days instead."
>
> **Claude's response:**
>
> Original formula: =IF(AND(B2<0.70, C2<45), "At Risk", "On Track")
>
> Adjusted formula: =IF(AND(B2<0.70, C2<30), "At Risk", "On Track")
>
> **Result:** Changing 45 to 30 fixed the problem. Now the manager sees accurate flags rather than false alarms.
>
> **Why this worked:** They said exactly what to change (the 45-day cutoff) and why (too many false warnings).
>
> **Template:** "This formula [what it does now]. Change it to [what you want instead]."

TIP

When requesting spreadsheet help, mention which spreadsheet application you use (Excel, Google Sheets, Numbers). While formulas often work across platforms, some functions have different names or syntax. Specifying your tool ensures that Claude provides compatible solutions.

You don't need to understand how formulas work to use them effectively. Copy what Claude provides, test it with a few rows of real data, and verify that the results make sense. If something doesn't work, describe what you're seeing, and Claude can adjust the approach.

Working with Different File Types

Documents arrive in whatever format the sender chooses, not necessarily the format you need. Suppose you receive a PDF when you need editable text or a complex diagram that you need to understand. Claude supports multiple file types, so the format is less likely to limit how you work with information.

REMEMBER

The examples in this section focus on uploading and analyzing existing files, which works on all plans, including the Free plan. Creating files in these formats requires a paid plan.

Processing PDFs, Word docs, and spreadsheets

Different file types require different handling, but from your standpoint, Claude treats them all the same. Upload the file, ask your question, and get your answer. The technical details of extraction and processing happen behind the scenes. Consider this scenario:

Situation: A sales consultant received three vendor proposals. One arrived as a Word document, one as a PDF, and one as a scanned PDF with no selectable text. The consultant needed to compare pricing structures, deliverables, and timelines across all three. Manually extracting this information from three different formats would take over an hour.

Prompt: "I'm uploading three vendor proposals (A, B, and C) in different formats. Extract and compare pricing structure, deliverables included, project timeline, and payment terms. Show me where they differ significantly."

Claude's response: It processed all three files regardless of format and created a comparison of the requested items.

Result: The consultant immediately saw that Vendor B's hourly estimate was significantly lower than the competitors' but lacked the support that Vendor A included. This comparison informed their vendor selection meeting.

Why this worked: The prompt focused on the information that mattered (pricing, deliverables, timeline, terms) rather than on file-format technicalities. Claude handled format differences automatically while extracting comparable information.

Template: "I'm uploading [number] [document types] in different formats. Extract and compare: [key point 1], [key point 2], [key point 3]. Show me where they differ significantly."

Extracting text from images

Sometimes information exists only as an image, such as a screenshot of an error message or a picture of a form someone filled out by hand. You need the text, but retyping wastes time and introduces errors. Here's what this means in action:

Situation: A team lead photographed project notes from a whiteboard session that included action items, responsible parties, and deadlines. The meeting wrapped up, someone erased the board, and now they need those notes in a shareable format. The photo showed 15 action items, each with a name and date.

Prompt: "Extract all the action items from this whiteboard photo. For each item, tell me what needs to be done, who's responsible, and the deadline."

Claude's response: It read the handwritten text from the photo and created a structured list:

- Update client presentation: Sarah, Feb 15
- Review budget forecast: Mike, Feb 12
- Schedule vendor meeting: Jennifer, Feb 18
- Complete security audit: David, Feb 22

Result: The team lead pasted this list into their project tracker. What would have required manual transcription of handwritten notes took seconds. The structured format made it easy to assign tasks in their project management system.

Why this worked: The prompt specified what information to extract (task, person, deadline) rather than just requesting that Claude "transcribe this." Claude organized unstructured visual information into a usable format.

Template: "Extract all the [type of information] from this [image type]. For each item, tell me: [field 1], [field 2], and [field 3]."

Understanding charts and diagrams

Visual information communicates differently from text. Charts show trends, diagrams illustrate relationships, and flowcharts map processes. Sometimes you need to understand what a visualization shows without recreating it or manually interpreting it. Take this case:

Situation: A marketing director received the agency's annual performance review deck. It contained six charts showing campaign reach, channel engagement rates, cost-per-acquisition trends, and shifts in brand awareness. The executive team wants key takeaways for tomorrow's strategy session, but decoding all six visualizations would take more than two hours.

Prompt: "I'm uploading six charts from our annual marketing review. For each chart, tell me: what's the main trend, what's surprising or noteworthy, and what it suggests about our marketing strategy."

Claude's response: It analyzed each visualization as requested and provided new findings.

Result: The marketing director used these insights directly in the strategy session. They understood which channels were working, where costs were rising, and how brand perception had shifted, all without spending time manually interpreting complex visualizations or risking misinterpretation of the data.

Why this worked: The prompt asked for interpretation (trends, notable points, implications) rather than just description. Claude extracted meaning from visual data, not just details.

Template: "I'm uploading [number] charts/diagrams about [topic]. For each one, tell me what's the main [trend/relationship/process], what's surprising or noteworthy, and what it suggests about [your domain/question]."

REMEMBER

Image and diagram analysis capabilities are available on all Claude plans, including the Free plan, although Free plan users have more limited usage allowances. Paid plans (Pro, Max, Team, and Enterprise) offer higher usage limits and priority access during peak times.

TIP

When uploading images of text, charts, or diagrams, a higher resolution produces better results. If Claude has trouble with an image, try taking a clearer photo or using a higher-quality scan. Good lighting and focus matter more than expensive equipment.

IN THIS CHAPTER

» Generating fresh ideas when you're stuck

» Creating social media and marketing content efficiently

» Planning meals and travel itineraries with less effort

Chapter 14

Creating Content for Work and Life

You need to write a social media post, and then create slides for tomorrow's presentation. What about that marketing email you've been avoiding? Content demands never stop, and each piece must be engaging enough to hold people's attention. Even experienced creators can hit the wall. You wind up staring at a blank document, recycling ideas, or settling for mediocre output because you've run out of time and inspiration.

Claude changes this dynamic. It's not about replacing your creativity or judgment. It's about having an AI partner that generates ideas on demand, drafts content you can refine, and helps you break through creative blocks instantly. This chapter shows you how to use Claude to make creating content easier in your work and personal life.

Generating Good Ideas

Coming up with fresh ideas is harder than writing about them. You can write a great social post or outline a strong presentation if you have something interesting to say. The blank page is the real challenge. You need fresh angles and interesting approaches that stand out. When you're brainstorming alone, you exhaust your best ideas quickly and start repeating yourself.

REMEMBER

Claude works best when you give it constraints, context, and a clear definition of success.

Brainstorming without running out of ideas

Solo brainstorming has a natural limit. You think of five ideas, realize three are variations of the same concept, dismiss the other two as impractical, and find yourself stuck. Your brain keeps returning to what feels familiar. You need someone (or something) to push beyond your first instincts and suggest angles you wouldn't consider.

Here's an example of how this unfolds:

Situation: A content marketing manager needed ideas for a quarterly email campaign. They'd been promoting their company's project management software the same way for two years, and engagement was declining.

Prompt: "I need 15 fresh angles for promoting project management software to small creative agencies. Our usual messaging focuses on efficiency and deadline tracking, but that's getting stale. The agencies we work with have 5–20 people, mostly designers and writers who resist structure."

Claude's response: It generated options the marketer hadn't considered. It positioned the software as protection against creative burnout (structure frees creative time), framing it as a client confidence builder (professionalism attracts better clients) and highlighting how it reduces the "where did we leave that?" conversations that derail creative flow. The marketing manager chose three angles and created their most successful campaign in two years.

Why it worked: The manager specified the audience's values (creative, resistant to structure), the constraint (avoiding stale efficiency messaging), and the quantity (15 options). The specificity helped Claude generate targeted ideas rather than generic suggestions.

Template: "I need [number] fresh angles for [goal/topic] to [specific audience]. Our usual [approach] [what you've been doing], but that's getting stale. [Relevant context about audience or situation]."

Pushing past your first (boring) ideas

Your first ideas are rarely your best. They're the obvious answers everyone else is also thinking. The good ideas are hiding beyond that initial burst. But solo brainstorming seldom gets you there because you run out of energy before you reach any interesting territory.

See how this works in practice:

Situation: A nonprofit director needed fundraising ideas for a youth literacy program. Their first brainstorm yielded the predictable options: read-a-thon, book drive, gala dinner. All fine. All forgettable.

Prompt: "Take these three fundraising ideas for a youth literacy program — read-a-thon, book drive, and gala dinner — and push each one in an unexpected direction. How can we make each concept fresh enough so that people will remember it?"

Claude's response: It transformed each idea:

- » The read-a-thon became a 24-hour livestream with some guest appearances by celebrity authors.
- » The book drive became a community book swap, where donors received a book for every book they donated.
- » The gala became a dinner and readings featuring local celebrities performing passages from children's books.

Result: The director combined elements from two suggestions and exceeded their fundraising goal.

Why this worked: Instead of asking for entirely new ideas, the director gave Claude something concrete to work from and asked for a transformation. "Push . . . in an unexpected direction" permitted Claude to be creative, while "fresh enough so that people will remember it" set a clear success criterion.

Template: "Take these [number] [topic] ideas for [goal] — [list your ideas] — and push each one in an unexpected direction. How can we make each concept [specific quality you need]?"

Finding angles others miss

The competitive advantage in content isn't having unique information. Everyone has access to the same facts. You get the benefit when you see those facts from angles your audience hasn't considered yet. Finding those angles when you're absorbed in a topic can be difficult because it's harder to see with fresh eyes what's surprising or interesting to outsiders.

Here's an example in practice:

Situation: A financial advisor wanted to write about retirement planning but knew the topic was oversaturated. Every blog post, podcast, and video covered the same ground: Start early, maximize contributions, diversify investments. Accurate advice, but their audience had heard it countless times.

Prompt: "I'm writing about retirement planning for people in their 30s. The standard advice to start early, maximize contributions, and diversify is everywhere. What angles on retirement planning haven't been covered extensively?"

Claude's response: It suggested angles that reframed familiar territory. These were retirement planning as career insurance that gives you the freedom to take risks; the psychology of why people who start at 35 often end up better off than those who start at 25 and stop; and how retirement planning changes if you don't want a traditional retirement.

Result: The advisor wrote about career insurance and increased their usual engagement.

Why this worked: The advisor acknowledged what was already covered extensively and asked specifically for surprising angles. They identified their audience's age (30s) and what they wanted to avoid (standard advice everyone's heard). Claude could focus on genuinely fresh perspectives rather than rehashing basics.

Template: "I'm [writing/creating content] about [topic] for [audience]. The standard advice [list what's been covered extensively] is everywhere. What angles on [topic] haven't been covered extensively?"

Writing Social Media and Marketing Content

Social media and marketing content need to work hard in a limited space. You're competing for attention against everything else your audience could look at, and you need to engage them fast. The challenge isn't just writing well. It's writing with purpose, adapting tone for different platforms, and staying consistent across everything you create.

Writing posts that get responses

Posts that get likes, shares, and responses aren't accidents. They pull people in and make them want to interact. The challenge is creating that pull consistently when you're posting several times a week and running out of fresh ideas.

This is an example of how this works in practice:

Situation: A small business owner sold handmade ceramics and regularly posted on Instagram, but engagement remained flat. The posts looked nice but generated minimal response. They displayed the products, mentioned new items, and occasionally shared workshop photos. All were pleasant; all were forgettable.

Prompts: "I sell handmade ceramics. Here are my last three Instagram posts: [pasted]. They're getting low engagement. Rewrite them to be more engaging while staying authentic to a small, independent maker. My audience is people who appreciate craftsmanship and sustainability."

Claude's response: It rewrote the product announcement to focus on the decision point that made each piece unique ("This mug almost didn't make it; the glaze was running too thick. But that 'flaw' created this watercolor effect that I love more than the planned result. Sometimes the best pieces are the ones that surprise you."). The new items post became a question that invited responses ("What matters more to you: a piece that's absolutely perfect, or one that has character from being handmade?"). The workshop photo turned into a brief story about learning to trust the process when a batch wasn't turning out as planned.

Engagement increased immediately. People responded to the questions, shared the posts about embracing imperfection, and several buyers mentioned that the captions influenced their purchases.

Why this worked: The business owner provided examples of their current posts (showing the style that wasn't working), specified what needed to change (to be more engaging), defined their authentic voice (a small, independent maker), and identified their audience's values (craftsmanship, sustainability). Claude could rewrite with a specific direction rather than guessing what *more engaging* meant.

Template: "I [describe what you do/sell]. Here are my last [number] [platform] posts: [paste the posts]. They're getting low engagement. Rewrite them to be more engaging while staying authentic to [your voice/brand]. My audience is [who they are and what they value]."

Tailoring content for each platform

The same message doesn't work across all platforms. LinkedIn audiences expect a different tone and depth than Instagram audiences. X rewards brevity and directness, while Facebook allows more story development. Each platform needs a different approach, but figuring out how to adapt your message without losing your point takes hours you don't have.

Here's an example of this in practice:

Situation: A career coach was launching a new workshop on career transitions. They'd written a detailed announcement covering the curriculum, their background, and why they created the program. It was perfect for their email newsletter. But they needed versions for LinkedIn, Instagram, and Facebook, each requiring a different approach while conveying the same essential information.

Prompt: "Here's my workshop announcement for email: [pasted the full announcement]. Create three versions: one for LinkedIn that emphasizes professional development and is appropriate for a business audience, one for Instagram that's more personal and visually friendly with a storytelling approach, and one for Facebook that balances personal connection with practical details."

Claude's response: It produced three distinct versions:

- The LinkedIn post opened with statistics and positioned the workshop as a professional investment.
- The Instagram post told a brief story about the coach's own career transition and used a conversational, mobile-friendly format.
- The Facebook post blended a personal story with practical details and included a clear call to action to register.

Each maintained the core message while fitting the platform's culture.

Why this worked: The career coach provided the source material (full email announcement), specified exactly what each platform needed (tone, approach, audience expectations), and made clear what needed to stay consistent across all versions (the essential information). Claude adapted rather than invented, maintaining message integrity while matching platform requirements.

Template: "Here's my [content type] for [original platform]: [paste content]. "Create [number] versions: one for [platform] that [specific requirement], [repeat (number) of times]."

Maintaining brand voice and consistency

Your brand voice is how people recognize your content before they see your name. It's the consistent personality in everything you publish that makes people trust you. But keeping that voice consistent when three different people are writing? That's where things get complicated.

Here's an example of how to maintain your brand's voice:

Situation: A growing startup consisted the founder, a marketing coordinator, three people creating content, and a contractor who wrote blog posts. Customers could tell which person wrote what because each had a distinct style. The team needed consistency without forcing everyone to write the same way.

Prompt: "Here are three examples of our best content that captured our brand voice: [pasted three pieces]. Analyze what makes these work and create a style guide that describes our voice in terms that other writers can follow. Include specific dos and don'ts with examples."

Claude's response: It identified patterns — the brand used active voice consistently, led with the reader's problem before introducing solutions, avoided jargon except when immediately explained, and used humor sparingly. It noted that the brand made bold statements but always backed them with evidence, and never used phrases like *game-changing* or *revolutionary.* The resulting guide gave the team specific, actionable direction.

Result: The contractor said the guide was the first one to help them match an existing voice, rather than describe abstract qualities like *friendly and professional.*

Why this worked: The team provided multiple examples of content that worked (showing the voice in action), asked for an analysis of patterns (not just a description), and requested specific dos and don'ts with examples (making it actionable for other writers). Claude could extract concrete guidelines rather than vague characteristics.

Template: "Here are [number] examples of our best content that captured our brand voice: [paste examples]. Analyze what makes these work and create a style guide that describes our voice in terms that other writers can follow. Include specific dos and don'ts with examples."

Building Presentations and Slide Content

Presentations combine writing, structure, and visual thinking. You need to organize information logically, write content that works when spoken aloud, and create slides that support rather than distract from your message. Each element requires different skills, and getting all three working together proves challenging.

Outlining compelling presentations

A persuasive outline makes sure your presentation flows logically and builds to a satisfying conclusion. Without that structure, even great individual slides feel disconnected. You jump between topics, repeat points, or reach the end without a clear resolution.

REMEMBER

The outline is where you figure out what to say and in what order, before you commit the time and effort to create slides.

Here's an example:

Situation: A sales trainer needed to create a presentation on handling difficult client conversations for a team of 25 account managers. They knew the key points they wanted to cover: staying calm under pressure, asking clarifying questions, and knowing when to escalate. But they couldn't figure out how to structure those elements into a narrative that built itself naturally.

Prompt: "I need to create a 30-minute presentation for account managers on handling difficult client conversations. The key skills are staying calm under pressure, asking clarifying questions, and knowing when to escalate. My audience deals with these situations weekly but doesn't have formal training. Create an outline that builds these skills in a logical sequence."

Claude's response: It structured the presentation around a framework. It opened with why difficult conversations escalate, showing the warning signs the sales trainer's team already recognized intuitively. Then it taught techniques in the order they'd use them: staying calm first, asking clarifying questions next, and escalating last. The outline closed with a decision tree the team could reference later during client conversations. The outline turned scattered skills into a coherent system.

Why this worked: The trainer specified the time constraint (30 minutes), identified the key skills to cover, described the audience's experience level (deals with situations weekly but lacks training), and asked for logical sequencing. Claude could structure around learning progression rather than just listing topics.

Template: "I need to create a [length] presentation for [audience] on [topic]. The key [skills/points/concepts] are [list them]. My audience [relevant context about their knowledge or experience]. Create an outline that [specific structural requirement]."

Writing slide text that works

Slide text isn't the same as document text. You're writing for an audience that's hearing you speak while reading your slides. Too much text and they read instead of listening. Too little and the slides don't reinforce your points. You need text that supports your spoken message without competing with it.

Here's an example of how to apply this:

Situation: A technology director was presenting a cybersecurity policy update to department heads. Their first-draft slides were dense paragraphs explaining each policy point in detail. When they practiced, they found themselves either reading the slides word-for-word (boring) or talking about topics that weren't on the slides (confusing).

Prompt: "Here are my cybersecurity policy slides with full paragraph text: [pasted the slides]. Rewrite the slide text to be speaker-friendly: each slide should have one clear headline and 3 to 4 bullet points that support what I'll say out loud without being complete sentences I need to read verbatim."

Claude's response: It transformed the paragraphs into a slide-ready format. The original slide had a paragraph explaining password requirements: multifactor authentication, 90-day rotation, and approved password managers. Claude turned the slide into a headline (New Password Requirements) and three bullets, one for each key fact.

Result: The director could speak naturally about why each requirement mattered while the slide showed the key facts.

Why this worked: The director provided the content (full paragraphs), specified the format needed (headline and 3 to 4 bullets), and explained the functional requirement (support spoken content without being read verbatim). Claude could restructure the presentation medium rather than summarize.

Template: "Here are my [topic] slides with full paragraph text: [paste content]. Rewrite the slide text to be speaker-friendly: each slide should have [structure you need] that [functional requirement]."

Creating speaker notes and scripts you can use

Speaker notes keep you on track without sounding like you're reading a script. You need enough detail to remember your key points, but not so much text that you're glancing down every five seconds. The challenge is writing notes that give you confidence without making you sound wooden.

Situation: A department manager was preparing a presentation of quarterly results to senior leaders. They'd created slides with data visualizations and key metrics but needed notes to help them speak confidently about what the numbers meant and what actions they were taking.

Prompt: "Here are my quarterly results slides: [pasted the slides]. Create speaker notes for each slide that cover what the data shows, why it matters, and what we're doing about it. Keep each slide's notes to 3 to 4 sentences that I can glance at while presenting."

Claude's response: It wrote notes that gave the manager structure without being a script. For the slide showing decreased response times, the notes read: "Response time down 15 percent from last quarter. This came from the new triage system we implemented in July. The improvement means we're handling 50 more requests weekly with the same team size. Next quarter, we're expanding this approach to our west coast team."

Result: The manager could glance at the notes and speak naturally while hitting all the key points.

Why this worked: The manager pasted the slides (giving Claude context), specified what each note needed to cover (what, why, action), and set a length constraint (3 to 4 sentences for glancing while presenting). Claude created speaking guides rather than scripts.

Template: "Here are my [presentation topic] slides: [describe or paste slide content]. Create speaker notes for each slide that cover [list the points you need to hit]. Keep each slide's notes to [length] that I can [how you'll use them]."

Making Recipes, Meal Plans, and Travel Itineraries

Content creation isn't limited to work issues. Things such as planning what to eat and organizing travel require the same kind of structured thinking and decision-making. Claude helps with these tasks by coming up with options that fit your constraints and organizing details you'd otherwise spend hours researching and collecting.

Planning meals for your dietary needs

Meal planning with dietary restrictions or nutritional goals turns a simple task into a challenge. You need meals that fit your constraints and ingredients you can find that match your cooking skill level and sound appealing. Planning a week of meals that check all those boxes quickly exhausts your limited recipe knowledge.

Here's an example of how that works in practice:

Situation: A parent needed to plan lunches for a child with multiple food allergies (no dairy, eggs, tree nuts, or soy). School lunches weren't safe, and they were out of ideas beyond sunflower-butter sandwiches and veggie sticks. They needed a variety of food that was safe, kid-approved, and practical to pack.

Prompt: "Create a week of school lunch ideas for a 7-year-old with allergies to dairy, eggs, tree nuts, and soy. Each lunch needs a protein, a vegetable or fruit, and a grain or starch. The lunch needs to be safe at room temperature for 4 hours and appealing to a kid who likes mild flavors. Use brand names if appropriate."

Claude's response: It created five distinct lunches. Each lunch included brand names of allergy-safe products.

Result: The parent could shop confidently knowing that the specific products were safe.

Why this worked: The parent specified the exact allergies (letting Claude avoid all problematic ingredients), described the lunch requirements (protein, vegetable and fruit, grain and starch), added practical constraints (safe at room temperature for 4 hours), considered the child's preferences (mild flavors), and requested specific brands for specialty items (making shopping practical). The specificity helped Claude create truly usable meal plans.

Template: "Create [number] of [meal type] ideas for [person with specific situation]. Each [meal] needs [nutritional requirements]. The [meal type] needs to [practical constraints] and [preference constraints]. Use brand names if appropriate."

Creating detailed travel itineraries

Travel planning means researching destinations, coordinating timing, and balancing must-see spots with realistic schedules. An organized itinerary will help you make the most of your limited time without the pre-trip stress.

Here's an example of an itinerary Claude planned for a couple visiting New York:

Situation: A couple was planning their first trip to New York City. They would be there three full days. They'd identified several attractions but couldn't figure out how to organize them efficiently by neighborhood, museum hours, or priority.

Prompt: "We have three full days in New York City in October. We want to see the Statue of Liberty, Central Park, the Metropolitan Museum of Art, Times Square, and the 9/11 Memorial. We're moderate walkers, prefer to start days around 9 am, and want to end each day with dinner at a restaurant. One person has mobility limitations and can't walk for long periods in a single day. Create a day-by-day itinerary that groups activities logically and includes realistic timing."

Claude's response: It organized the three days by neighborhood to minimize transit time and distributed walking-heavy activities across multiple days. Day 1 covered the Statue of Liberty and the 9/11 Memorial (both in lower Manhattan). Day 2 tackled Central Park and the Met (both Upper East Side, walkable). Day 3 covered Times Square with a lighter afternoon. Each day included approximate timing, subway directions, and restaurant recommendations.

Why this worked: They listed specific attractions, identified constraints (October timing, moderate walking, mobility limitations), and specified what the itinerary needed to accomplish. Claude could optimize for their needs rather than creating a generic itinerary.

Template: "We have [duration] in [destination] in [time of year]. We want to see [list attractions/activities]. We're [activity level], prefer to [timing preferences], and want to [specific requirements]. [Any constraints or limitations]. Create a day-by-day itinerary that [specific structural requirement]."

REMEMBER

Content creation becomes manageable when you have an AI partner who generates options and helps you break through blocks. The examples in this chapter show patterns you can use repeatedly:

- Be specific about your audience and constraints.
- Provide examples of what works and what doesn't.
- State exactly what you need from Claude.

You'll still make creative decisions, but you'll spend less time staring at blank pages and more time developing good options into great final content.

IN THIS CHAPTER

» Researching, writing, and publishing in one workflow

» Analyzing data and creating presentations

» Solving problems from definition to implementation

Chapter 15
Looking at Complete Workflow Examples

Do you treat Claude like a search engine? You ask a question, get an answer, and close the tab. Ask for a draft and copy it into Word for editing. Get research insights, paste them into your outline. Copy analysis results into a spreadsheet. In this workflow, every step requires manual transfer. You become the connection between disconnected outputs, losing context and momentum with every switch.

Claude's real power comes into play when you keep everything combined in one conversation. Research flows naturally into outlining. Outlines become drafts. Drafts get refined through editing. You see this pattern repeat itself in visualizations. Data exploration reveals patterns. Those patterns become charts. Charts turn into presentations. Problem-solving generates options. Options become action plans.

Each stage builds on what came before. You maintain the focus of your thinking without manually transferring context between tools or losing track of where you started.

This chapter presents three complete workflows. You see how keeping everything in one conversation produces better results faster than jumping between tools and losing the focus of your thinking.

Exploring Research-to-Publication Workflows

The gap between needing to write something and having it ready to publish used to take days or weeks. You'd gather research, organize notes, draft content, fact-check, revise, and format. Each step was separate with its own timeline. Research-to-publication workflows substantially compress this process by keeping everything in a single continuous conversation, where each step naturally builds on the last.

Gathering information from multiple sources

Traditional research can fragment your thinking. You open browser tabs, read articles, take notes, switch between sources, and try to remember what each one said. By the time you finish reading, you've forgotten half of what you learned. The scattered information never transforms into a clear understanding.

Claude's Research feature completely changes this. It requires a paid plan (Pro, Max, Team, or Enterprise). Research uses a sophisticated multi-agent architecture where Claude investigates your question from multiple angles simultaneously, and then combines findings into a structured report with citations. Free plan users have access to basic web search for quick questions but don't have the full multisource investigation that Research delivers for publication-quality work.

To turn on Research:

1. **Click or tap + at the bottom left of the conversation window, next to where you type your messages, as shown in Figure 15-1.**

   A menu pops up showing available features.

2. **Click or tap Research, as shown in Figure 15-2.**

   The text switches from gray to blue when active.

Claude now knows you want deep research with multiple sources instead of a quick answer, and the toggle stays on for your entire conversation unless you turn it off.

FIGURE 15-1: Click or tap + to display a drop-down menu.

FIGURE 15-2: Click or tap Research to enable the feature.

TIP

The Research feature uses multiple parallel AI agents to simultaneously investigate different angles. While one agent examines current industry trends, another searches for case studies, and a third analyzes expert opinions. Then it combines these threads into a single report. Session length varies. It will run long enough to explore complex questions in depth and return a synthesized overview with citations to the main sources used.

For example, a marketing director needed to write a competitive analysis for their executive team. They started their Research session with a clear prompt: "Research how major retail brands adapted their customer loyalty programs in 2024 – 2025. Focus on what worked and what failed."

After several minutes, they had a detailed report analyzing changes at six major retailers, industry trends, specific program features that increased engagement, and cautionary examples of approaches that backfired. The report included citations to news articles, company announcements, and industry analysis. What might have taken a couple of days of manual research fit into one round using Research.

Here are some ways to effectively use Claude's Research feature for publication:

- **Start broad, then narrow.** Begin with "Research [topic] over [timeframe], focusing on [specific angle]." Let Research map the landscape before you commit to a specific direction.
- **Request source diversity.** Ask Research to draw from academic sources, industry publications, company announcements, and news coverage, when available, for the topic. Different source types reveal different aspects of the story.
- **Specify what you'll do with findings.** Tell Research, "I'm writing a [type of piece] for [audience]" to emphasize information relevant to your publication goal.
- **Build on initial findings.** After reviewing the Research report, ask follow-up questions: "Now research the three most successful programs in detail" or "Find specific metrics on engagement changes."

Creating structured outlines and drafts

Research findings don't automatically become organized writing. The path to a coherent draft usually involves staring at a variety of notes, wondering how to structure everything.

For example, a consultant had used the Research feature to explore changing workplace technology adoption patterns. They had excellent information but no structure. They asked Claude: "Based on this Research report, create an outline for a 2,000-word article for HR executives. They need to understand what's changed, why it matters, and what they should do differently."

Claude analyzed the Research findings and proposed a structure: an opening hook using the most surprising statistic, three main trends with evidence for each, implications for HR strategy, and actionable next steps. The outline revealed that one trend split into two distinct patterns that needed separate sections, and that the "what to do differently" section required more specific tactical guidance than the Research report provided.

They approved the outline with minor adjustments, and then asked: "Write the first draft of this article using this outline. Include the statistics and examples from the Research report. Make the tone professional but accessible, not academic."

Claude generated a complete first draft in conversational yet authoritative language. Of course, it wasn't perfect, but it gave the consultant something to improve rather than a blank page to fill. The draft reduced two days of writing to two hours of editing.

Here are some ideas about how to efficiently move from research to a structured draft:

- **Request structure before content.** Ask "Create an outline for [type of piece] covering [topics] for [audience]." Review the structure before investing time in full drafting.
- **Specify the structural logic.** Different structures serve different purposes. "Should I organize this chronologically, by importance, or by topic?" helps you choose the right approach before you write.
- **Include constraints upfront.** Tell Claude about word counts, required sections, tone requirements, and audience needs so the draft matches publication requirements.
- **Iterate on the structure first.** If the outline reveals problems, fix them before drafting. A consultant realized their outline buried the most important finding in the third section. They restructured before drafting, saving themselves from having to rewrite later.

The transition from outline to draft works best when you're clear about what you need. Instead of "Write this," try "Using this outline and research, write a 1,500-word article for executives who need to understand [topic] well enough to make decisions. Include specific examples but keep it scannable with clear section headers."

TIP

Save successful outlines as templates for future projects. For example, a research analyst discovered that a particular three-part structure worked perfectly for market analysis reports. They now start every similar project by asking Claude to "Create an outline following this three-part structure" and to adapt the proven format to new topics. The template doesn't limit their thinking; it accelerates it.

The research-to-outline-to-draft workflow can compress what used to take a week into a day. Don't worry that you're cutting corners. What you're doing is removing the friction between steps, keeping your thinking connected, and focusing your energy on editing rather than creating.

Editing, fact-checking, and finalizing

First drafts often contain good ideas wrapped in uneven prose. The real writing happens during revision, when you transform adequate into excellent. Traditional editing means reading your own work repeatedly, trying to spot problems your brain automatically skips over when you write. You know what you meant to say, so you struggle to see what you actually said.

Here's an example. A policy analyst drafted a white paper on education funding. They knew it needed work but couldn't identify the specific problems. They prompted Claude: "Read this draft and identify sections where the argument loses clarity, claims that need stronger evidence, paragraphs that try to say too much at once, and transitions that feel abrupt."

Claude highlighted that

- The introduction buried the main argument in the third paragraph
- Two sections made claims without supporting data
- Four paragraphs each covered multiple distinct points that should be separated

This feedback gave clear revision targets. The analyst wasn't guessing what felt off; they knew exactly what to fix.

After making the revisions, they systematically addressed fact-checking. They asked: "Verify these specific claims in paragraphs 4 and 7, using current sources when web search is enabled. Flag anything outdated, contested, or that needs additional support."

Claude checked the current information for each claim and confirmed that the statistics were accurate. It suggested revised wording that incorporated more up-to-date context, which the analyst then reviewed against primary sources before updating the draft.

For the final pass, they focused on polish: "Review this for sentences longer than 25 words that could be simplified, passive voice that weakens impact, jargon that needs explanation or replacement, and sections where tone shifts inappropriately."

Claude identified long sentences that could be split for clarity, passive constructions where the active voice would be stronger, and four terms that needed brief explanations for non-specialist readers.

The analyst made the changes, transforming a competent draft into polished work ready for publication.

Here are some ways you can use Claude for effective editing and finalization:

- **Edit in stages, not all at once.** First pass: structure and argument. Second pass: evidence and accuracy. Third pass: clarity and polish. Trying to fix everything simultaneously overwhelms you and Claude.
- **Ask for specific problems, not general improvement.** "Make this better" yields vague suggestions. "Identify where my evidence doesn't support my claims" yields actionable fixes.
- **Verify time-sensitive information.** Statistics, policies, company information, and current events change. Ask Claude to check anything that could be outdated since your initial research, and then confirm important facts using authoritative or primary sources before publishing.
- **Read Claude's edits before accepting them.** Claude identifies problems accurately but doesn't always know your audience or publication standards. Use the feedback to guide your revisions, rather than automatically accepting every suggestion.
- **Check for consistency across long documents.** Ask "Do I use consistent terminology throughout? Does the tone match across all sections? Are examples at similar levels of detail?"

For example, a business writer discovered that their 20-page report used *customer* in some sections, *client* in others, and *account holder* in the conclusion. Claude caught the inconsistency that readers would have noticed but that the writer, immersed in the content, had missed.

The editing workflow succeeds because it separates different types of problems. When you try to check structure, facts, clarity, and polish simultaneously, you end up catching none of them well. When you focus on one type of problem at a time, you systematically improve the work.

REMEMBER

Publications require accuracy. Use Claude to identify what needs verification, but verify the information yourself through authoritative sources. Claude helps you identify what to check and provides current information, but the final fact-checking responsibility remains with you, the author. You are ultimately responsible for how you interpret the model's output and for any real-world decisions or publications that rely on it.

The complete research-to-publication workflow turns scattered tasks into a connected set of steps. Each step happens in the same conversation, building on what came before and maintaining momentum from the initial question to the final publication.

Reviewing Data-to-Insights Workflows

Numbers can tell stories, but only if you can extract the narrative from the existing rows and columns. Traditional data analysis can trap you in spreadsheets for hours. You upload files, create Excel pivot tables, build charts, adjust formatting, and hope you haven't missed the insight hiding in the numbers. Data-to-insights workflows move you from raw information to a clear understanding without getting lost in the mechanics.

Uploading and exploring data files

Interestingly, the first barrier to data analysis is not complexity but getting started. You have a CSV file with customer data or a spreadsheet tracking monthly metrics. Opening it reveals hundreds of rows and dozens of columns. Where do you even begin? Here's an example of how to handle this.

A retail manager received quarterly sales data across 50 store locations. The Excel file contained 12 columns and 600 rows of transaction information. The manager needed to prepare a presentation for the regional director but felt overwhelmed staring at the raw numbers.

The manager uploaded the file to Claude and prompted, "What's in this data? Give me an overview of the structure, the information you captured, and any initial observations about patterns or anomalies."

Claude examined the file and explained: "This dataset tracks 600 transactions across 50 stores, capturing date, store ID, product category, units sold, revenue, and customer type." It also made a list of initial observations. This overview gave the manager immediate direction. They knew which questions to ask next without spending an hour just understanding the data structure.

Here are some ideas about how to explore uploaded data effectively with Claude:

- **Start with structure, not analysis.** Ask "What information does this data contain?" before jumping into specific questions. Understanding the landscape prevents wasted time analyzing the wrong things.
- **Request initial patterns.** Claude spots obvious trends, outliers, and anomalies during initial examination. These observations often reveal your most important questions.
- **Clarify what success looks like.** Tell Claude, "I need to present findings to [audience] who cares about [specific outcomes]." This type of prompt focuses exploration on relevant insights rather than interesting but useless observations.
- **Check data quality immediately.** Ask, "Are there missing values, inconsistencies, or data quality issues I should address first?" Cleaning data before analysis saves you from building insights on flawed foundations.

A financial analyst uploaded transaction records and, during Claude's initial exploration, discovered that 15 percent of entries lacked cost center codes. The analyst fixed the data quality issue before analysis, preventing incorrect budget allocations that would have required extensive corrections later.

File upload works on all Claude plans (Free, Pro, Max, Team, Enterprise). You can upload common file types such as PDFs, Word documents, text files, spreadsheets, and images on any plan.

What you can do with uploaded files depends on your plan. Free plan users can analyze data and create visualizations that appear in the chat window. These charts and graphs help you spot patterns and understand your data, but they stay within your Claude conversation.

Paid plan users (Pro, Max, Team, or Enterprise) get code execution, which adds the capability to create downloadable files. (For more information about enabling code execution, see Chapter 6.) Claude can build Excel spreadsheets, PowerPoint presentations, Word documents, and PDFs that you save to your computer and use in other programs. For current details on supported file types and size limits, check Anthropic's documentation at `https://support.claude.com`.

Analyzing patterns and creating visualizations

Raw data becomes useful only when you spot patterns that inform decisions. A list of numbers stays a list until you see the trend, identify the outlier, or recognize the correlation that changes your strategy. Here's how this works in practice.

The retail manager had their data overview and wanted a deeper understanding. They prompted: "Compare performance across store locations. Which stores are underperforming and why? Create visualizations showing the key differences."

Claude analyzed the data systematically and created three visualizations: a bar chart comparing store performance, a line graph showing sales trends over the quarter, and a scatterplot revealing the correlation between staffing hours and revenue.

The analysis revealed that underperforming stores operated in perfectly good locations. The issue might be that they reduced weekend staffing, which missed peak sales periods. The scatterplot made the pattern impossible to miss: every store with below-average weekend coverage showed proportionally lower revenue.

The manager followed up by prompting: "Calculate how much revenue we're losing due to understaffing and create a cost-benefit analysis for adding weekend staff at the five underperforming locations."

Claude calculated lost revenue potential, estimated staffing costs, and showed that adding one weekend employee per underperforming location would generate $45,000 additional quarterly revenue at a cost of $18,000. For this team, the analysis helped move from "stores are underperforming" to a concrete, data-backed staffing recommendation that could solve the problem.

Here are some ways to have Claude help you move from data to actionable insights:

- **Ask questions that drive decisions.** Instead of "Analyze this data," ask "Which factors most influence [outcome I care about]?" Decision-focused questions yield decision-enabling insights.
- **Request visual thinking.** Tell Claude, "Show me this pattern visually" or "Create charts that make the key insight immediately obvious." Visualization often reveals patterns that tables of numbers obscure.
- **Compare specific segments.** Ask Claude to compare groups, time periods, categories, or locations. "How do weekday sales compare to weekend sales by product category?" yields more actionable insight than general averages.

» **Quantify the effect.** After identifying patterns, ask: "What's the business effect of this pattern?" Numbers become compelling when you translate them into dollars, time, or customer outcomes.

» **Iterate on visualizations.** If a chart doesn't communicate clearly, request adjustments: "Make the underperforming stores more visually distinct" or "Add a trend line showing the decline over time."

For example, a marketing analyst discovered that the initial bar chart of campaign performance looked cluttered and confusing. The analyst prompted Claude to "Create a cleaner visualization focusing only on the top 5 and bottom 5 campaigns, with clear labels showing ROI percentages." The revised chart made the message immediately clear for the executive presentation.

Claude creates interactive visualizations and charts directly in the interface via Artifacts, available on all plans, including Free. Team and Enterprise plans can also use Connectors to integrate with external services such as Google Drive, Slack, or Asana, enabling Claude to access and visualize data from those sources directly. (For Connector availability and further details, see Chapter 6.)

Presenting results and recommendations

Analysis doesn't create value until it informs action. You can identify every pattern in your data, but if stakeholders don't understand the findings or know what to do with them, the analysis effort achieves nothing.

For example, the retail manager you met earlier had compelling analysis but needed to present it to executives who would not wade through detailed data. The manager asked: "Create an executive summary of these findings as a Word document. Focus on what we discovered, why it matters, specific recommendations, and expected effect. Keep it to one page with a supporting visualization."

Claude generated a document with four clear sections: the problem (inconsistent store performance driven by staffing gaps), the evidence (quantified revenue loss with visualization showing the correlation), the recommendation (add weekend coverage at five specific locations), and the expected outcome ($27,000 net quarterly gain, 15 percent revenue increase at affected stores).

The one-page summary included a single, powerful chart: a scatterplot of the staffing-revenue relationship, with the five underperforming stores highlighted. The visual made the case instantly clear without requiring executives to process tables of numbers.

The manager then requested: "Create a PowerPoint presentation with 5 slides covering the same content, formatted for a 10-minute presentation to the regional director."

Claude produced slides following a presentation logic: an opening slide stating the problem, a data-driven analysis showing the pattern, a quantification of the financial effect, a clear recommendation with implementation steps, and expected results. Each slide communicated a single main point, avoiding the common mistake of cramming too much information into a single slide.

Here's how to transform analysis into presentation-ready deliverables:

- **Specify your audience explicitly.** "Create this for executives who need to make decisions quickly" yields different content than "Create this for analysts who want to verify methodology." Know who reads it and what they need from it.
- **Request an appropriate format.** Use one-page summaries for quick decisions, detailed reports for stakeholders who need a complete methodology, and presentations for group discussions. Match the format to how you will use the information.
- **Lead with conclusions, not process.** Decision-makers need "Here's what we found and what to do" before "Here's how we analyzed it." Save methodology details for appendices or follow-up questions.
- **Make specific, actionable recommendations.** "Improve weekend staffing" is vague. "Add one sales associate at stores 12, 23, 34, 41, and 47 for Saturday and Sunday shifts, estimated cost $18K quarterly, projected return $45K" enables immediate action.
- **Include the "so what" explicitly.** Never assume people will extrapolate effect from raw findings. State directly: "This means we're leaving $100K annually on the table" or "This change would improve customer retention by 12 percent."

A consultant learned this lesson the hard way. They presented a detailed analysis to a client, who responded, "This is interesting, but what should I do?" The consultant revised the presentation to start with "Stop doing X and start doing Y. Here's why." supported by the analysis rather than building toward conclusions the client had to infer.

TIP

Save successful presentation structures as templates. An operations director discovered that a specific four-slide format worked perfectly for process improvement recommendations. The director now asks: "Present this analysis following the structure we used for the warehouse optimization Project," and adapts the proven format to new topics. The template ensures consistency and speeds creation.

The complete data-to-insights workflow connects steps that traditionally lived in different tools. Upload and explore reveals what you have. Pattern analysis and visualization show what it means. The results presentation communicates what to do. Keeping the steps in a single conversation maintains context, enables iterative refinement, and delivers presentation-ready insights from raw data in hours rather than days.

REMEMBER

Data analysis requires judgment about what matters and what to ignore. Claude helps you spot patterns and create visualizations, but you decide which insights are meaningful for your specific context. The technology accelerates analysis; your domain expertise determines which findings deserve action.

Examining Problem-to-Solution Workflows

Problems rarely arrive with clear boundaries and obvious answers. You face a messy situation with multiple factors, unclear priorities, and no guaranteed solution. Traditional problem-solving means struggling alone through the stages of definition, brainstorming, evaluation, and planning. Each step feels disconnected from the last. Problem-to-solution workflows keep everything connected in one focused conversation.

Defining and breaking down complex problems

The hardest part of solving problems is not finding answers but understanding what you need to solve. You jump into solutions before clarifying the real issue. For example, a consultant spent weeks implementing a fix for low team productivity, only to discover the problem was unclear priorities, not work methods.

A nonprofit director faced declining donor retention. Fewer people renewed annual memberships each year, but the director could not pinpoint why. The director asked Claude: "Our donor retention dropped from 65 percent to 48 percent over two years. I think it's our messaging, but I'm not sure where to focus. Help me break this down."

Claude responded with questions that revealed the structure hiding in the mess: "Let's separate causes from symptoms. The 17-point drop is the symptom. What changed two years ago? Have you surveyed lapsed donors? Which donor segments declined the most? What touchpoints exist between initial donation and renewal?"

Through this questioning, the director realized three distinct problems masked as one. First-time donors never felt connected to the mission (onboarding problem). Multiyear donors felt taken for granted (engagement problem). Major donors received the same generic updates as small donors (segmentation problem). The director had been treating all three as a single messaging issue.

Claude then helped break each problem into components. For the onboarding problem: timing of the first follow-up, content of the welcome series, opportunities for early engagement, and measurement of connection strength. What felt like an overwhelming retention crisis became a list of specific, addressable issues.

Here's how to define and break down problems effectively:

- **Start with symptoms, then dig for causes.** Describe what you observe: "Sales are down" or "Team morale is low." Then ask: "Help me identify the underlying causes creating this symptom."
- **Separate what you know from what you assume.** Tell Claude: "Here's what the data shows. Here's what I suspect but haven't verified. Help me distinguish facts from assumptions I need to test."
- **Break multipart problems into distinct issues.** Ask: "Is this one problem or several problems that look connected? Help me separate these into distinct challenges I can address individually."
- **Identify root causes, not just proximate triggers.** Request: "Walk me through the chain of causation. What causes this immediate problem? What causes that? Keep going until we reach the root."
- **Map stakeholders and constraints.** Explain: "Who gets affected by this problem and the solution? What constraints limit our options?"

A technology director learned this approach while troubleshooting a system outage. Instead of jumping to fix the immediate error, the director asked Claude to map the chain: the immediate error, the configuration change that triggered it, the process failure that allowed the risky change, the training gap that created the process failure, and the organizational priority that deprioritized training. Fixing just the error would have left four underlying causes unaddressed.

The value of proper problem definition is not philosophical precision but practical efficiency. When you clearly define the problem, solutions become obvious. When you misidentify the problem, even perfect execution fails because you're solving the wrong thing.

Generating and evaluating options systematically

Once you understand the problem, you need options. Most people generate two or three obvious ideas, and then choose one. This shallow exploration misses better solutions that require a bit more thinking.

The nonprofit director needed solutions for the three distinct retention problems. For the onboarding issue, the director asked: "Generate 8 to 10 different approaches to help first-time donors feel connected to our mission within their first 30 days. Range from simple to ambitious."

Claude generated options across multiple categories: immediate connection (personal thank-you calls from beneficiaries), education approaches (video series showing impact), engagement opportunities (volunteer sessions for new donors), community building (monthly virtual meetups), milestone recognition (30-day check-in with impact report), feedback loops (survey about their motivations), surprise touchpoints (handwritten notes from leadership), ambassador programs (connecting new donors with long-term supporters).

The director had been fixating on better email newsletters. The systematic exploration revealed that newsletters addressed none of the three core problems. New donors needed a human connection, not more content. Multiyear donors needed appreciation, not information. Major donors needed personalized engagement, not generic updates.

Next came evaluation. The director asked: "Evaluate these onboarding approaches based on implementation cost under $5,000, measurable effect within 6 months, staff time required under 10 hours monthly, and scalability as we grow."

Claude analyzed each option against these criteria, revealing that personal thank-you calls combined with 30-day impact reports scored highest. Calls cost minimal money (volunteer time), created measurable effect (track follow-up donations), required manageable staff time (training volunteers), and scaled easily (more volunteers as donations grow).

Here's how to generate and evaluate options systematically:

» **Push past your first three ideas.** Ask for 8 to 10 options to force exploration beyond the obvious. The best solution often hides in options 5 to 8, after you've exhausted familiar territory.

- **Request categorical variety.** Specify: "Give me conventional options, creative options, low-cost options, and high-effect options." This prevents generating ten variations of the same basic approach.
- **Make evaluation criteria explicit before analysis.** Define what matters: "Evaluate based on cost, implementation speed, risk level, and long-term sustainability." Claude then judges options consistently against the same factors.
- **Look for combination solutions.** Ask: "Could we combine elements from different options to create something better than any single approach?" Often, the best solution mixes pieces from multiple options.
- **Test assumptions about constraints.** Question: "I said we can't spend more than $5,000, but what if that constraint is wrong? What options open up at $10,000 or $50,000?" Sometimes constraints you accept as fixed are actually negotiable.
- **Consider the implementation sequence.** Request: "Which option should we try first to learn the most? Which builds the capabilities we need for other options?"

A product manager used this systematic approach when deciding how to address user complaints about a complex feature. The manager generated options (simplify the interface, improve documentation, add tutorials, redesign the workflow, remove the feature), evaluated against criteria (user satisfaction impact, development time, risk of breaking other features), and tested the assumption that users needed the feature at all. The analysis revealed that 80 percent of users never touched the feature, and the other 20 percent had workarounds. The best option was to remove it, freeing up development resources for features people wanted.

The systematic approach works because it separates idea generation from idea evaluation. When you generate and judge simultaneously, you reject promising options before fully considering them. When you generate broadly first and then evaluate methodically, you make better choices.

Documenting decisions and implementation plans

Good decisions fail without good implementation. You choose the right solution but lose momentum translating that choice into action. Documentation turns decisions into outcomes by creating clear accountability and next steps.

The nonprofit director chose the solution but needed an implementation plan. The director asked: "Create an implementation plan for launching personal thank-you calls and 30-day impact reports. Include timeline, responsible parties, resources needed, success metrics, and potential obstacles."

Claude structured the plan systematically:

- *Timeline:* Week 1 (recruit volunteers, create call scripts, design impact report template), week 2 (train callers, test process with 10 donors), week 3 (launch full program, make calls within 48 hours of donation), week 4 (send 30-day reports, track response), month 2 (analyze results, adjust approach).
- *Responsible parties:* Development director (overall ownership), volunteer coordinator (recruiting and training), communications lead (impact report design), database manager (tracking and measurement).
- *Resources needed:* $800 for call-training materials, $1,200 for impact report design, 15 hours of staff time for setup, 3 to 5 volunteer hours weekly for calls.
- *Success metrics:* 60 percent of new donors complete the welcome call, 30-day retention improves to 55 percent, and second-gift rate increases by 15 percent.
- *Potential obstacles:* Volunteer availability (mitigation: recruit backup callers), donor phone preferences (mitigation: offer a call or email option), staff capacity during the busy season (mitigation: phase the launch around major campaigns).

The plan transformed "We should do thank-you calls" into specific actions with clear owners and deadlines. More importantly, identifying obstacles upfront allowed proactive solutions rather than scrambling when problems arose.

Here's how to document decisions effectively:

- **Capture the decision context.** Record: "We chose option B because it best balanced X, Y, and Z factors. We considered options A and C but rejected them because. . ." In the future, you will need to remember why this choice made sense.
- **Break implementation into discrete steps.** Ask: "What needs to happen first, second, third? What can happen simultaneously? What must happen sequentially?" Parallel work accelerates timelines.
- **Assign specific ownership.** Avoid "the team will handle" or "someone should do." Name people: "Jordan leads training, Alex creates templates, Sam measures results."

- **Define done clearly.** Specify: "This step completes when we have X deliverable meeting Y criteria, approved by Z person." Vague completion criteria drag out work.
- **Build in checkpoints.** Request: "Create a plan with review points at 25 percent, 50 percent, and 75 percent completion. What should we check at each point?" Catching problems early prevents costly pivots later.
- **Document the decision rationale.** Ask Claude to "Summarize why we chose this approach, what we expect to achieve, and what would indicate we need to revise." Six months later, when someone questions the decision, you will have the reasoning recorded.

A project manager discovered the value of thorough documentation when inheriting a stalled initiative. The previous manager decided to rebuild a key system but provided no rationale for the decision. The new manager spent three weeks reverse-engineering the decision to determine why it made sense and whether circumstances had changed. With proper documentation, those three weeks would have taken three minutes.

TIP

Create decision documentation that your future self will thank you for. A facilities director developed a simple template: Problem, Options Considered, Choice Made, Why This Choice, Implementation Steps, Success Measures, Decision Date, Decision Owner. Every significant decision follows this format, stored in a shared drive. When questioned later about past choices, the director pulled up documentation showing how and why the decisions were made. The template prevented relitigating settled decisions.

The complete problem-to-solution workflow connects understanding, ideation, evaluation, and implementation. Define the problem clearly so you solve the right thing. Generate options systematically so you find the best solution, not just the first solution. Evaluate against explicit criteria so choices reflect priorities. Document thoroughly so decisions become action. Each step builds on the last, maintaining momentum from "We have a problem" to "We solved it."

Problem-solving with Claude works best as a conversation, not an assignment. Claude helps you think through problems more systematically, generates options you might not consider, and structures implementation plans. But you bring domain knowledge, organizational context, and judgment about what matters in your situation. This combination produces better solutions than either could achieve alone.

4 Mastering Advanced Features

IN THIS PART . . .

Turn any conversation into something you can use.

Get current facts and explore any topic in depth.

Tackle your hardest problems by using extended thinking.

Hand off entire tasks to Cowork, Claude's desktop agent.

Find out why Claude misses the mark and how to fix it.

IN THIS CHAPTER

» Recognizing when conversations need to become tangible

» Requesting the right artifact type for your goal

» Refining artifacts through specific, iterative requests

Chapter 16
Working with Artifacts

When you ask Claude a question, you usually get a text response in the chat box. Claude explains concepts, offers advice, or helps you think through problems. But some tasks need something you can interact with, save, and use outside the conversation. *Artifacts* are standalone outputs that appear in a separate panel alongside your chat. They're the deliverables, not just the discussion about them.

This chapter shows you the different artifacts from Claude, how to recognize when you need an artifact instead of text, how to request the type that best matches your goal, and how to refine artifacts through conversation until they meet your needs. You learn to create tools, documents, and visualizations that extend beyond chat and are ready to use in your real work.

REMEMBER

Artifacts work across all Claude subscription tiers: Free, Pro, Max, Team, and Enterprise plans. You don't need to upgrade to access this feature. The tier differences appear in usage limits, not feature access. Free plan users get fewer messages per session before hitting rate limits. Pro and Team users get higher message caps and faster response times, which matters when you're revising complex artifacts.

Introducing Artifacts

An artifact might be a HyperText Markup Language (HTML) page (code that displays text, images, links, and interactive elements in a web browser), a calculator, a formatted document ready to download, or an interactive data visualization you can adjust and export to use outside of Claude. You might create a quiz that provides immediate feedback or a form that collects information. Each artifact exists as an entity, separate from the conversation.

REMEMBER

Unlike chat responses that scroll away as the conversation continues, artifacts stay in their own dedicated space on the right side of your screen. You can view them while continuing to chat with Claude on the left. You can test and refine them through conversation, and then export them when they're ready. The artifact is visible and accessible throughout your session.

Enabling artifacts

Artifacts work automatically when your request suggests a need for a standalone or interactive output. Most users never need to touch the artifact setting because it's enabled by default. But you can verify that the feature is turned on in Settings if Claude doesn't create artifacts when you expect them. A quick look at these settings will confirm whether the feature is active:

1. **If the sidebar is hidden, display it by clicking or tapping the sidebar icon in the upper-left corner of the screen (and shown in the margin).**
2. **Click or tap your profile icon (your initials) and then select Settings.**

   Your profile icon is in the lower-left corner in the web and desktop apps and in the upper-right corner in the mobile app.
3. **Click or tap Capabilities.**

   At the top of the Capabilities screen, under the Artifacts heading, are two toggles: Artifacts and AI-Powered Artifacts.
4. **Make sure the Artifacts and AI-Powered Artifacts settings are toggled on so that Claude can create artifacts in response to your requests, as shown in Figure 16-1.**

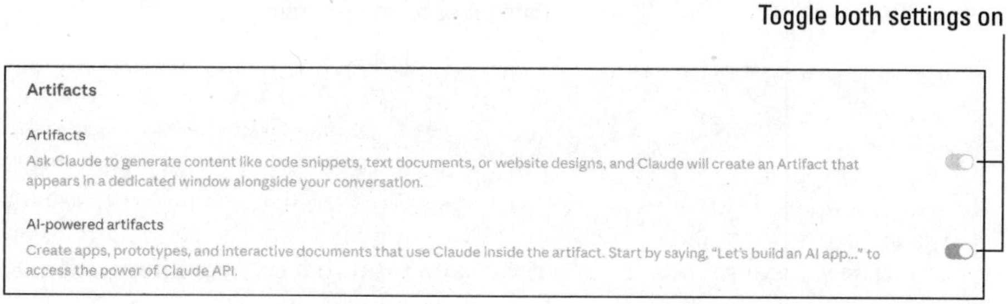

FIGURE 16-1: Enabling artifacts.

Exploring artifacts

Before you create your first artifact, it's helpful to explore what's possible by seeing what others have built. Claude provides three ways to discover artifacts and understand their potential.

You need to open Claude to access the Artifacts section in your sidebar. This dedicated space provides access to Anthropic-created example artifacts and templates organized by category, including Learn Something, Life Hacks, Play a Game, Be Creative, and Touch Grass, as shown in Figure 16-2.

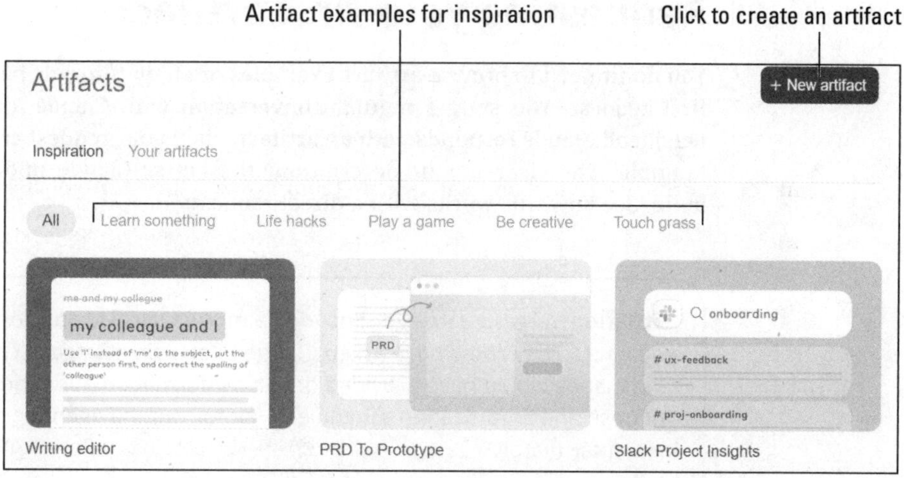

FIGURE 16-2: The Artifacts sidebar shows curated examples organized by category.

When you're ready to create your own, click or tap the New Artifact button in the upper-right corner. Claude displays available artifact categories and templates to help you choose a starting point, as shown in Figure 16-3.

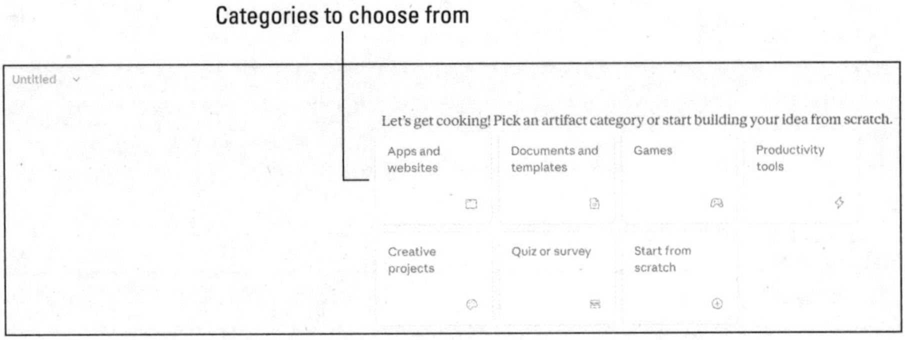

FIGURE 16-3: Clicking New Artifact displays creation options and templates.

The interface presents different artifact types and starting points, each designed for a specific purpose. Templates have the structure already in place. For example, a budget template includes categories for expenses, fields for planned versus actual spending, and automatic variance calculations. Starting from a template can save you time.

TIP

Select Start from Scratch when you have something specific in mind that doesn't match existing templates.

Requesting your first artifact

You don't need to browse artifact examples or study tutorials before making your first request. You start a regular conversation with Claude, describe what you need, and Claude responds with an artifact when your request calls for something tangible. The clearer your description, the better Claude understands what to build. See how this works with a direct request:

Situation: A real estate agent needed a mortgage calculator for client meetings. They could have asked Claude to explain mortgage calculations, and Claude would have provided detailed information about principal, interest, and amortization schedules. Helpful, but the agent needed the actual calculator.

Prompt: "Create an interactive mortgage calculator with fields for home price, down payment, interest rate, and loan term. Show monthly payment, total paid over the life of the loan, and total interest. Use a purple color scheme with the Calculate Payment button."

Claude's response: It built a calculator with the requested inputs. The purple Calculate payment button can add all expenses, as shown in Figure 16-4.

Result: The agent could immediately test the calculator with different numbers, adjust the design, and export it for client use. The artifact worked as a standalone tool, ready to use outside the conversation.

Template: "Create an interactive [calculator type] with fields for [input 1], [input 2], [input 3], and [input 4]. Show [result 1], [result 2], and [result 3]. Use [color scheme] with [button text] button."

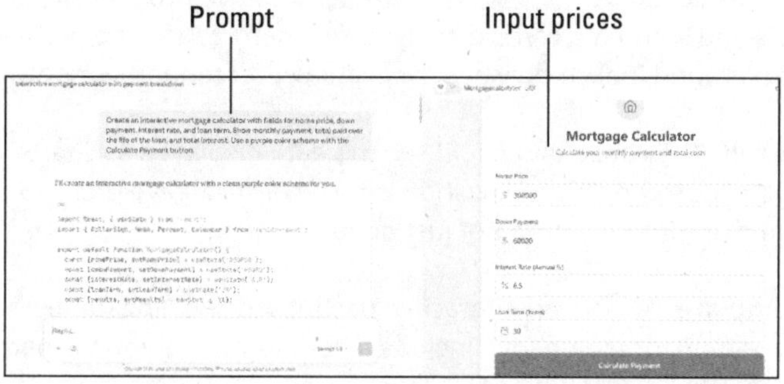

FIGURE 16-4: Artifacts appear on the right while chat continues on the left.

TIP

A conversation with Claude explores ideas and provides guidance. Artifacts turn those conversations into tangible outputs you take with you. You're not just learning about something or discussing possibilities. You're creating something that exists outside Claude and serves a specific purpose.

Recognizing When You Need an Artifact

How do you know when you would benefit from an artifact? Watch how this plays out:

Situation: A marketing consultant needed to present Q4 results to a client. They had revenue data for five product categories, but explaining numbers in conversation wasn't having an effect. The client wanted to see trends and compare categories visually. The consultant went to the Apps and Websites artifact (refer to Figure 16-3) and input the following prompt.

Prompt: "Create an interactive dashboard showing Q4 revenue by product category for Acme Corp. Include a header with the company name and date range, a total revenue summary ($8.38M, up 1.8 percent from Q3), a bar chart comparing five categories, and cards highlighting the top performer (Electronics) and growth leader (Software, up 21.5 percent). Use a dark theme with purple accents."

TIP

Sometimes, after you enter your prompt, Claude will tell you what it will build before building it. If it meets your requirements, you can say, "Build it."

Claude's response: It generated a professional dashboard with all the requested elements. The bar chart showed five product categories side-by-side and summary cards displayed key metrics, and the purple-highlighted background looked polished for client presentations, as shown in Figure 16-5.

Result: The consultant could see the data displayed as charts, adjust the view, and export the finished dashboard. The artifact gave them something they could use immediately, not just discuss.

Template: "Create an interactive dashboard showing [time period] [metric] by [category] for [company]. Include a header with [company name] and [date range], [primary summary metric], [chart type] comparing [data series], and cards highlighting [key insight 1] and [key insight 2]. Use [theme] with [accent color]."

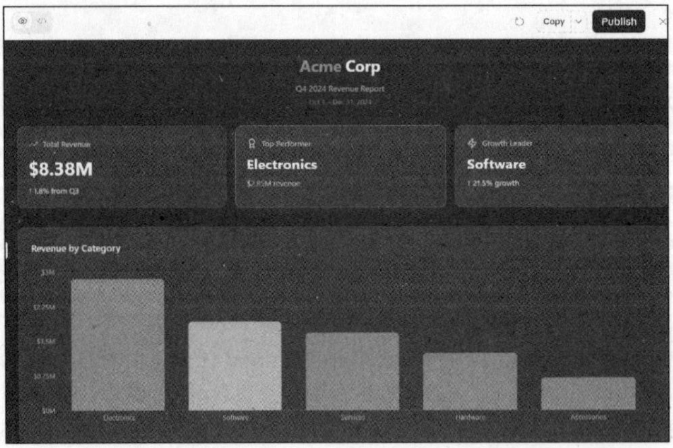

FIGURE 16-5: A dashboard of Q4 revenue by product.

You'll begin to recognize when you need an artifact rather than a conversation. Some requests work better as a text exchange, such as getting advice, brainstorming ideas, and refining your thinking. Other requests need something you can interact with, modify, and take with you.

Seeing what artifacts do that conversations can't

Artifacts create standalone outputs that exist separately from the chat. When you ask Claude to build a calculator, design a form, or create a formatted document, the result appears in its own workspace where you can test it, use it, and see it in action.

Artifacts work best when you need to:

- » Test something interactive (calculators, tools, forms).
- » See formatted output (documents with styling, reports with structure).
- » Export finished work (visualizations, templates, web components).
- » Iterate on working versions (add features, fix problems, adjust behavior).

Understanding when Claude creates artifacts automatically

Claude may recognize requests that are better suited to an artifact and respond with a standalone output rather than conversational text.

For example, a project manager asked: "Build a budget tracker that compares planned versus actual spending across five categories." Claude responded with a working calculator instead of a description, which can happen when a request strongly implies hands-on use.

The following requests typically produce artifacts:

- » Building tools and calculators ("Create a tip calculator with options for party size")
- » Creating formatted documents ("Write a business proposal with an executive summary, three key sections, and a conclusion")
- » Making visualizations ("Generate a timeline showing major events in the Civil Rights Movement")
- » Designing interactive components ("Build a color picker that shows hex codes")

REMEMBER

You don't need to memorize these categories or request artifacts every time. When your request clearly implies a need for something functional or formatted, Claude may respond with an appropriate artifact.

Knowing when to request specific artifact formats

Sometimes you'll want to specify the artifact format when your request could go either way. If you ask for help with a presentation, Claude might offer advice in the conversation. If you ask Claude to "create slides for a presentation on cyber-security basics," you're more likely to get a formatted document artifact.

For example, a financial advisor prompted, "Help me explain compound interest to clients." Claude responded with suggestions for analogies, key points to emphasize, and common misconceptions to address. Helpful, but the advisor wanted something tangible to share.

They clarified their prompt: "Create a one-page explainer document on compound interest with real-world examples and a simple visual." The formatted document appeared as an artifact. The specificity triggered artifact creation: they asked for a particular format (one-page document), included structural elements (examples and visuals), and implied that they needed finished output, not just ideas.

When you want an artifact but get conversation instead, add specifics about format, structure, or interactivity:

- "Create a . . ." or "Build a . . ." signals you want something produced, not just discussed.
- "Make this interactive" or "with working buttons" indicates that functionality is required.
- "As a formatted document" or "as a calculator I can export" clarifies that you need a standalone output.

TIP

You'll develop an instinct for this. If Claude's response doesn't give you something you can use, refine your request to specify the format you need. The conversation should be flexible; you can always adjust your approach based on what you get.

Choosing the Right Artifact Type

You'll encounter different situations that call for different artifact types. For example, a financial advisor needs a calculator that runs numbers. A teacher needs a formatted lesson plan. A data analyst needs charts that visualize trends. Matching your request to the right artifact type helps Claude create exactly what you need.

Four main artifact types handle most requests:

- Interactive tools
- Formatted documents
- Data visualizations
- Web components

Creating interactive tools and calculators

A small business owner needs to estimate monthly expenses for different scenarios. They asked Claude: "Create a calculator that shows monthly costs based on the number of employees, office size, and operational hours." An interactive calculator appeared on the right side of the screen.

The calculator included input fields for the number of employees, average salary, square footage, rent per square foot, weekly hours, and utility costs. The owner experimented with scenarios. The calculator enabled them to model different business sizes without having to recalculate anything manually.

Interactive tools work when you need something users can manipulate, test, or experiment with repeatedly. Interactive artifacts include input fields, controls, and calculated results that respond to user inputs, as shown in Figure 16-6.

If you find yourself thinking "I want to try different numbers" or "Users need to interact with this," request an interactive tool.

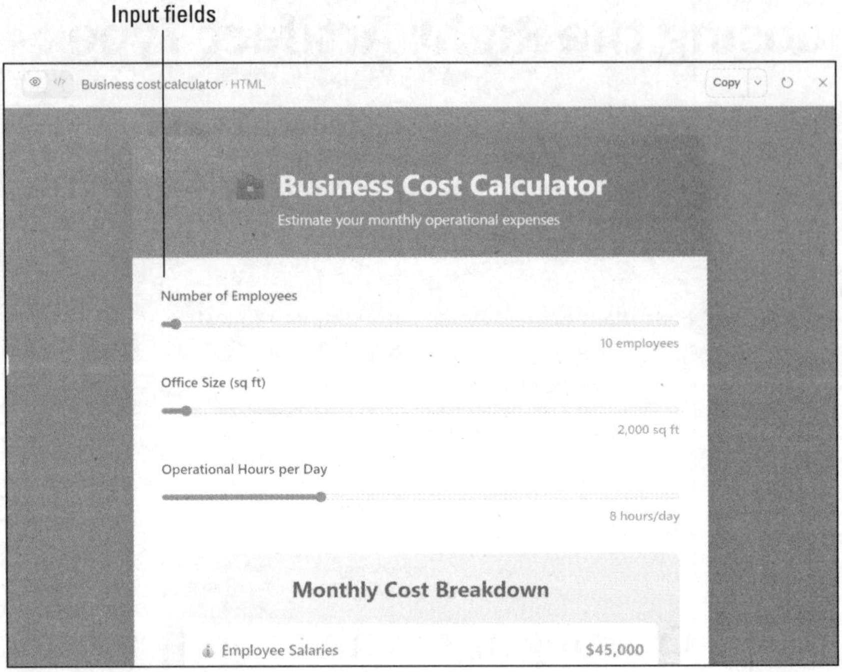

FIGURE 16-6: Interactive calculators include fields you can update.

Building formatted documents and reports

Documents need more than just words on a page. Headers create hierarchy, sections organize information, and formatting guides the reader's eye. When you need content that looks polished and professional, formatted document artifacts deliver structure and visual appeal that plain text can't match. Here's how that looks in practice:

Situation: A consultant needed to present findings about remote office workers to a client but wanted more than plain text. They went to the Documents and Templates category (refer to Figure 16-3).

Prompt: "Create a one-page executive summary about remote office workers with sections for key findings, recommendations, and next steps. Use professional formatting with clear section headers and bullet points."

Claude's response: It generated a formatted document with three sections: Key Findings (about remote work effectiveness), Recommendations (collaboration tools, manager training, policies), and Next Steps (survey, platform research, training development).

Result: Professional typography with clean hierarchy made it ready for printing, as shown in Figure 16-7.

Template: "Create a one-page executive summary about [topic] with sections for [section 1], [section 2], and [section 3]. Use professional formatting with [structural elements]."

Formatted executive summary

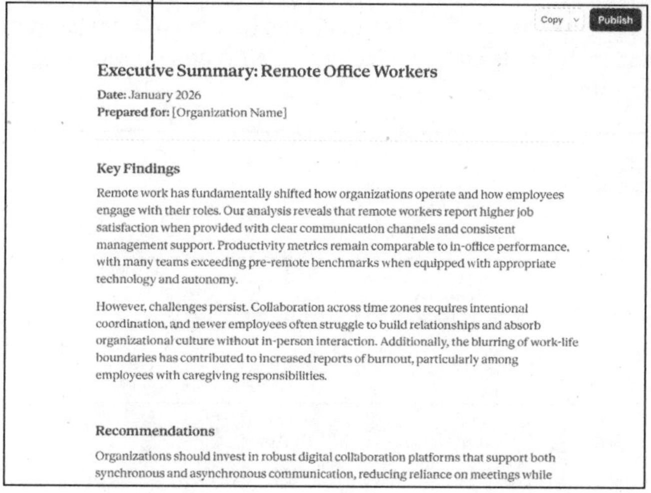

Executive Summary: Remote Office Workers

Date: January 2026
Prepared for: [Organization Name]

Key Findings

Remote work has fundamentally shifted how organizations operate and how employees engage with their roles. Our analysis reveals that remote workers report higher job satisfaction when provided with clear communication channels and consistent management support. Productivity metrics remain comparable to in-office performance, with many teams exceeding pre-remote benchmarks when equipped with appropriate technology and autonomy.

However, challenges persist. Collaboration across time zones requires intentional coordination, and newer employees often struggle to build relationships and absorb organizational culture without in-person interaction. Additionally, the blurring of work-life boundaries has contributed to increased reports of burnout, particularly among employees with caregiving responsibilities.

Recommendations

Organizations should invest in robust digital collaboration platforms that support both synchronous and asynchronous communication, reducing reliance on meetings while

FIGURE 16-7: Document artifacts maintain professional formatting.

Formatted documents work when presentation matters as much as content. If you're thinking "This needs to look polished" or "I need clear sections," request a formatted document.

Making data visualizations and diagrams

Numbers tell stories, but charts reveal patterns you might never spot in spreadsheets. Consider what happens when a project manager needs to spot patterns:

Situation: A project manager tracked task completion across four team members over six months.

Prompt: "Create a bar chart showing tasks completed per month for Bob, Sharon, Tim, and Jane from January through June. Use a different color for each person with a legend. Generate realistic sample numbers that show variation in performance across team members.

Claude's response: It displayed a chart with monthly clusters of four colored bars (blue for Bob, green for Sharon, amber for Tim, pink for Jane), as shown in Figure 16-8. The visual immediately revealed that Sharon consistently completed the most tasks (18 to 28 per month), while Tim's output varied significantly (7 to 18 per month), patterns that were invisible in the raw numbers.

Template: "Create a [chart type] showing [what you're measuring] for [person 1], [person 2], [person 3], and [person 4] from [start month] through [end month]. Use different colors for each person with a legend. Use sample data showing [desired pattern]."

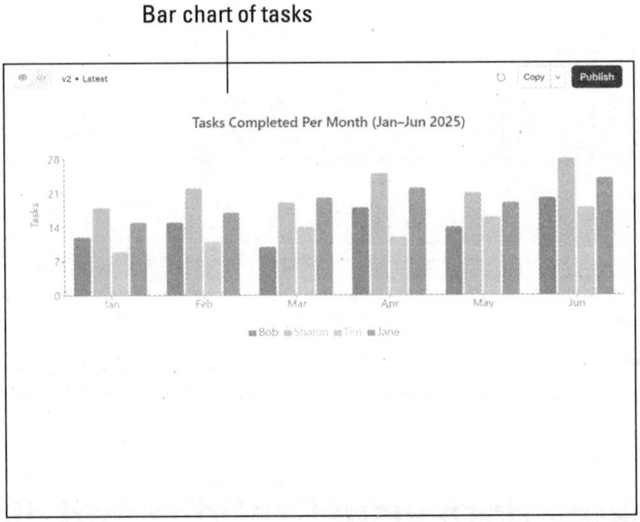

FIGURE 16-8: Bar chart showing task completion.

Data visualizations work when patterns, trends, or relationships matter more than individual numbers. Charts that compare values across categories, timelines that show event sequences, graphs that reveal trends over time, or diagrams that illustrate processes all communicate faster visually than in text. If you're thinking "I need to see this" or "The pattern matters," request a visualization.

Designing web components and layouts

Web components combine visual design with interactive functionality, letting you create polished elements for websites or presentations. Here's how that works in practice:

Situation: A real estate agent wanted an attractive contact form for their website. They chose the Web Apps and Templates category (refer to Figure 16-3) and asked Claude to do the following.

Prompt: "Design a contact form with fields for name, email, phone, and message. Use a clean layout with a blue submit button and labels above each field."

Claude's response: It built a clean vertical form with four fields (Name, Email, Phone, Message), each with its label positioned above the input. The fields used subtle gray borders that turned blue when clicked or tapped. The prominent blue Submit button spanned the width of the form, as shown in Figure 16-9.

Template: "Design a [form type] with fields for [field 1], [field 2], [field 3], and [field 4]. Use [layout description] with a [color] [button text] button and labels [placement]."

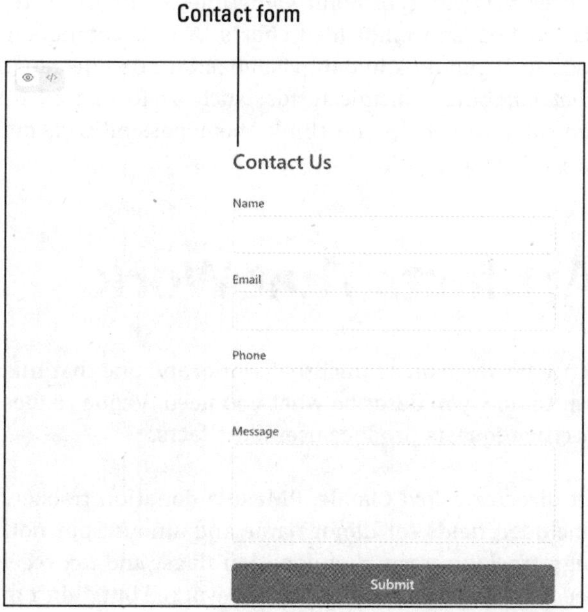

FIGURE 16-9: Contact form with four fields.

Web components work when you need styled, interactive elements for websites or presentations. Landing page sections, interactive widgets, styled forms, or display components that combine layout and functionality all benefit from web component artifacts. If you're thinking "This goes on a website" or "I need this styled and functional," request a web component.

Matching your goal to the right type

You don't need to master these categories or analyze which type fits perfectly. Claude recognizes your intent from your request. When you ask for "a calculator," it creates an interactive tool. When you ask for "a formatted report," Claude creates a document. When you ask for "a chart showing," Claude makes a visualization.

TIP

If you're unsure which type you need, focus on what you want to accomplish:

- "I need to calculate something repeatedly" suggests an interactive tool.
- "I need to present information professionally" suggests a formatted document.
- "I need to see patterns in data" suggests a visualization.
- "I need something styled for my website" suggests a web component.

The boundaries between types blur sometimes. A financial report might include both formatted text and embedded charts. A web component might consist of both interactive elements and data visualization. Claude can often accommodate requests that combine multiple needs, such as formatted text with embedded visuals. The categories help you think about possibilities, not create rigid rules about what's allowed.

Requesting Artifacts That Work

The difference between an artifact that works and one that misses the mark often comes down to how you describe what you need. Vague requests produce generic results. Specific requests produce useful artifacts.

A nonprofit director asked Claude, "Make a donation tracker." The artifact that appeared included fields for donor name and amount but nothing else. It lacked the campaign tracking, recurring donation flags, and tax receipt notes the organization needed. The calculator technically worked but didn't match the workflow.

The director tried again: "Create a donation tracker with fields for donor name, amount, date, campaign name, and donation type (one-time or recurring), as well as a notes field for tax receipt information. Calculate total donations automatically and show a breakdown by campaign."

This time, the tracker included everything the team needed. The specificity made it immediately useful.

Describing what you want clearly

Clear descriptions tell Claude not just what you're building, but what it needs to do. "Make a calculator" leaves Claude guessing about which calculations matter. "Create a mortgage calculator that shows monthly payment, total interest paid, and amortization schedule when I enter loan amount, interest rate, and term" gives Claude the complete picture.

Think about the specific information you need to enter and the specific results you want to see. The extra detail takes seconds to add but transforms the generic into something useful.

Providing the right context and constraints

Context helps Claude make smart choices about structure, layout, and functionality. A teacher requested: "Create a quiz about photosynthesis." They received 10 questions covering various aspects of the topic, but some were too advanced for their sixth-grade students, and the format didn't align with their classroom needs.

Next, the teacher provided context: "Create a quiz about photosynthesis for sixth-grade students. Include five multiple-choice questions focusing on the basic process, light, water, carbon dioxide, and glucose production. After each answer, show whether it's correct and explain why briefly." The quiz matched their students' level and gave them immediate learning feedback, not just right/wrong answers.

Context includes:

- **Your audience:** Who uses this?
- **Your limitations:** Any limits on size, format, or complexity?
- **Your use case:** Where or how will this be used?

TIP

A budget calculator for personal use differs from one for a small business. A presentation slide for executives differs from one for a technical team. These details guide Claude's choices about what to include and how to present it.

Testing and troubleshooting initial versions

The first version of an artifact rarely gets everything perfect. That's normal. Test your artifact immediately to spot what needs adjustment.

Try using your artifact. Enter real data. Click the buttons. Look at the results. You'll quickly spot missing features, unclear labels, confusing layouts, or calculations that don't match your needs.

When something doesn't work right, describe the problem and what you want instead. "The calculator isn't working" gives Claude little to fix. "The calculator shows $1,500 for a monthly payment when I enter a $200,000 loan at 6 percent for 30 years, but it should show closer to $1,200. Please check the formula." This prompt pinpoints the issue.

You're not expected to get the artifact picture perfect on the first try. The conversation lets you refine and adjust until the artifact matches your needs. Testing and iteration are part of the process, not a sign that something went wrong.

Refining Artifacts through Iteration

Artifacts improve through conversation. You start with a working version, use it, spot what needs adjustment, and refine through clear requests. This iterative process transforms basic artifacts into exactly what you need.

For example, a freelance designer created a project invoice template but realized after reviewing it that several elements needed adjustment. The template worked but felt incomplete. Rather than starting over, the designer refined it through specific requests, each improving a different aspect. The invoice template included basic fields such as client name, project description, hours worked, and rate. The designer realized they needed more: "Add a field for project number, a section for expenses with individual line items, and automatic calculation of subtotal, tax, and total amount due."

Claude modified the template to incorporate these features based on the request. The core structure stayed intact while new functionality appeared where needed.

Adding features and improvements

Sometimes the first version gets you close but needs more elements to be complete. Here's how that works in practice:

Situation: A home cook wanted consistent recipe formatting.

First prompt: "Create a recipe card for Chocolate Chip Cookies with a warm, inviting design. Include: recipe title at top, 10 ingredients in a two-column grid, numbered step-by-step instructions, and a helpful tip at the bottom. Use a brown and cream color scheme."

Claude's response: It generated a recipe card with title, ingredients in two columns, numbered instructions, and a tip. After reviewing it, she realized essential info was missing.

Second prompt: "Add three fields at the top between title and ingredients: Prep time (15 min), Cook time (10 min), and Servings (24 cookies). Display these horizontally, keeping the same color scheme."

Claude's response: Claude added a horizontal info bar showing the three fields in brown boxes with cream text, creating a cohesive bridge between title and ingredients, as shown in Figure 16-10.

First template: "Create a recipe card for [Recipe Name] with [style]. Include: recipe title at top, [number] ingredients in [layout], [numbering style] instructions, and [optional element] at bottom. Use [color scheme]."

Second template: "Add [number] fields at [location] between [element A] and [element B]: [Field 1] ([value]), [Field 2] ([value]), and [Field 3] ([value]). Display these [orientation] keeping the same [what to preserve]."

TIP

Adding features works best when you describe what you want added and where it fits. "Add more fields" leaves Claude guessing which fields and where they belong. "Add a priority drop-down list above the notes field with options for High, Medium, and Low" gives clear direction.

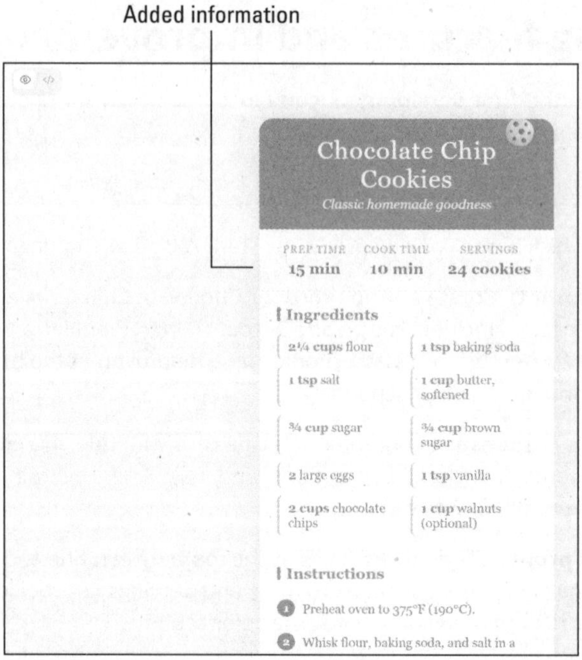

FIGURE 16-10: A recipe card showing added fields for prep time, cook time, and servings.

Fixing problems and adjusting behavior

Sometimes artifacts work mostly right but have specific issues. Take this case:

Situation: A bookstore owner created an inventory tracker that incorrectly calculated reorder quantities. The formula added when it should have subtracted, showing they needed to order 100 books when they had 100 in stock. The owner identified the problem as follows.

Prompt: "The reorder calculation is wrong. It's adding current stock plus the minimum stock level, but it should be minimum minus current. For example, if the minimum is 50 and the current is 30, the reorder should show 20, not 80. Fix the formula to minimum minus current equals reorder amount. When current exceeds minimum, show 0."

Claude's response: Claude corrected the formula to: reorder quantity = maximum of 0 or (minimum stock – current stock). Now entering minimum: 50, current: 30 correctly shows reorder: 20. When current: 60, it shows reorder: 0.

Template: "The [function] is [specific problem]. It's [wrong behavior] but should be [correct behavior]. For example: if [condition 1] and [condition 2], [result] should show [correct value], not [wrong value]. Fix [element] so it [correct description]. When [edge case], show [edge case behavior]."

Remixing existing artifacts for new uses

Successful artifacts often serve as starting points for related needs. See how this works:

Situation: A consultant used a client feedback form effectively for months and then needed a similar form for employee surveys. Rather than building from scratch, they asked Claude for a refinement.

Prompt: "Take the client feedback form and modify it for employee surveys. Replace 'Client Satisfaction' with 'Job Satisfaction,' 'Service Quality' with 'Workplace Environment,' 'Communication Effectiveness' with 'Management Communication.' Add these new sections: Professional Development (rating 1 to 5) and Work-Life Balance (rating 1 to 5). Keep the same rating scale format, same color scheme, same layout structure, same submit button styling."

Claude's response: It created the employee survey using the same structural foundation, but renamed all three sections and added two new sections. Each used the same 1 to 5 rating scale with comment boxes.

Result: The remix took minutes instead of rebuilding from scratch.

Template: "Take the [existing artifact] and modify it for [new purpose]. Replace '[original 1]' with '[new 1],' '[original 2]' with '[new 2],' '[original 3]' with '[new 3].' Add these new [components]: [new component 1] ([specs]) and [new component 2] ([specs]). Keep the same [structural element], same [visual element], same [interactive element]."

REMEMBER

The refinement process should mirror conversation. You see what works, notice what doesn't, and ask for specific changes. Each iteration brings the artifact closer to your ideal version without requiring a restart. This flexibility makes artifacts powerful. They evolve with your needs rather than forcing you to work around limitations.

Using Artifacts beyond the Conversation

Artifacts become more valuable when you can use them outside your conversation with Claude. Export them to share with others, integrate them into your existing tools, or describe successful artifacts in new discussions to recreate or adapt similar outputs.

Exporting artifacts for external use

A marketing manager created a social media content calendar as a formatted document. They needed to share it with their team, who didn't have access to the manager's conversation with Claude.

The manager exported the calendar as a PDF and emailed it. Their team could view, print, and reference the calendar without needing to see the conversation that created it.

Note that export options vary by artifact type. Interactive tools and web components export as HTML files that you can open in any browser or embed in websites. Formatted documents are exported as standard document files or as PDFs that you can edit in word processors, as shown in Figure 16-11. Data visualizations can be exported as image files for inclusion in presentations or reports.

FIGURE 16-11: Click or tap the Copy button to save the artifacts, which you can edit outside Claude.

In most cases, exports preserve much of the artifact's structure and appearance, though functionality may vary by format.

Here's how artifacts move from conversation to real-world use:

Situation: A financial advisor wanted to build a retirement calculator for offline client meetings.

Prompt: "Create a retirement calculator projecting nest egg growth. Include inputs for current age, retirement age, current savings, monthly contribution, and expected annual return. Show years until retirement, total contributed, investment growth, and final nest egg at retirement. Use green accents for growth."

Claude's response: It created a calculator showing Years Until Retirement: 30, Total Contributed: $230,000, Investment Growth: $388,511, Final Nest Egg: $618,511.

Result: The advisor clicked Copy (refer to Figure 16-11) and saved the calculator as HTML. They could then open the calculator on their laptop during client meetings without an internet connection.

Template: "Create a [calculator type] projecting [what]. Include inputs for [input 1], [input 2], [input 3], [input 4], and [input 5]. Show [result 1], [result 2], [result 3], and [result 4]. Use [color/theme]."

Bringing successful artifacts into new Projects

When you start a new conversation with Claude, you can describe artifacts you've created previously and ask Claude to recreate or adapt them. For example:

Situation: A teacher made an effective vocabulary quiz format consisting of multiple-choice questions with immediate feedback and explanations. Weeks later, they started a new conversation for a different subject.

Prompt: "I previously created a vocabulary quiz format with multiple-choice questions, immediate right/wrong feedback, and brief explanations for each answer. Create the same format for geometry terms."

Claude's response: It built the new quiz matching the successful structure from the teacher's description.

Result: The teacher didn't need to access the original conversation or export files describing what worked; they could simply replicate the format for different content.

Each artifact can serve as a foundation for future work, whether in the same conversation or new ones. This flexibility means you're not just creating one-time outputs; you're building a toolkit of useful formats and structures that you can adapt and reuse.

Exploring Claude Design for Visual Projects

Do you need more than a standard artifact, such as polished pitch decks, marketing materials, UI mockups, or interactive prototypes? Check out Claude Design, which is available in preview for Pro, Max, Team, and Enterprise subscribers. You describe what you want and refine it through conversation, inline comments, or direct edits.

Claude Design can apply your team's design system for visual consistency and exports to PDF, PowerPoint, HTML, or directly to Canva. It's currently in research preview, so features may change.

IN THIS CHAPTER

» **Recognizing when you need current information**

» **Searching the web for quick facts**

» **Investigating complex topics with research mode**

Chapter 17
Accessing Current Information

Claude is trained on a large collection of text, including books, articles, code, and other written material. But that training happens at a specific point in time, which means Claude's knowledge has a cutoff date. Ask about a historical event, and Claude can usually provide a detailed explanation. Ask about yesterday's stock price, and Claude needs help.

This chapter shows you how Claude accesses current information when its training data doesn't cover the time frame in question. You learn when to trust built-in knowledge, when to search for fresh data, and how to use both together for comprehensive answers.

Breaking Free from the Knowledge Cutoff

Claude's knowledge comes from data it was trained on up to a certain point in time, called a knowledge cutoff. Different Claude models can have different cutoffs, and Anthropic may update these models over time. To see the current cutoff for the model you're using, ask it directly.

Claude may have seen some information from shortly before its knowledge cutoff and may be missing newer developments that happened after it. Its answers tend to be more reliable for topics that were well covered before that cutoff and less dependable for recent events.

For example, a financial analyst asked Claude in late January 2026, "What was the Amazon stock price at market close yesterday?" Claude couldn't answer from its training data because this question fell beyond the model's knowledge cutoff, so it needed to look up the latest price on the web.

The same analyst asked, "What were the key factors that historically affected that stock price?" Claude answered this immediately from training data. Historical patterns and established relationships don't change daily, so the knowledge cutoff doesn't matter.

TIP

When working with Claude, quickly test whether you need current data. If you're asking about facts that change frequently (prices, news, current events, recent appointments), you'll need a web search. If you're asking about established knowledge (historical events, scientific principles, general how-to advice), Claude's built-in knowledge handles it.

Distinguishing a web search from research

Claude offers two ways to access current information. Many people confuse them because both involve looking up fresh data, but they work differently and serve different purposes:

- **A web search retrieves specific current facts.** Think of this approach as asking Claude to check what's happening right now. Web search is available in all Claude plans, but availability can change. When web search is enabled, Claude often decides on its own when a question needs current information.
- **Research mode conducts comprehensive multisource investigations.** Think of research mode as asking Claude to spend significantly longer than a normal chat message investigating a complex question from multiple angles, and then writing a detailed report with citations. Research mode requires a paid plan (Pro, Max, Team, or Enterprise). Behind the scenes, research mode breaks your request into multiple lines of inquiry and then synthesizes what it finds into a structured report with citations.

Here's how they differ in practice:

- **Web search example:** "What's the current stock price of Microsoft?" Claude searches quickly, finds the latest trading data, and tells you the price and recent movement in a few seconds.
- **Research example:** "Research how cloud computing revenue has grown across major tech companies over the past three years. Focus on what market share shifts occurred and what different customer segments drove growth." Claude can spend significantly longer than chat searching multiple sources (quarterly earnings reports, industry analyst research, market share data, technology trend analysis), analyzes patterns across sources, and typically includes citations to the sources that informed key points, so you can check the underlying material and dig deeper where needed.

TIP

In Chapter 15, you looked at the research feature and how it fits into complete publication workflows. This chapter focuses on web search for everyday quick lookups and on research strategies beyond publication projects.

Knowing when current data matters

Not every question needs current data. Reaching for web search or research mode when Claude's built-in knowledge has the answer wastes time and sometimes produces less accurate results.

For example, a consultant asked Claude with web search enabled, "What are best practices for running effective meetings?" Claude searched the web and returned recent blog posts with generic meeting tips. The consultant was expecting something more useful.

The consultant tried again without web search: "What are evidence-based best practices for running effective meetings? Draw on research about meeting effectiveness and organizational behavior." Claude provided a comprehensive answer based on established research about meeting structure, participation patterns, and decision-making processes. The second response proved more useful because meeting effectiveness principles don't change weekly. Established research beats recent blog posts.

You need current research data when you're asking about:

- Recent events ("What happened at yesterday's Apple event?")
- Current prices or rates ("What's the exchange rate for USD to EUR?")

- Breaking news ("What are today's major headlines about the snowstorm?")
- Time-sensitive verification ("Is this policy still in effect?")
- Recent changes ("What changed in the latest tax law?")
- Current positions ("Who is the current CEO of Netflix?")

You don't need current data when asking about:

- Historical facts ("What happened during the 2008 financial crisis?")
- Established concepts ("How does compound interest work?")
- Scientific principles ("Why does gravity affect time?")
- General how-to advice ("How do I write a compelling introduction?")
- Stable definitions ("What is machine learning?")
- Completed events ("Who won the 2020 World Series?")

Just because something involves recent work doesn't mean you need current data. If you're writing a marketing plan for a 2026 product launch, you need Claude's strategic knowledge about marketing planning (no search needed), but you'd want web search or research mode to verify current competitor positions or recent market trends.

Using Web Search for Quick Information

Web search gives Claude access to current information for quick lookups. You turn on the feature, ask your question, and Claude uses web search when your query requires fresh data. It works on all plans and handles everyday "I need to know this current fact" situations.

Turning on web search

Web search is in the same menu where you enable other Claude features. Here's how to activate it:

1. **Click or tap + in the chat input area.**

   A drop-down menu appears, as shown in Figure 17-1.

2. **Click or tap Web Search.**

   A check mark appears to the right of the option.

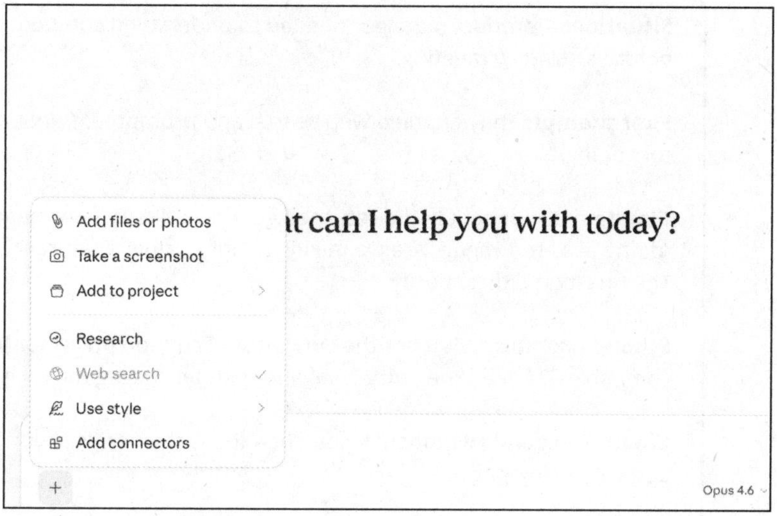

FIGURE 17-1: Enabling the web search feature.

Web search stays on for your entire conversation unless you turn it off. Once enabled, Claude automatically decides when to search based on your questions. You usually don't need to tell Claude, "Search the web for this." But if you prefer, you can still explicitly ask Claude to use web search — as well as ask Claude to avoid it.

For example, a marketing manager enabled web search and asked, "What are the latest social media advertising costs?" Claude recognized that this question required current data and searched automatically. The manager's next question was, "What makes social media ads effective?" Claude answered from training data, without searching, because advertising effectiveness principles don't change daily.

TIP

Keep the web search on during work sessions when you might need current information. It doesn't slow down responses when not needed, and Claude searches only when your query requires fresh data. This prevents the "I forgot to enable search" moment when you need current facts.

Asking questions that trigger search

Claude automatically searches when questions require current information, but how you phrase the question affects the quality of the results. Clear, specific questions yield better answers than vague ones. Here's how that plays out:

> **Situation:** A product manager needed to understand competitor pricing before a strategy meeting.
>
> **First prompt:** They enabled web search and prompted, "What are competitors doing?"
>
> **Claude's response:** Claude returned generic industry information because "doing" was too vague. Are we talking about pricing? Features? Marketing? The question didn't specify.
>
> **Second prompt:** "What are the current subscription prices for [named companies]? I need the entry-level and mid-tier pricing for each."
>
> **Claude's second response**: It searched for each specific product and found current pricing pages.
>
> **Why this worked:** The specific question told Claude exactly what to search for (product names and pricing tiers), making it easy to find and compare the right information.
>
> **Template:** "What are the current [specific metric] for [specific companies/products]? I need [specific details] for each."

Here are some more ways to ask questions that yield good search results:

- **Current events:** "What did [specific company/organization] announce about [topic] in the past week?"
- **Price checking:** "What is the current price of [specific product/service] from [specific retailer]?"
- **Fact verification:** "Is [specific claim] accurate? What are current authoritative sources saying about [topic]?"
- **Breaking news:** "What are today's major developments regarding [specific event/topic]?"

Web search excels at retrieving specific current facts. The more focused your request, the more useful the results.

Getting current news, prices, and data

When checking current news, specify your time frame and focus. "What's in the news about artificial intelligence?" returns too much information across too many topics. "What did Google announce about AI products this week?" provides targeted, up-to-date information.

Here's an example:

> **Situation:** A retail manager needed competitor pricing before a Monday meeting. On Saturday evening, they prompted.
>
> **Prompt:** "What are the current weekend sale prices at Target, Walmart, and Best Buy for 35-inch 4K TVs? Include brand and regular price if shown."
>
> **Claude's response:** Claude searched each retailer's current site, found weekend promotions, and returned specific prices with brand names.
>
> **Template:** "What are the current [time-specific] prices at [specific retailers] for [specific product category]? Include [specific details needed]."

When you are verifying time-sensitive facts, ask for verification from authoritative sources:

- "Has the [health entity] changed its guidance on [specific health topic] in the past six months? What are the current official recommendations?"
- "Is the [specific policy/regulation] still in effect as of today? Have there been recent changes?"

To get current data and statistics:

- "What is today's [specific data point: stock price, exchange rate, commodity price]?"
- "What are the latest official [statistics: unemployment rate, inflation figures, census data] released by [government agency]?"

Looking at what web search handles well and not so well

Web search answers questions where current facts matter. It doesn't replace Claude's analytical abilities or domain expertise.

Here's what web search handles well:

- » Current prices, rates, and market data
- » Recent news and announcements
- » Today's weather and conditions
- » Current policies and regulations
- » Recent appointments and changes
- » Time-sensitive facts
- » Verification of recent claims

Here's what web search doesn't handle well:

- » Analysis and interpretation (Claude does this from training)
- » Strategic advice (Claude's expertise doesn't need fresh data)
- » Complex reasoning (Claude uses reasoning, not web data)
- » Creative work (Claude's creativity comes from training, not search)
- » Synthesis across multiple concepts (Claude handles this without search)
- » Domain expertise on stable topics (Claude knows this already)

For example, a financial planner, with web search enabled, prompted, "Based on today's market conditions, should I recommend that my clients shift their portfolio allocation?"

Claude searched for current market data (which was appropriate), but the strategic advice about portfolio allocation came from Claude's training in financial planning principles (which was also relevant). The web search provided the current context, but Claude's expertise provided the analytical framework.

REMEMBER

Web search retrieves facts; Claude interprets them. When you need both current information and expert analysis, web searches provide the facts, and Claude's training provides the expertise to understand what those facts mean for your situation.

Using Research Mode for Deep Investigation

The research feature handles questions that require a comprehensive investigation across multiple sources. While web search checks individual facts, research mode explores complex topics from various angles and synthesizes findings into structured reports.

To select research mode:

1. **Click or tap + in the chat input area (refer to Figure 17-1).**
2. **Select Research so that a check mark appears to the right of the item.**

Knowing when research mode beats web search

Choose research mode over web search when your question needs more than quick facts. To explore multiple sources, research mode can take much longer than a normal chat, so save it for questions worth that investment.

Imagine this scenario:

Situation: A consultant needed to understand how nonprofits adapted their fundraising strategies during 2024–2025. They tried web search first, which returned individual articles but didn't synthesize patterns. They switched to research mode.

Prompt: "Research how major nonprofits adapted their fundraising strategies during 2024–2025. Focus on what changes worked, what failed, and what patterns emerged across different organization types. I need this for a strategic planning presentation to nonprofit board members."

Claude's response: After many minutes of investigating multiple sources (nonprofit industry publications, case studies, annual reports, news coverage), Claude delivered a comprehensive report organized into sections:

- Major shifts in fundraising strategy (with specific examples from eight organizations)

- What worked: Successful adaptations (data-backed examples of effective changes)
- What failed: Approaches that backfired (cautionary tales with specifics)
- Patterns across organization sizes (small versus large nonprofit differences)
- Key recommendations based on evidence

Result: Each major point included citations to the sources used, allowing the consultant to verify findings and dig deeper into specific examples.

Why this worked: The prompt specified the time period, the aspects to examine (what worked/failed), the patterns to look for, and how the information would be used (for a board presentation). This guided research mode toward relevant sources and useful organization.

Template: "Research how [industry/organization type] adapted their [specific function/strategy] during [time period]. Focus on [specific aspects to examine]. I need this for [how you'll use it]."

Use research mode instead of web search when you need:

- Multisource investigation of complex topics
- Pattern identification across different sources
- Comprehensive reports with citations
- Analysis of how something evolved over time
- Comparison of approaches or perspectives
- Deep dives into industry trends or changes

Use web search instead of research mode when you need:

- A single current fact quickly
- Today's news on a specific topic
- Current pricing or availability

» Quick verification of a claim

» Fast answers to straightforward questions

Connecting research mode to Google Workspace

If you connect research mode to Google Workspace, you can search your connected Google Workspace accounts and the web, giving you access to your organization's documents, emails, and calendar, as well as public information. Research mode must be enabled and Google Workspace must be connected through Claude's integrations. (For details on how to connect Google Workspace, see Chapter 6.)

A project manager used research mode with Google Workspace connected to ask, "Research how our customer feedback has evolved over the past six months. Compare what customers told us in support tickets and feedback emails against what industry trends show customers want from products like ours."

The analysis revealed that customers mentioned speed issues more frequently than industry reports suggested, indicating a specific product problem rather than a general market trend. When you connect research mode to Google Workspace, you can search your organization's emails and documents you've granted access to, along with relevant public web sources, and then summarize what it finds across both.

TIP

When you connect Google Workspace to research mode, specify whether you want Claude to search your organization's information, web sources, or both. "Research this using only our internal emails and documents" keeps the investigation internal. "Research this using both our internal information and current industry sources" combines your data with public information.

Getting comprehensive reports with citations

Research mode reports include citations that identify the sources that informed each major point. These citations let you verify findings and explore sources that interest you.

For example:

Situation: A business development manager was researching partnership opportunities.

Prompt: "Research the three fastest-growing companies in manufacturing AI over the past 18 months. For each, find their primary product focus, recent funding rounds, key partnerships, and what analysts say about their growth trajectory."

Claude's response: Research mode delivered a structured report with sections for each company. The report included citations like the following:

- Funding information cited in TechCrunch and Crunchbase articles from specific dates
- Product focus cited in company announcements and industry analysis
- Partnership details cited in press releases and news coverage
- Growth analysis cited to analyst reports and market research

Result: The manager could click any citation to read the original source, verify information, or gather additional details Research didn't include in the summary.

Template: "Research the [number] [superlative] [type of companies/products/trends] over [time period]. For each, find [specific information point 1], [specific information point 2], [specific information point 3]."

When reviewing reports created by research mode:

- Check citations for major claims you plan to use.
- Note which sources appear most frequently. (These can be the most relevant.)
- Look for where sources agree (high confidence) versus disagree (requires judgment).
- Use citations as starting points for deeper investigation of topics that matter most.

Research reports synthesize information from multiple sources, but you remain responsible for how you use findings. Review citations for important claims, verify critical facts against authoritative sources, and apply your domain expertise to interpret what the research means for your specific situation.

Reviewing research strategies beyond publication workflows

Chapter 15 showed how research mode fits into research-to-publication workflows. Research mode also solves other investigative challenges that require a comprehensive understanding. Here are some prompts you can try:

- **Competitive intelligence:** "Research how [competitor] has evolved their pricing strategy over [time period]. What changes did they make, when did they make those changes, and what do industry analysts say about why they did so?"
- **Market understanding:** "Research the key factors driving growth in [specific market segment] since [date]. What's changing, who's benefiting, and what risks do experts identify?"
- **Problem investigation:** "Research what solutions companies in [industry] have tried for [specific problem]. What worked, what failed, and what patterns emerge?"
- **Trend analysis:** "Research how [specific trend] has developed over [time period]. Track major milestones, identify key drivers, and show how expert perspectives have shifted."
- **Due diligence:** "Research [company/product] focusing on leadership team backgrounds, funding history, customer reviews, and any controversies or concerns mentioned in news coverage."
- **Opportunity assessment:** "Research whether [potential opportunity] makes sense given current market conditions. What are competitors doing? What do industry experts predict? What risks should I consider?"
- **Learning about emerging topics:** "Research [new technology/trend] from multiple angles, including what it is, why it matters, who's leading development, what criticisms exist, and what realistic timelines experts suggest."

Combining Claude's Knowledge with Fresh Data

A powerful approach is to combine Claude's built-in expertise with current information from web search or research mode. When you share fresh data, Claude draws on its training to analyze trends and provide context.

Trusting built-in knowledge versus verifying current facts

Claude's training includes extensive knowledge that remains accurate and useful. You don't need to verify everything through web search. The key is recognizing what changes over time versus what stays stable.

Here's how you recognize the difference:

Situation: A product manager asked Claude about the pricing strategy for a new software product. They weren't sure whether they needed web search enabled or could trust Claude's existing knowledge.

First prompt: "I'm pricing a new project management tool for small teams (5 to 10 people). What pricing models work well for software tools in this category, and what factors should influence my pricing decision? I'll follow up with questions about current competitor pricing."

Claude's response: It drew on training data to explain pricing models (freemium, per-user, tiered, value-based), factors affecting pricing decisions (customer willingness to pay, cost to serve, competitive positioning, feature differentiation), and psychological pricing strategies (anchoring, grandfathering). This knowledge doesn't expire; pricing strategy principles remain stable.

Second prompt: With web search enabled, the manager asked: "What are the current per-user monthly prices for [software companies] for teams of 5 to 10 people?"

Claude's response: It searched for current pricing and returned specific tiers and costs for each competitor, which change periodically.

Why this worked: The manager separated questions about stable principles (pricing strategy) from questions about changing facts (current competitor prices). Claude's training handled strategy; web search handled current prices.

Template: Start with principle-based questions that draw on Claude's training: "What are the key considerations for [decision/strategy]? What approaches work well in [situation]?" Then follow up with web search for current specific facts: "What are the current [specific data points] for [specific examples]?"

This separation helps you use each source of information appropriately.

Blending training data with search results

You can combine Claude's built-in knowledge with fresh search results to get surprisingly accurate answers. Claude explains the principles from its training, and then searches for today's specific data and applies those principles to your situation right now.

This two-step process gives you more than either source alone. You get the underlying framework that makes sense of the data, along with the current reality that informs your decision. Claude doesn't just tell you what's happening today; it helps you understand what it means for your context.

For example:

Prompt: A logistics manager prompted: "What should I know about the relationship between ocean freight rates and inventory planning? Then search for current shipping rates from Asia to the US and help me understand what it means for our Q2 inventory strategy."

Claude's response: Claude explained the relationship between container costs, order lead times, bulk purchasing economics, and cash flow considerations — all from training data. Then Claude searched for current shipping rates, found the specific pricing trends and capacity constraints, and analyzed what these particular conditions meant for Q2 planning, given the principles just explained.

Template: "Explain the relationship between [factor A] and [factor B]. Then search for current information about [factor A] and help me understand implications for [factor B]."

Here are some prompts for analysis combining expertise and current data:

- "What are the key factors that determine [outcome]? Then search for the current state of those factors and analyze what they suggest for [situation]."
- "Explain what makes [strategy] effective. Then search for how [specific company] is currently executing that strategy and evaluate their approach."

Building reports that use both sources

Comprehensive reports often need both Claude's analytical expertise and current factual information. Structure these requests to separate analysis from fact-gathering. Here's how this works in practice:

Situation: A technology director needed to recommend whether or not to switch the company's project management platform. The decision required both software evaluation expertise and current information about available tools and pricing.

Prompt: "I need to decide whether we should switch from our current project management software. First, explain the key factors that determine whether a company should migrate to a new project management platform. Then use a web search to find current information on leading project management tools and their pricing, recent feature updates across major platforms, user satisfaction trends, and integration capabilities with Slack and Microsoft Teams. Finally, synthesize this into a preliminary migration recommendation."

Claude's response: It explained the factors that informed the migration decision, specifically training, total cost of ownership, feature gaps versus current needs, migration complexity, team adoption risk, integration requirements, scalability, vendor stability. Then Claude searched for current platform-specific information and found updated pricing structures, recent feature launches including AI capabilities, customer review trends on G2 and Capterra, and detailed integration documentation for Slack and Teams.

Claude combined both sources into an analysis that applied migration frameworks to current market conditions, highlighting that several platforms had recently added AI-powered task automation that could address the client's workflow bottlenecks, while migration costs had decreased due to improved data export tools released in the past six months.

Why this worked: The prompt separated "explain frameworks" (training data) from "find current facts" (web search) and from "synthesize" (analysis combining both). This structure lets Claude use each information source appropriately.

Template: "I need to [decision/analysis]. First, explain [relevant framework/principles]. Then use [web search/research mode] to find current information about [specific current fact 1], [specific current fact 2], [specific current fact 3]. Finally, synthesize this into [deliverable]."

TIP

When building comprehensive analyses, explicitly structure your request in stages: explain principles/frameworks, gather current facts, and synthesize into recommendations. This approach prevents Claude from searching for information it already knows while ensuring that fresh data informs the analysis.

Here are some more templates to try:

- **Strategic decisions needing current context:** "Explain what determines success for [strategy/initiative]. Search for how [relevant factors] have changed recently. Analyze what this means for [my specific situation]."
- **Recommendations requiring current data:** "What framework should I use to evaluate [decision]? Search for current conditions regarding [key factors]. Recommend an approach for [my situation] based on both the framework and current conditions."
- **Comprehensive understanding:** "Teach me the fundamentals of [topic]. Then search for the most significant recent developments in [topic]. Explain how recent developments change or confirm what the fundamentals suggest."

IN THIS CHAPTER

» Deciding when to use extended thinking for more reliable reasoning

» Using research mode for comprehensive investigations

» Choosing the right model and mode for different types of tasks

Chapter 18
Using Extended Thinking and Research Mode

Sometimes a quick answer isn't good enough. When you're tackling a problem with multiple moving parts or decisions that affect other choices, you need more than an instant response. You need extended analysis, not a snap answer.

That's exactly what the extended thinking mode delivers. It provides a way to tell Claude to take more time to process a problem before responding. You can toggle it on when the situation calls for deeper analysis and leave it off when speed matters more.

For example, a financial analyst faced a complex valuation problem involving multiple scenarios, interdependent variables, and regulatory constraints. Their usual approach with Claude produced decent answers, but they sensed Claude was not fully working through the complexity.

Then they toggled the extended thinking icon on and asked the same question. Claude took nearly a minute reasoning through each scenario before responding. The difference was striking: instead of a quick answer that missed edge cases, the analyst received a thorough analysis that anticipated complications they hadn't even considered.

This chapter introduces Claude's advanced reasoning and research capabilities, which are available on Pro, Max, Team, and Enterprise. You learn when extended thinking helps Claude work through genuinely complex problems, how research mode conducts comprehensive investigations using current information, and how to choose the right model and mode for different situations.

You also learn when *not* to use these advanced features, and why standard chat remains the best choice for most everyday work.

Understanding Extended Thinking

Most conversations with Claude happen in standard mode, where Claude reads your prompt and generates a response in a continuous stream. Extended thinking mode works differently. When you enable it, Claude pauses before responding, taking time to break down the problem, exploring approaches, and reasoning through complications before presenting its answer.

Learning what extended thinking does differently

Think of standard mode as asking a knowledgeable colleague for a quick answer. They draw on their expertise and respond immediately. Extended thinking is more like asking that same colleague to sit down, work through the problem step by step, and show you their reasoning before giving a final recommendation.

When extended thinking is active, Claude may take longer to respond, from a few seconds to over a minute. The time spent scales with the difficulty of the task.

You may see an on-screen indicator that shows Claude is reasoning before responding. The exact presentation varies by model and interface and may change over time. In Figure 18-1, the extended thinking icon is selected and the Extended Thinking window in its collapsed state. (You can't see the thinking taking place when the window is closed.)

After the thinking phase completes, you can expand a section above the response to see a summary of Claude's reasoning process, as shown in Figure 18-2. (Some models show a condensed summary of the thinking, while others display the full thinking process in more detail.)

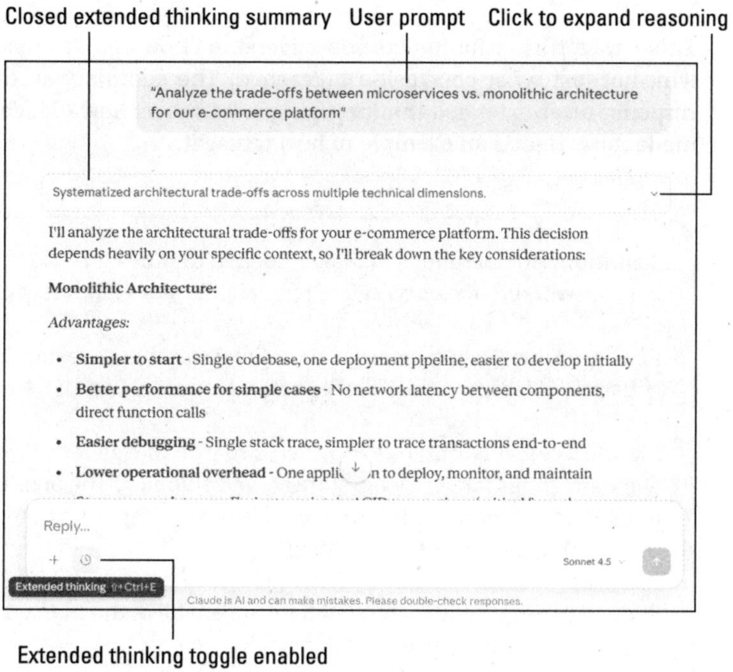

FIGURE 18-1: The Extended Thinking summary window in its collapsed state.

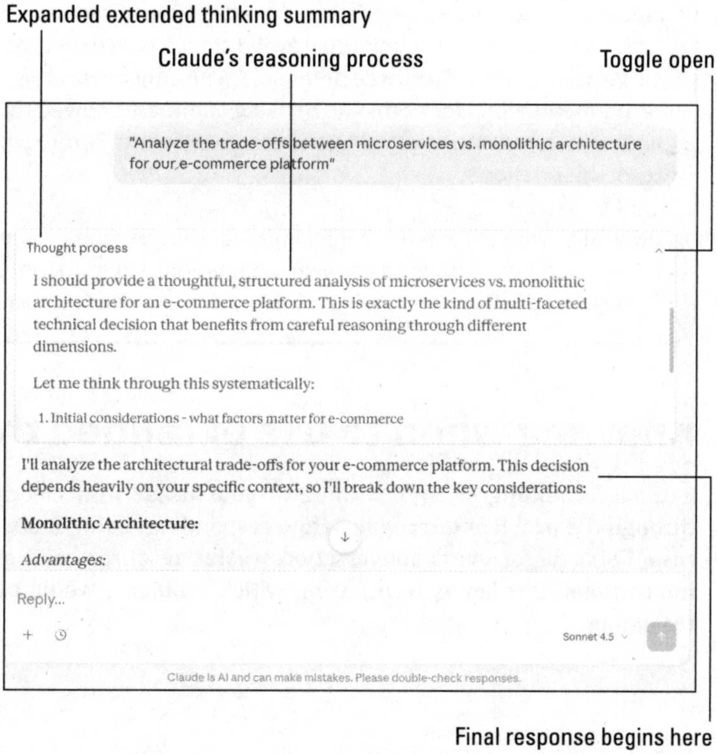

FIGURE 18-2: The Extended Thinking summary in its open state.

Either way, this visibility lets you understand how Claude approached your problem, not just what conclusion it reached. The summary section above Claude's response after extended thinking completes shows how Claude weighed competing factors. Here's an example of how to use it:

> **Situation:** An operations manager needed to redesign a warehouse layout to balance worker efficiency, safety regulations, and equipment constraints.
>
> **First prompt:** "Help me design an optimal warehouse layout for a 50,000 square foot facility with 12 workers, forklift traffic, and OSHA requirements."
>
> **Claude's response:** Claude provided a reasonable generic layout with standard zones for receiving, storage, and shipping. The answer was fine, but it didn't account for information it had about specific traffic patterns or the unusual L-shape of the building.
>
> **Second prompt:** With extended thinking enabled, the manager asked the same question with extended thinking turned on.
>
> **Claude's response:** After about 45 seconds of thinking, Claude produced a layout that considered forklift turning radii at specific intersections, positioned high-turnover items to minimize travel distance based on order frequency patterns, and identified three potential OSHA concerns with specific recommendations for each. The thinking summary showed that Claude had considered and rejected two alternative layouts before settling on the recommendation.
>
> **Why this worked:** Extended thinking gives Claude time to simulate the workflow, identify conflicts between competing requirements, and reason through tradeoffs rather than defaulting to a standard template.

Knowing when to use extended thinking

Extended thinking consumes more of your usage limits because Claude works through the problem internally before responding, using more tokens in the process. Using it for every conversation wastes resources and slows down simple interactions. The key is recognizing which problems would benefit from deeper reasoning.

Here are signs that your task may benefit from extended thinking:

- Multiple interdependent decisions where early choices affect later options
- Tradeoffs between several valid approaches
- Technical problems in which missing edge cases could cause failures
- Strategic questions that require balancing different stakeholder priorities
- Situations where understanding the reasoning matters as much as the conclusion

Standard mode remains the most efficient for:

- Straightforward questions with clear answers
- Writing tasks where creativity matters more than analytical rigor
- Quick information retrieval or summarization
- Conversational interactions and brainstorming
- Tasks where speed matters more than exhaustive analysis

Here's another example of extended thinking in practice:

> **Situation:** A tax accountant began using extended thinking for everything after seeing impressive results on a complex estate-planning question. But when they used it to draft a simple client email, they waited 30 seconds for Claude to think about something that didn't require deep reasoning.
>
> **Result:** Now the accountant reserves extended thinking for genuinely complex tax scenarios and uses standard mode for routine communications.
>
> **Template:** "I need to analyze [situation] considering [factor 1], [factor 2], and [factor 3]. These factors sometimes conflict. Help me think through the tradeoffs and recommend an approach."

Reading and using insights from the thinking process

When Claude uses extended thinking, you get more than just a better answer. You get visibility into how Claude approached the problem. This transparency helps you evaluate whether Claude understood your situation correctly and catch reasoning errors before they affect outcomes.

The thinking summary reveals not just what Claude concluded but also how it weighed your priorities against one another. Here's an example of Claude ranking priorities:

> **Situation:** A product manager asked Claude to prioritize features for the next release of a mobile app.
>
> **Prompt:** "We're planning our Q2 release for our fitness tracking app. Help me prioritize these eight features considering development effort, user impact, and our goal of improving retention among users who've been active for 3+ months."
>
> **Claude's response:** The reasoning summary showed that Claude initially ranked a feature highly for engagement, and then adjusted its recommendation after recognizing the company's specific retention goals.

TIP

When reviewing extended thinking outputs, pay attention to what Claude considered and rejected, not just what it recommended, so that you can check the reasoning itself.

Accessing Research Mode for Deep Dives

While extended thinking helps Claude reason more carefully about problems, research mode helps Claude gather current information. In research mode, Claude actively investigates your question by consulting multiple sources and synthesizing the findings into a structured report.

TIP

Research mode is available in Pro, Max, Team, and Enterprise plans, though availability might expand in the future. Check your plan's features to confirm access.

Starting research mode conversations

In the Claude web app, look for the Research option near the text input area or in the mode controls, as shown in Figure 18-3. When you activate it, Claude treats your next message as a research request and investigates your question using current web sources. That is, Claude understands that your next message should trigger an investigative process rather than an immediate response.

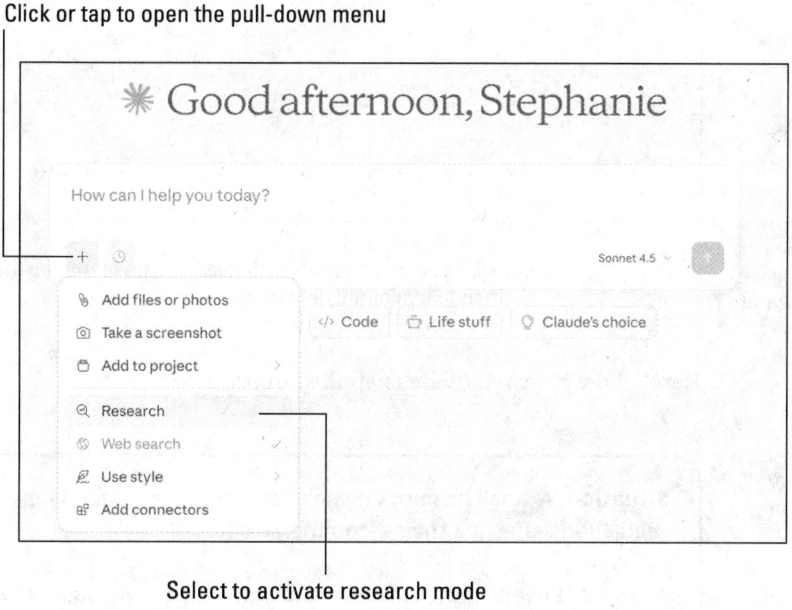

FIGURE 18-3: Select Research to start research mode.

The research mode progress indicator displays Claude's investigation steps during the multi-minute research process, as shown in Figure 18-4. Research mode may take several minutes for complex topics as Claude gathers, cross-checks, and synthesizes information.

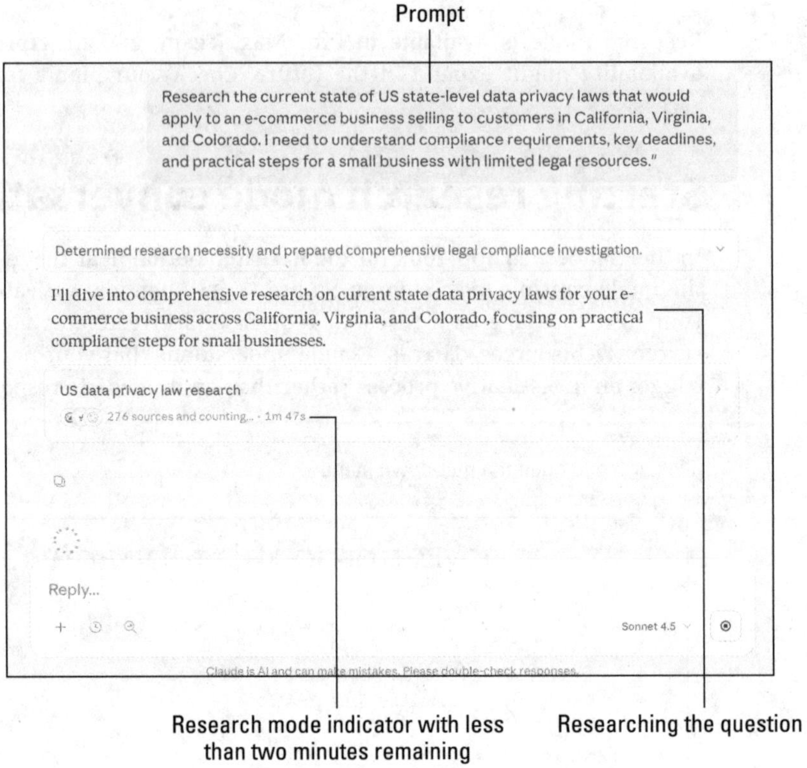

FIGURE 18-4: The research mode progress indicator.

Here's how research mode is applied in practice:

Situation: A small business owner needed to understand new data privacy regulations affecting their e-commerce site.

Prompt: "Research the current state of US state-level data privacy laws that would apply to an e-commerce business selling to customers in California, Virginia, and Colorado. I need to understand compliance requirements, key deadlines, and practical steps for a small business with limited legal resources."

Claude's response: Over several minutes, Claude searched regulatory websites, legal analysis publications, and compliance guides. The research mode indicator showed Claude examining multiple sources, cross-referencing requirements, and building a synthesized report. Claude prepared a structured report covering each state's requirements, a comparison table highlighting key differences, specific compliance deadlines, and a prioritized action list for small businesses. Each major claim was linked to its source.

TIP

Research mode doesn't just search the web. When you've connected applications such as Google Workspace, Jira, or Confluence to Claude (available on Pro, Max, Team, and Enterprise plans), research mode can also investigate across these sources. Claude might search your company's Confluence documentation while checking current regulations online, synthesizing internal knowledge with external information into a unified report.

Template: "Research [topic] with focus on [specific angle]. I need to understand [key question 1], [key question 2], and [practical implications for my situation: describe context]."

Understanding how research differs from regular chat

Regular conversations draw on Claude's training knowledge, which has a cutoff date and doesn't include events or changes since that date. Research mode accesses current web information, making it essential for topics where recency matters.

Regular chat is better for:

- Conceptual explanations that don't depend on current data
- Creative work and brainstorming
- Quick document summaries and simple Q&A about uploaded files
- Quick back-and-forth conversations
- Topics where Claude's training knowledge is sufficient

Research mode is better for:

- Current events, recent developments, or breaking news
- Market data, pricing, or competitive analysis
- Regulatory changes or policy updates
- Technical documentation that may have been updated
- Any question where you'd want current sources cited

The distinction between training knowledge and current information becomes obvious when the stakes are high:

Situation: A marketing consultant was preparing a competitive analysis. Their regular Claude conversations provided solid strategic frameworks but relied on outdated information about competitor pricing and features.

Claude's response: Claude found current pricing pages, recent press releases about new features, and industry analyst reports from the past month.

Result: The distinction between "generally accurate but dated" and "current and verified" was significant for the consultant's presentation to the client.

REMEMBER

Research mode uses your plan's limits more intensively than regular chat because Claude actively searches, retrieves, and processes information from multiple sources. For quick questions where Claude's existing knowledge is sufficient, standard chat is more efficient. See Chapter 2 for details on plan limits, options, and upgrading.

Getting comprehensive reports on complex topics

Research mode shines when you need Claude to investigate a topic thoroughly rather than answer a quick question. The reports Claude produces include citations linking to original sources, allowing you to verify claims and dig deeper into specific areas.

When you frame your research request around your specific decision-making criteria, Claude organizes its investigation accordingly. In the following situation, we see that in practice:

Situation: An investment club needed to evaluate a potential stock purchase.

Prompt: "Research [Company Name] for a potential long-term investment. I need to understand their competitive position, recent financial performance, major risks, and analysts' views on the stock. We're value investors focused on companies with sustainable competitive advantages."

Claude's response: For about 18 minutes, Claude examined SEC filings, analyst reports, industry publications, and financial news. The research mode progress indicator showed Claude breaking the question into components: competitive analysis, financial metrics, risk factors, and analyst sentiment.

Claude produced a detailed report organized by the investor's priorities, with specific data points cited to sources, a discussion of competitive factors, recent earnings results with context, risks including management concerns from recent proxy statements, and a summary of analyst ratings with links to the underlying reports.

Why this worked: The investor asked for research structured around their investment philosophy (value investing, sustainable advantages), so Claude organized findings to address those specific criteria rather than producing a generic company overview.

WARNING

Research mode produces comprehensive reports, but it comes with important caveats. Claude may occasionally misattribute quotes or generate citations that don't match their claimed source. Always verify critical claims, especially those you plan to share with others or use for important decisions. The citations Claude provides make verification straightforward. You can click or tap through to the source and confirm that the information appears as Claude reported it.

TIP

When requesting research, tell Claude how you plan to use the findings. A report for internal decision-making needs a different depth than one you'll present to clients. Specifying your use case helps Claude adjust the level of detail and formality.

Choosing the Right Model and Mode for Your Task

Claude isn't a single model. Anthropic offers multiple models optimized for different needs, and understanding their differences helps you work more efficiently.

Understanding model differences

Three model tiers serve different purposes. Anthropic updates these models regularly, so specific capabilities may evolve, but the fundamental tradeoffs between speed, cost, and depth remain consistent:

- **Claude Haiku** is fast and efficient and is best for quick drafts, simple questions, and high-volume tasks.
- **Claude Sonnet** balances capability and speed and is ideal for most professional work, analysis, and writing.
- **Claude Opus** provides the deepest reasoning and is best for complex, high-stakes problems where accuracy matters most. Opus 4.7 introduces adaptive thinking, which automatically adjusts how deeply the model reasons based on the complexity of your task. Instead of running at a fixed thinking depth every time, Opus now spends more time on hard problems and less on simple ones, so you get better results without managing anything yourself.

TIP

Haiku is like quick, junior-level help, Sonnet is like a capable professional, and Opus is like a senior expert who takes time to think carefully.

The best approach matches model capability to task complexity rather than defaulting to the most powerful option for everything.

Situation: A consulting firm developed different workflows for each model tier:

- *Haiku workflow:* Initial drafts of client communications, quick research summaries, formatting and restructuring documents, and brainstorming sessions where the volume of ideas matters.
- *Sonnet workflow:* Client deliverables requiring professional quality, analysis of business problems, code review and development, and any task going directly to clients.
- *Opus workflow:* Complex strategy recommendations, multifactor analysis where errors have significant consequences, and final review of high-stakes deliverables.

Why this worked: The consulting firm matched model capability to task complexity, using faster models for routine work and reserving deeper reasoning for situations that require it.

Comparing speed versus deep thinking

The tradeoff between response speed and reasoning depth appears at multiple levels: model choice (Haiku versus Sonnet versus Opus) and mode choice (standard versus extended thinking). Understanding when each combination makes sense helps you work efficiently.

Speed-optimized combinations:

- **Haiku in standard mode:** Fastest possible responses for simple tasks
- **Sonnet in standard mode:** Quick responses with good capability for most work

Depth-optimized combinations:

- **Sonnet with extended thinking:** Strong analysis with reasonable speed
- **Opus with extended thinking:** Deeper reasoning for the most complex problems automatically with Opus 4.7's adaptive thinking. The model decides how much reasoning a task needs rather than applying the same depth to everything. As a result, you're less likely to waste time waiting for Claude to overthink a simple question.

Knowing when faster is better prevents the trap of overengineering every interaction:

Situation: A data scientist discovered that they were overusing Opus with extended thinking. Every question, even simple ones, triggered a minute of thinking. Opus 4.7 addresses this problem directly with adaptive thinking. The model now calibrates its reasoning depth to match the task, so you no longer need to manually toggle thinking on and off for different types of questions. The scientist restructured their workflow: Haiku for quick data formatting questions, Sonnet for analysis interpretations, and Opus with extended thinking for only complex statistical methodology questions.

Why this worked: Their work improved because they spent less time waiting and more time testing hypotheses and building on insights.

Switching between models strategically

Most users don't need to switch models frequently because Sonnet handles the vast majority of tasks well. But recognizing when to switch can improve both efficiency and outcomes.

Switch to Haiku when:

- You need rapid iteration on drafts you'll heavily edit.
- The task is simple, and you're paying for unused capability.
- You're doing high-volume work like processing many similar items.
- Response time matters more than maximum quality.

Switch to Opus when:

- Standard Sonnet responses feel superficial for the task complexity.
- You're making decisions with significant consequences.
- The problem requires holding many factors in consideration simultaneously.
- You've tried Sonnet, and the results aren't meeting your needs.

REMEMBER

With Opus 4.7, adaptive thinking means the model does much of this calibration for you. It automatically reasons more deeply on complex tasks and responds quickly on simple ones.

Start complex projects with Sonnet to draft initial approaches and explore the problem space quickly. Switch to Opus for final review and validation of critical decisions. This pattern gives you speed during iteration and depth for decisions that matter. You can even ask Opus to review work that Sonnet produced earlier in your conversation.

Following is a template you can use for model selection. Ask yourself: "If this task were done by a junior, mid-level, or senior expert, which level is needed?" Haiku corresponds roughly to capable but quick work, Sonnet to thoughtful professional work, and Opus to senior expert deliberation.

Using standard chat for most tasks

After learning about extended thinking and research mode, some users fall into the trap of using advanced features for everything. This approach wastes resources and unnecessarily slows work.

Standard chat remains the right choice for:

- Conversations where you're exploring ideas
- Writing tasks where Claude's initial output is a starting point
- Questions Claude can answer with its training knowledge
- Back-and-forth refinement of any project
- The majority of your daily Claude interactions

REMEMBER

If you're using extended thinking for every draft, you're adding 30-60 seconds of waiting to each request. Standard mode works equally well for initial drafts you'll revise anyway. Save extended thinking for content requiring complex argument structures or technical accuracy, where Claude's reasoning path matters.

Launching research mode for a thorough investigation

Research mode is ideal when your question depends on current information or when you need Claude to survey a topic rather than answer from existing knowledge.

Effective research requests include:

- A clear topic or question to investigate
- Specific angles or sub-questions to address
- Context about how you'll use the findings
- Any constraints on sources or approach

For example, you might use research mode as follows: "Research current best practices for remote employee onboarding at technology companies. Focus on what's changed since 2023, common challenges companies report, and specific tools or approaches that have strong evidence of effectiveness. I'm redesigning our onboarding program for a 50-person startup."

This prompt clearly defines the scope (remote onboarding at tech companies), the time frame (changes since 2023), the key questions to explore (challenges and tools), and the context needed to tailor the results (a startup environment).

IN THIS CHAPTER

» Setting up and running your first task

» Assigning tasks from your phone with Dispatch

» Letting Claude use your computer's app directly

Chapter 19

Taking Control with Claude's Desktop Agent Cowork

Skills and Connectors stretch what Claude can do inside a conversation. What they can't do is reach into your computer, run a sequence of tasks from start to finish, and hand you the result while you step away. Those tasks require a different tool category called an autonomous desktop agent. That's what Cowork is.

Cowork runs Claude as an *autonomous desktop agent.* You describe an outcome, give Cowork access to a folder, and let it work. While you focus on something else, Claude reads your files, plans its approach, executes the steps, and delivers results: a formatted spreadsheet, a synthesized report, and an organized folder.

This chapter walks you through what Cowork can do. You learn how to run your first task, how to use Projects to give Claude persistent memory of your work, how to assign tasks from your phone with Dispatch, and how the computer use feature extends Claude's reach to apps without a direct integration. You also find where Cowork falls short, so you know when to rely on it and when to stick with regular chat.

REMEMBER

Cowork is available on all paid plans: Pro, Max, Team, and Enterprise. It requires the Claude desktop app on macOS or Windows.

Understanding What Cowork Does

Cowork isn't a smarter chat window. It's a different tool category. You hand off an entire workflow and return with a finished result. This section explains what Cowork does that regular Claude chat can't, and how to recognize the tasks worth handing off.

Seeing how Cowork differs from regular chat

Skills and Connectors extend what Claude can do inside a conversation. Cowork takes a different approach. It runs Claude as an autonomous desktop agent that works through multistep tasks on your computer while you focus on other work.

The idea behind Cowork is simple. You describe an outcome, give Claude access to a folder, and let it work. Cowork directly accesses your local files, plans its own approach, executes it, and delivers results. You don't have to watch in real time.

In a regular chat, every response is part of a conversation. With Skills in chat, Claude still produces files one request at a time. Cowork handles the entire sequence on its own. It reads the files, cross-references them, produces a summary, formats it for distribution, and saves the result.

Here's what Cowork can do that regular chat can't:

- **Work with your files directly:** No uploading. Cowork reads from and writes directly to a folder on your computer.
- **Run complex jobs from start to finish:** Instead of walking you through steps, Cowork handles the entire sequence and hands you the result.
- **Deliver files, not summaries:** You get a finished Word doc, spreadsheet, or report, not a description of one.
- **Work in parallel:** For complex tasks, Claude coordinates multiple workstreams simultaneously, completing them faster than a step-by-step approach would allow.

Knowing when to hand off a task

Cowork earns its place with tasks that are complex, repetitive, or time-consuming enough that you'd rather not manage them step by step. Good candidates include organizing and renaming large batches of files, pulling data from multiple sources into a single report, processing a folder of documents to extract consistent information, and running weekly or daily tasks on a schedule.

Regular chat is still the right tool when you want to think through a problem, draft something quickly, or ask a question. Use Cowork when you want to hand off work and come back to a result.

TIP

Not sure whether a task belongs in Cowork? Ask yourself: Would I describe this to an assistant and walk away, or would I stay involved through every step? If you'd walk away, it's a Cowork task.

Getting Started with Cowork

Your first Cowork task is closer than you think. All you need is the desktop app, a folder on your computer, and a clear description of what you want to do. This section walks you through the setup, your first task, and how to stay in the loop while Claude works.

Setting up and running your first task

Cowork requires a paid plan (Pro, Max, Team, or Enterprise) and runs as a desktop application on macOS and Windows.

To get started with Cowork:

1. **Download and install the Claude desktop app at `https://claude.com/download`, as shown in Figure 19-1.**
2. **In the Claude desktop app, click the task list icon to open Cowork in the left sidebar.**

   The interface switches to task mode.
3. **In the task description field, shown in Figure 19-2, describe the outcome you want.**

   Be specific, for example: "Review all the client intake forms in this folder, extract the key information from each, and produce a single summary spreadsheet with one row per client."

4. **Click the Work in a Project button, and then select the folder for Claude to work in.**

   This will be the folder Cowork reads from and writes to.

5. **Read the Allow Claude to Change Files in [Folder Name] dialog box carefully, and then click Allow.**

6. **Click Let's Go to confirm.**

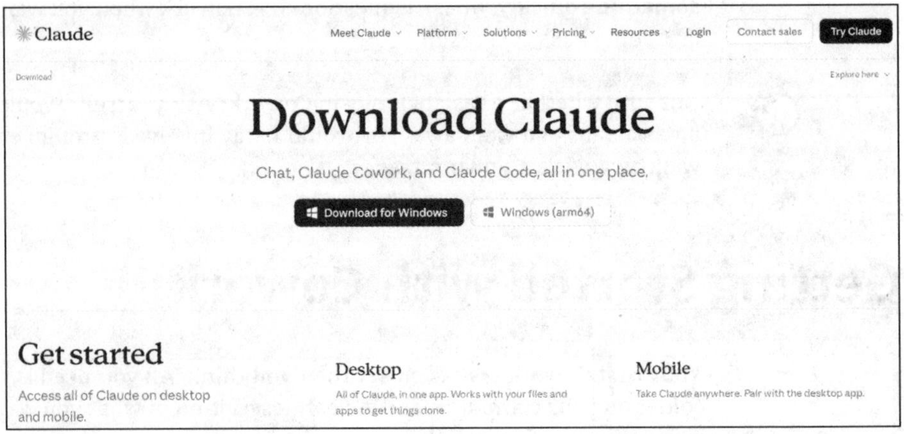

FIGURE 19-1: Get the Claude desktop app here.

FIGURE 19-2: Type your task in Cowork's prompt field.

Claude does the work in the background so you can move on to other tasks. To stop a task in progress, click Stop or Cancel in the sidebar.

TIP

When you're learning Cowork or testing a new task, point it to a copy of your folder rather than to the original folder. Once you're confident that the task runs as you want, switch back to the original files.

WARNING

Claude will move, rename, and delete files if you tell it to. That's the point, but it's also a risk. Before you use Cowork for anything important, back up your files. Cowork will always prompt you for permission before permanently deleting any files, but after a file is gone, Cowork can't undo the deletion.

Monitoring progress and steering mid-task

After you start a task, you don't have to step away entirely. Cowork gives you a running view of what Claude is doing, and you can step in at any point.

Before Claude begins work, it may ask you a few clarifying questions through an interactive prompt in the task window. These questions help Claude nail down the format you want, who the output is for, and any scope decisions it can't safely assume. Answering these questions takes a minute and typically gets you a much closer first result. If you see a question prompt after you click Let's Go, that's normal. Claude is making sure it understands the job before it starts.

To monitor Claude's progress, check the sidebar. As the task runs, Claude displays a visual task checklist in the task window, with each step marked as pending, in progress, or completed. This gives you a real-time view of where Claude is in the sequence, not just a general status message. The sidebar also lists the tools and files in use. If the sidebar isn't visible, click the panels icon in the upper-right corner of the Cowork window.

You can redirect Claude mid-task by typing additional instructions in the task field. If Claude is heading in the wrong direction, you can redirect it without canceling the job. When the task finishes, Claude saves its outputs to the folder you designated. Claude also presents your output files as clickable cards in the session view. Click any card to open the file directly.

TIP

If Claude's approach doesn't match what you had in mind, redirect it early. A mid-task correction is faster than canceling and restarting with a rewritten prompt.

REMEMBER

The Claude desktop app must remain open throughout a task. If you close the app or your computer goes to sleep, the task stops. Claude won't automatically know where to pick back up.

Organizing Work with Projects

Running one-off tasks in Cowork is useful. Running the same kind of task repeatedly, without re-explaining yourself every time, is where Projects come in. This section covers how to create a Project, how to write instructions that persist across sessions, and how global and folder-level settings shape every task Claude runs.

Creating a Cowork Project

Running a single task in Cowork is straightforward. But when you want to run the same kind of task repeatedly or pick up a long-running Project where you left off, you use Cowork Projects.

A Project in Cowork is a persistent workspace that holds everything Claude needs for recurring or complex work: the files it can access, the links it should reference, standing instructions for how you want things done, and a memory of what you've worked on together. When you open a Project, Claude already knows the context. You don't have to re-explain your preferences, your file structure, or how you like your reports formatted.

A standalone Cowork session is like hiring a skilled temp: they do the work well and leave. That's also why a standalone session starts fresh every time. It has no memory of what you worked on yesterday or last week. A Cowork Project is like working with someone who's been on your team for a month. They know your systems, your standards, and your quirks.

To create a Cowork Project, do the following:

1. **Open the Claude desktop app and click Cowork in the left sidebar.**
2. **In the left sidebar, click Projects, then click the + button.**

   The screen shown in Figure 19-3 appears.
3. **Choose how you want to create the Project.**

   You have three options:

   - *Start from Scratch:* Set up a new folder with instructions and files.
   - *Import a Project:* Bring into Cowork a Project you already built in claude.ai Chat, including its files and instructions.
   - *Use an Existing Folder:* Designate a folder already on your computer.

4. **In the Name field, type a name for the Project.**

   Use something descriptive, such as Weekly Reports, Client Intake, or Content Pipeline.

5. **Under Instructions, type any standing guidance you want Claude to follow every time it works in this Project.**

   For example, you might type your preferred output format, terminology, or quality standards.

6. **Click Create.**

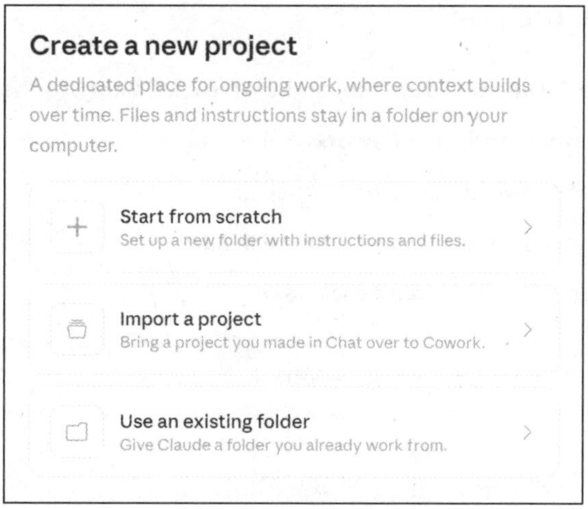

FIGURE 19-3: You can start from scratch, import a Project, or use an existing folder.

From this point, every task you run inside that Project inherits its context. Claude's outputs go to the folder you designated, and the memory of what you've done persists from session to session.

TIP

Use a Project any time you find yourself typing the same background instructions at the start of a Cowork session. If you've explained your file-naming convention or output format more than twice, that information belongs in a Project's standing instructions.

REMEMBER

Cowork Projects store memory in the Project workspace. That memory lives on your local machine, not on Anthropic's servers. If you change computers or reinstall the desktop app, that memory doesn't transfer automatically.

Setting global and folder instructions

One of the quiet frustrations with any AI tool is having to re-explain yourself. Your preferred output format, the terminology your team uses, and the fact that you always want a summary row at the top of a spreadsheet: typing all that at the start of every session adds up.

Global instructions apply to every Cowork session, regardless of which folder or Project you're working in. Use them for standing preferences that never change: your role, your preferred tone for written outputs, the file naming convention you use, or any background about your work that's always relevant.

To set global instructions:

1. **Open the Claude desktop app, and then click Cowork in the left sidebar.**
2. **Go to Settings, and then Cowork.**

   The screen shown in Figure 19-4 appears.
3. **In the Global Instructions section, click Edit.**
4. **Type your instructions and click Save.**

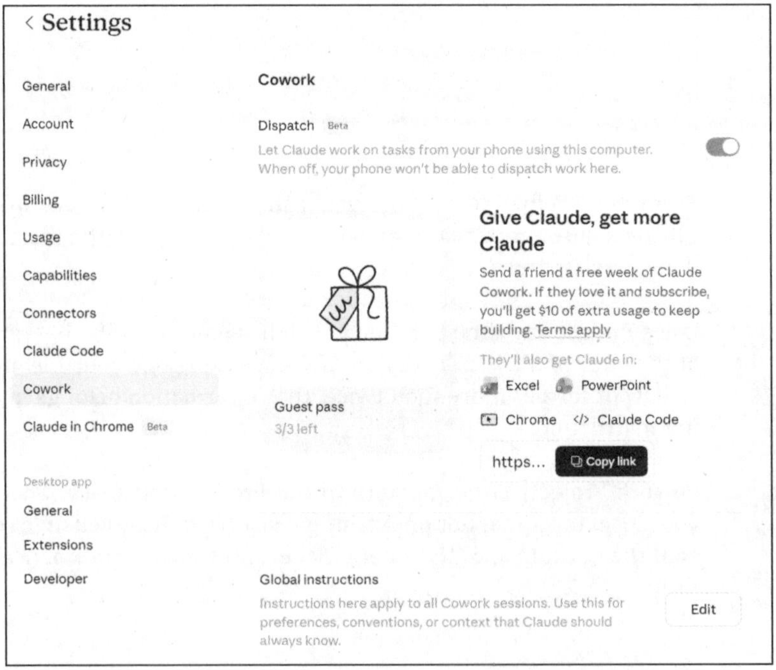

FIGURE 19-4: The Global instructions edit field.

Claude will read those instructions at the start of every Cowork session.

Folder instructions work the same way but apply only when Claude works in a specific folder. A client folder might specify the client's preferred terminology and reporting format. A content folder might specify word counts and style guidelines. Claude can also update folder instructions on its own during a session. If you share something important mid-task, Claude can save that as a note for next time.

TIP

Start your global instructions with a brief description of your role and what you primarily use Cowork for. Something like: "I'm a project manager at a consulting firm. I use Cowork mainly for client reporting, meeting prep, and file organization." That text orients Claude immediately and shapes everything it produces.

REMEMBER

Global instructions and folder instructions stack rather than override each other. If your global instructions say to write in plain English and your folder instructions say to use formal legal language for a specific client, Claude applies the folder instructions in that context. More specific instructions always win.

Assigning Tasks from Your Phone with Dispatch

Dispatch connects your phone and your desktop in a single continuous thread. This section covers how to set up Dispatch and how to write tasks that give Claude everything it needs to get started.

Setting up Dispatch on your devices

Dispatch gives you a single, continuous conversation with Claude that follows you between your phone and your desktop. You send a task from your phone on the way to the office. Claude does the work on your desktop. You sit down at your computer, and the result is waiting.

This approach differs from simply using the Claude mobile app. In a regular Claude chat, your phone conversations remain separate from your desktop conversations. With Dispatch, they form a single, connected thread, and Claude has access to your local files, your Connectors, and everything you've configured in Cowork, even when you're not sitting at your computer.

Before you start, you need the following:

- A Pro or Max plan
- The latest version of the Claude desktop app on your macOS or Windows computer
- The latest version of the Claude mobile app on your phone
- A desktop that is awake, and the desktop app running when you want Claude to work

To set up Dispatch, do the following:

1. **Download or update the Claude desktop app at `https://claude.com/download`.**
2. **Download or update the Claude mobile app on your phone.**
3. **Open Cowork on either your desktop or phone and click Dispatch in the left sidebar.**

   The Dispatch welcome screen appears, as shown in Figure 19-5, introducing its three core capabilities: control from your phone, work with apps and files, and schedule tasks, before you click Get Started.
4. **Click Get Started.**

   The Pair with the Claude mobile app screen appears, as shown in Figure 19-6.
5. **Scan the QR code with your phone's camera to download the Claude mobile app and pair it with your desktop.**

   This connection is what makes Dispatch work across both devices.
6. **Sign in to the Claude mobile app on your phone, and then click I'm Signed In on My Phone in the Desktop App.**

   The Get Ready to Dispatch screen appears, as shown in Figure 19-7.
7. **Choose one of the three setup options:**
   - *Keep this computer awake:* This option is toggled on by default. Leave it on so Dispatch can run tasks without your computer going to sleep.
   - *Enable Claude in Chrome:* Lets Dispatch navigate, click, and fill in forms in your browser. Click Enable if you want this capability.
   - *All connectors Are On:* Confirms that Claude can use every connector you've already authenticated. A checkmark here means you're ready.
8. **Click Finish Setup.**

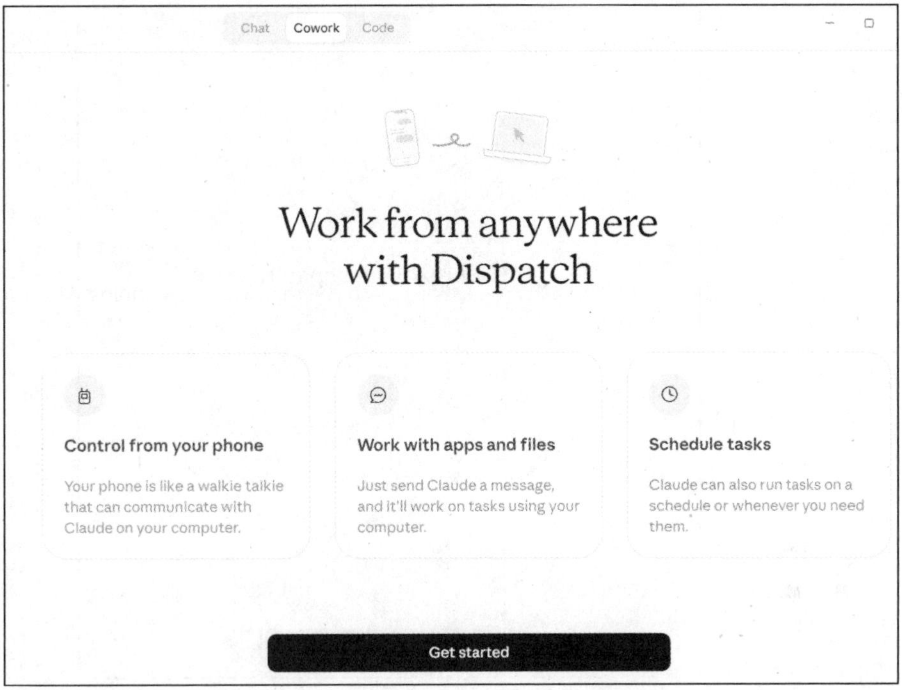

FIGURE 19-5: The Dispatch welcome screen.

FIGURE 19-6: Scan the QR code.

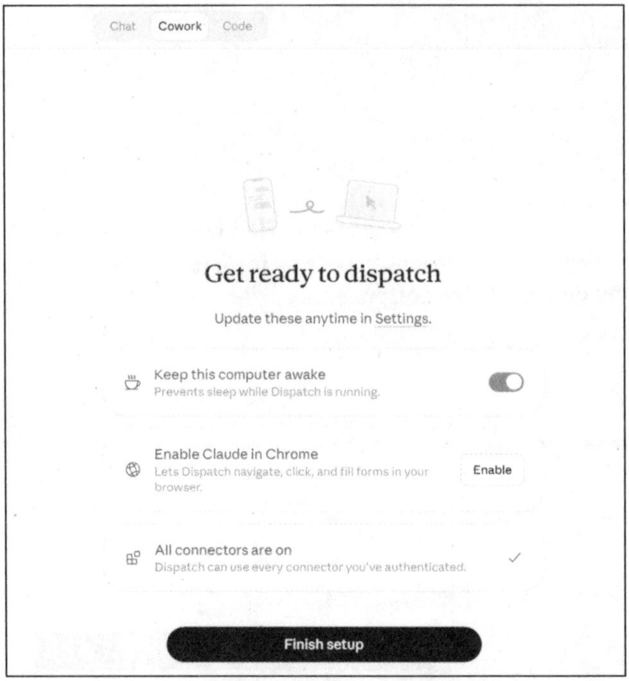

FIGURE 19-7: The Get Ready to Dispatch screen.

You can update any of these settings later by going to Settings and then Cowork.

WARNING

Dispatch works only while your desktop is awake and the Claude desktop app is open. If you send a task from your phone and your computer has gone to sleep, Claude can't start. Before you leave the office and plan to assign work remotely, make sure your desktop stays awake.

Sending tasks and retrieving results

Once Dispatch is set up, open it on your phone and describe the outcome you want, as you would from the desktop. Claude picks up the task, works on your computer, and sends the result back to the same thread. You get a push notification when the task is done or when Claude needs your input before it can continue.

You can hand Claude tasks that use everything on your desktop, including things you can't open on your phone. For example, you can ask Claude to pull data from a local spreadsheet and compile a summary report; have Claude search your Slack messages and email and then draft a briefing document; or tell Claude to organize files in a specific folder on your computer.

TIP

The clearest Dispatch tasks are outcome-focused: "Pull this week's metrics from the analytics folder and drop them into the weekly report template" gives Claude everything it needs. Vague requests like "do the reports" will result in a clarifying question before Claude starts.

REMEMBER

Dispatch is available on Pro and Max plans. If you don't see the Dispatch option in your Cowork sidebar, check that both your desktop and mobile apps are up to date. Team plan users should check with their admin; Dispatch may be available but off by default in your organization's settings.

Scheduled tasks and Dispatch are separate features. Scheduled tasks run automatically on a cadence you define. Dispatch is for tasks you assign on demand. You'll find each in its own section of the Cowork sidebar.

Letting Claude Use Your Computer

Most Cowork tasks involve reading and writing files in a folder you designate. A newer capability called *computer use* lets Claude go further by interacting with apps directly when no Connector exists. This section explains how the computer use feature works and how to enable it.

How computer use works in Cowork

Cowork has always worked by reading and writing files in folders you designate. The computer use feature takes it further. When Claude needs to complete a task and doesn't have a direct Connector for the app involved, it can use your computer the way you do: opening apps, navigating your browser, clicking buttons, and filling in fields.

Claude reaches for the most precise tool first. If a Connector exists for the app you need, Claude uses it. Connectors are faster and more reliable than screen interaction. If no Connector is available, Claude tries the browser next. Computer use, clicking and typing directly on your screen, is the fallback when nothing else handles the job.

The computer use feature is available on Pro and Max plans for both macOS and Windows. Check the Help Center for current availability on Team and Enterprise plans.

WARNING

Computer use runs outside the virtual machine that Cowork normally uses for file work. This means Claude is interacting with your desktop and apps, not an isolated sandbox. Claude asks for your permission before accessing each application, and some sensitive apps are blocked by default. Do not use the computer use feature with apps containing financial accounts, health records, legal documents, or other sensitive personal information.

TIP

Check the Connectors directory in your Claude settings regularly. As new Connectors are added, you may find that direct integrations can handle tasks you'd otherwise route through computer use. Connectors are faster and more reliable on any platform.

Enabling computer use on your computer

To turn on the computer use feature, you need the latest version of the Claude desktop app. Then follow these steps:

1. **Open the Claude desktop app, and then click Cowork in the left sidebar.**
2. **Go to Settings and then General (under Desktop App).**
3. **Find the Computer Use toggle and turn it on, as shown in Figure 19-8.**
4. **Open Cowork or Claude Code in the desktop app and start a session.**
5. **Ask Claude to do something that involves an app on your computer.**

   Claude asks for your permission to access the app before proceeding.

Start with simple tasks, like pulling data from a local dashboard or filling in a form in a web app, before asking the computer use feature to handle anything complex. Once you see how Claude navigates your screen for straightforward work, you'll have a good idea about where it will be reliable.

REMEMBER

When using the computer use feature, Claude takes screenshots to understand how to navigate. This means Claude can see anything visible on your screen or in the apps you've granted access to. Close files or apps with sensitive information before you start a computer use task.

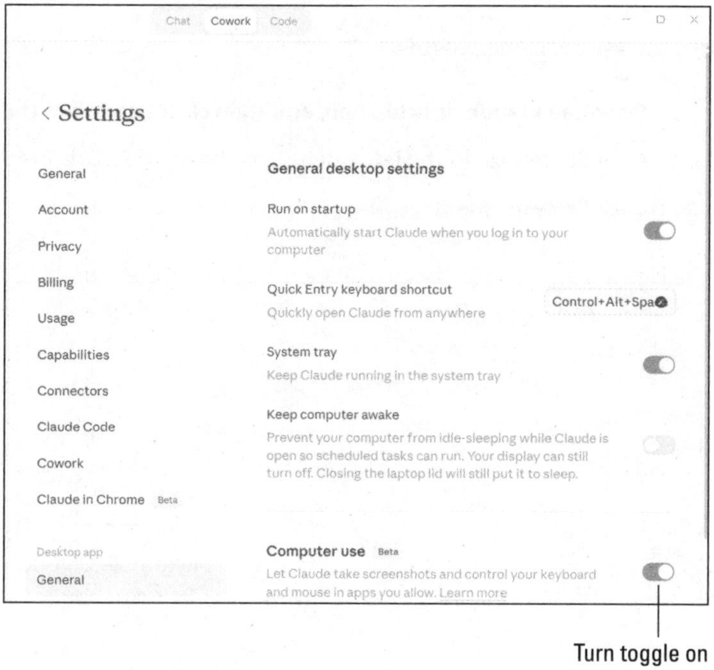

FIGURE 19-8: Turn on Computer Use toggle.

Automating Work with Plugins and Scheduled Tasks

Once Cowork is working well for you, plugins and scheduled tasks let you systematize that work. Plugins bring in ready-made workflows for specific roles and departments. Scheduled tasks run those workflows automatically on a schedule you set. This section covers how to find, install, and configure both.

Browsing and installing plugins

Plugins extend Cowork's capabilities by bundling Skills, Connectors, slash (/) commands, and subagents into a single package tailored to a specific type of work. Instead of manually assembling the pieces for a recurring workflow, you install a plugin to do the job.

Anthropic organizes available plugins by department and function: HR onboarding, design workflows, engineering code reviews, operations reporting, and more. If your organization runs a Team or Enterprise plan, your administrator can also build a private plugin marketplace: a curated set of plugins based on your company's specific tools, terminology, and processes.

To browse available plugins:

1. **Open the Claude desktop app, and then click Cowork in the left sidebar.**
2. **Click Customize in the left sidebar, as shown in Figure 19-9.**
3. **Click Browse plugins.**

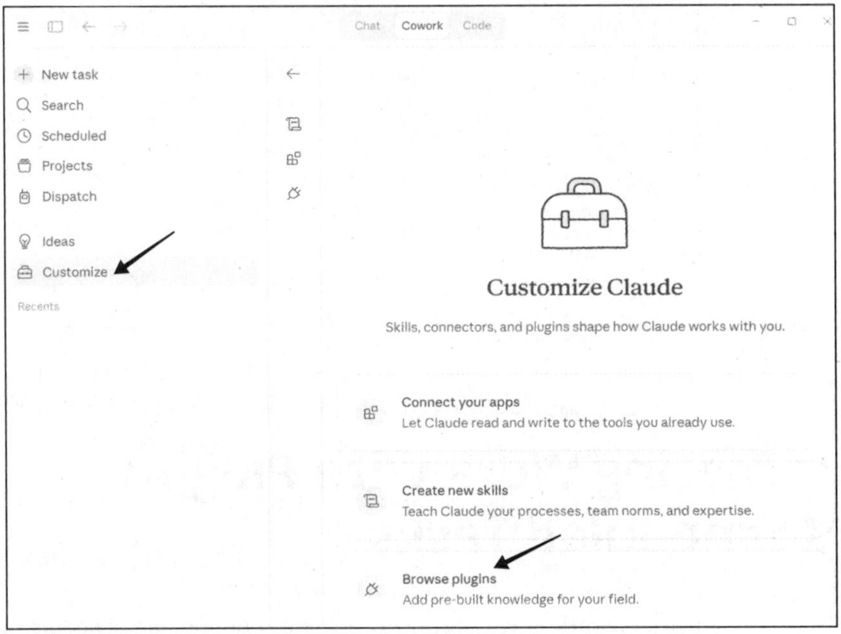

FIGURE 19-9: Check out the plugins you can install.

From here, you can install any plugin with a single click. Installed plugins appear in your Cowork sidebar and are available to any task you run.

TIP

Before building a custom workflow from scratch, browse the plugin directory. Department-specific plugins often cover the use case you have in mind, and they're faster to set up than assembling the same components manually.

TECHNICAL STUFF

If you're on a Team or Enterprise plan and want to build your own plugins, you can use the Cowork Plugin Create plugin, which walks you through the process. You can also start from Anthropic's templates and modify them to match your organization's needs.

Setting up scheduled tasks

Some work doesn't need a prompt every time. It just needs to happen on a schedule. With Cowork's scheduled tasks, you define the recurring work once and then Claude runs it automatically.

To schedule a recurring task, type **/schedule** in any Cowork task description, or click Scheduled in the Cowork sidebar. You can set the frequency, time, and specific folder or files involved.

Scheduled tasks work well for:

- Daily briefings that pull from your calendar and email
- Weekly reports compiled from folder contents
- Regular file organization and cleanup
- Recurring data pulls that feed a standing report template

Once you set the schedule, Cowork handles the rest. You can view, edit, and delete your scheduled tasks at any time from the Scheduled section in the sidebar.

REMEMBER

Scheduled tasks run only while your computer is awake and the Claude desktop app is open. If your computer goes to sleep before a scheduled task fires, that task won't execute until the next scheduled time.

TIP

Start with a simple scheduled task, such as a weekly folder summary, before automating anything consequential. Once you see how Claude handles it, you'll have a good feel for what to trust it with next.

Knowing Cowork's Limits

Cowork is powerful, but it has limits. Before you build workflows that depend on it, know what it can't do yet and what habits will keep your files safe.

What Cowork can't do yet

Cowork is a fast-moving product. Anthropic adds and updates capabilities frequently. Before building a business-critical workflow around a specific Cowork behavior, verify that it still works as expected.

Here are the current limitations:

- **Standalone sessions don't carry memory.** If you run a task outside a Project, Cowork starts fresh. It has no recollection of what you worked on in a previous session.

  TIP

  If you need continuity without setting up a full Project, keep a running notes file in the folder you give Claude access to and point it to that file at the start of each session.

- **Sessions are yours alone.** You can't hand a Cowork session to a colleague or pick it up on a different device. Whatever you start on your computer stays on your computer.
- **Cowork requires the desktop app.** There is no browser-only version of Cowork. You need the Claude desktop app installed and running on your macOS or Windows computer. You can assign tasks from your phone via Dispatch, but Claude completes the work on your desktop.
- **Cowork is not ready for regulated industries.** If your work requires a paper trail for healthcare, legal, finance, or any other compliance requirement, don't use Cowork. It doesn't currently log the actions it took or the reasons for them, so you can't prove what happened if someone asks later.
- **The app must stay open.** Cowork runs only while the desktop app is open. Close the lid or quit the app, and the task stops. If Claude is mid-task when the app closes, it won't know where to resume.
- **The computer use feature is available in Pro and Max only.** Even if you're on a Team or Enterprise plan, the computer use feature is not available at this time. Use Connectors and plugins for those workflows instead.

  TIP

  Connector availability in Cowork continues to expand. Check the Connectors directory in your Claude settings for the current list. What wasn't available when this was written may be there now.

Keeping your work safe

Cowork's power comes from the direct access it has to your files. That same access creates risk. A few habits will protect you.

- **Back up any folder before you point Cowork at it for the first time.** Cowork requires your permission before permanently deleting any files, but moves and overwrites happen without a separate confirmation. A backup before you start is cheap insurance.

» **Avoid granting access to folders containing sensitive information.** Create a dedicated working folder for Cowork and keep your sensitive material — such as financial documents, credentials, client records, or personal files — out of it.

» **Take extra care with scheduled tasks.** Scheduled tasks run automatically, which means Claude may work without you watching. Start with low-risk tasks before automating anything with real consequences, and review outputs after each run.

WARNING

Claude will move, rename, and delete files if you tell it to. Once files are gone or overwritten, Cowork can't undo that. Keep a current backup of any folder you give Cowork access to.

WARNING

Cowork doesn't handle regulated workloads. If your work requires compliance logging for healthcare, legal, or financial requirements, stick with standard Claude chat where your organization's admin controls apply.

Cowork shifts Claude from a conversational tool into a working one. The tasks that used to require your constant attention, file by file and step by step, are now things that you can describe once, hand off, and come back to. That's a big change in how you spend your time. Start with one task you've been putting off, let Claude take a run at it, and see what you get.

IN THIS CHAPTER

» Diagnosing why Claude misunderstands your requests

» Getting specific, useful responses instead of generic advice

» Improving quality when results fall short

Chapter 20
Fixing Common Problems

Problems with Claude's responses usually aren't random. They follow patterns you can learn to recognize and fix. When Claude completely misses what you need, gives you shallow or generic advice, or confidently states something you know is incorrect, specific prompt adjustments solve these issues better than regenerating the same flawed request.

This chapter shows you the most common problems people encounter with Claude. You learn to diagnose what's wrong rather than guessing and then administer the right cure.

When Claude Completely Misunderstands

You ask one thing and get an answer to a completely different question. Claude writes a formal business proposal when you need talking points for an informal meeting, or explains beginner concepts when you ask for advanced analysis. The response isn't bad; it's answering the wrong question.

TIP

This problem happens when your prompt contains signals pointing in different directions or when Claude lacks the context to interpret your request correctly. A missing detail about your situation or an unstated assumption can lead the response in an unintended direction.

Being more specific

Vague requests get vague interpretations. When you say, "Help me with this presentation," Claude doesn't know whether you need content, structure, talking points, or visual suggestions. Claude may interpret the request in a way you didn't intend. Here's an example:

Situation: A product manager needed help with a client presentation.

First prompt: "I'm presenting our new analytics feature next week. Help me prepare."

Claude's response: This first attempt failed. Claude gave them a generic presentation structure consisting of an introduction slide, a problem statement, a solution overview, benefits, and a conclusion. The response wasn't wrong, but it wasn't useful.

Result: The manager already had the structure. They needed help explaining complex analytics to non-technical stakeholders.

Second prompt: "I'm presenting our new analytics dashboard to executives who aren't technical. I need to explain predictive models without using jargon. The presentation is 15 minutes with 7 slides, which I already drafted. Help me simplify the explanation of how machine learning powers our forecasting feature."

Claude's response: It provided analogies, plain-language explanations, and suggestions for what to emphasize and what to skip.

Why this worked: The specificity about the audience (non-technical executives), the goal (simplify ML concepts), and the constraints (15 minutes, slides done) gave Claude the frame it needed.

When Claude misses your intent, check your prompt for what's unstated. Add the details you assumed Claude would know, such as your audience, your goal, your constraints, and what you've already done. Specificity prevents misinterpretation.

Adding missing context

Context changes everything. "Review this contract" means something different depending on whether you're the buyer or the seller, and whether it's a standard contract or one with unique clauses. Without context, Claude has to guess.

> **Situation:** A consultant asked Claude to review their statement of work (SOW).
>
> **First prompt:** "Look at this SOW and tell me what you think."
>
> **Claude's response:** It provided general feedback about clarity and structure. It mentioned that the deliverables seemed well-defined and that the timelines looked reasonable.
>
> **Result:** Claude's response was accurate but basically useless. The consultant wasn't asking for proofreading; they needed to know if the scope protected them from endless revisions.
>
> **Second prompt:** "I'm reviewing this SOW from a client perspective. I've had problems before with clients requesting unlimited revisions beyond the agreed scope. Look specifically for language that protects me from scope creep. Do the revision clauses give the client too much room to demand rework without additional fees?"
>
> **Claude's response:** It analyzed the specific clauses, flagged three areas where reasonable revisions lacked definition, and suggested the language to use to limit revision rounds.
>
> **Result:** The context about the consultant's past problems and what they were protecting against completely changed what Claude looked for.

Starting afresh with better framing

Sometimes the problem isn't what you said but what you said first. Your opening sentence or initial framing strongly influences how the request is interpreted. If that framing is wrong, everything after it gets filtered through the wrong lens. Here's an example in practice:

Situation: A marketing director wanted campaign ideas for a luxury product. Their initial prompt mentioned budget constraints first.

First prompt: "We have a limited marketing budget this quarter. Generate campaign ideas for our new luxury watch line targeting high-net-worth individuals."

Claude's response: It focused entirely on cost-effective tactics, specifically social media contests, influencer partnerships, and guerrilla marketing.

Result: These approaches don't match luxury positioning, where exclusivity and prestige matter more than reach.

Second prompt: "Our new luxury watch line targets high-net-worth collectors who value Swiss craftsmanship and limited editions. Price points start at $15,000. What campaign approaches maintain the exclusive positioning while reaching serious collectors?"

Claude's response: It suggested private trunk shows, partnerships with high-end galleries, limited edition announcements through luxury publications, and VIP preview events.

Result: Claude's second response use the same budget reality, but framing the luxury positioning first shaped appropriate solutions.

TIP

When your first attempt goes wrong, don't just add details. Check whether your opening prompt pointed Claude in the right direction. Sometimes you need to restart with a completely different angle.

Knowing When Responses Are Too Generic

Claude may give you advice that sounds reasonable but applies to everything and helps with nothing. "Build relationships with customers." "Focus on quality." "Communicate clearly." All true, and all useless. You need specific actions for your particular situation.

REMEMBER

Generic responses happen when Claude doesn't have enough detail to get specific or when your prompt accidentally invites broad advice. The fix isn't asking Claude to "be more specific; it's giving Claude the constraints and details that make specific answers possible."

Providing examples

Examples show Claude what level of detail you need and what format works for you. Without examples, Claude has to guess whether you want high-level strategy or step-by-step tactics. Here's an example:

Situation: A team leader needed onboarding improvements but got generic advice.

First prompt: "How can I improve onboarding for new team members?"

Claude's response: It suggested creating documentation, assigning mentors, scheduling check-ins, and setting clear expectations.

Result: Claude's response consisted of standard onboarding advice that appears in every management book. The team leader needed to add an example.

Second prompt: "Our current onboarding includes a welcome email with login credentials and a 30-minute orientation meeting. New developers then struggle to find information about our code review process, testing requirements, and deployment procedures. Here's what happened last time: An employee spent three days figuring out our workflow because it wasn't documented anywhere. Give me three specific onboarding additions that prevent this kind of time waste."

Claude's response: It provided concrete solutions in the form of a workflow diagram for the welcome email, a checklist of week one essentials covering code review and deployment, and a Slack channel archive of common new-hire questions.

Why this worked: The team leader's example showed Claude the specific type of problem to solve. Examples grounded the request in reality, showing Claude what they were dealing with rather than what they were theoretically asking about.

Adding constraints

Constraints are helpful. When you define what won't work, Claude can focus on what will. When you tell Claude, "Suggest marketing tactics," the universe of possible answers is huge. When you change that to "Suggest marketing tactics that require no paid advertising and can launch in two weeks," Claude has to get specific about which tactics fit. Here's an example:

Situation: A nonprofit director needed fundraising advice.

First prompt: "What are effective fundraising strategies for nonprofits?"

Claude's response: It listed annual campaigns, major donor cultivation, grant writing, events, monthly giving programs, corporate partnerships, and planned giving.

Result: Claude supplied a complete list of how nonprofits raise money, but none were actionable for their immediate needs.

Second prompt: "I run a small food bank with no development staff and no donor database. We need to raise $25,000 in the next three months to replace our refrigeration units. Our current donors give $50-$200 annually. What are three fundraising approaches that don't require hiring staff or expensive technology?"

Claude's response: It suggested a matched giving campaign where board members match donations dollar-for-dollar up to $12,500, a "sponsor a shelf" program at $500 per shelf for the new refrigeration units, and a grocery store partnership for point-of-sale donations.

Result: Each idea fit the director's constraints: no staff needed, no database required, achievable in three months.

Constraints aren't limitations; they're opportunities. They're guides that force you to apply specificity.

Requesting particular styles or formats

Format requests tell Claude how to package information. "Give me a list" produces different results than "Write this as talking points" or "Create a decision matrix." The same information, organized differently, serves various purposes. Here's an example:

Situation: An finance executive needed to explain a reorganization to their staff.

First prompt: "Explain our organizational restructuring to the team."

Claude's response: It wrote three paragraphs of explanation covering the reasons for change, new reporting structures, and the timeline.

Result: Claude's response was accurate but not usable. The executive needed to present this in a team meeting, not email it.

Second prompt: "Create talking points I can use in a 5-minute team meeting to explain our reorganization. Include why we're doing this (2 points), what's changing (3 key changes), what's staying the same (2 reassurances), and next steps (3 actions). Make each point one sentence that I can speak naturally."

Claude's response: It delivered effective, speakable points organized for verbal delivery. It was the same information but formatted as a verbal presentation.

Understanding Why You're Not Getting Quality Results

Sometimes the response addresses your question but the quality falls short. The analysis stays surface-level when you need depth, or the writing sounds off-tone. Something's missing, but you can't immediately identify what it is.

Quality problems usually trace to three sources:

- You asked for too much at once.
- You didn't provide enough information.
- You need a different approach.

Checking if you're asking too much at once

Claude handles complex requests well but has limits. When you ask for market analysis, competitive research, a content strategy, and an implementation timeline in a single prompt, quality suffers across the board. Claude tries to address everything and ends up giving shallow coverage to each piece. Here's an example:

Situation: A startup founder needed to identify their company's competitive advantages.

Prompt: "Analyze the meal kit market, identify our competitive advantages, suggest a content marketing strategy, and create a launch timeline for our new service."

Claude's response: It touched on all four areas but none deeply enough to be useful. The market analysis listed obvious players without insight into gaps. The competitive advantages repeated their pitch deck. The content strategy suggested blog posts and social media. The timeline was generic.

Result: The founder had to break the prompt into focused requests to get depth.

Second prompt: "Analyze the meal kit market specifically for families with dietary restrictions. What gaps exist in current offerings for gluten-free, dairy-free, and allergen-friendly options? Focus only on market analysis."

Claude's response: This single-focus prompt produced a detailed analysis of market gaps, customer pain points in existing services, and specific opportunities for an allergen-friendly positioning.

Result: The founder used that analysis to inform separate prompts for competitive advantages and content strategy.

REMEMBER

When results feel thin across the board, you've probably asked for too much. Break your request into single-focus prompts that let Claude go deep on one thing at a time.

Verifying that you gave enough information

Sometimes quality suffers because Claude doesn't have enough to work with. You ask for strategic advice, but you describe only symptoms, not the situation. You want writing feedback, but don't explain the audience or purpose.

Situation: A freelance consultant needed recommendations for a client's employee retention problem.

First prompt: "My client's employee retention is terrible. What should they do?"

Claude's response: It suggested better compensation, improved management training, career development programs, and workplace culture initiatives.

Result: Claude's responses were true but generic, like solutions in every retention playbook. The consultant needed to add context.

Second prompt: "My client is a 50-person tech startup. Their retention problem is specific to mid-level engineers with 2-4 years of experience who leave for larger companies. Exit interviews reveal they're leaving for better-defined career paths, more technical challenges, and concerns about startup instability. Compensation is already competitive with big tech. What retention strategies address these specific drivers?"

Claude's response: It suggested creating a technical career ladder with clear advancement criteria, establishing a senior engineer mentorship program pairing midlevel engineers with complex projects, and implementing quarterly presentations to reduce instability concerns.

Result: Each solution targeted a specific driver from the exit interviews.

Information quality determines solution quality. If you're getting generic answers, check whether you've given Claude enough specific details to guide the answer.

Trying different prompt approaches

Sometimes the problem isn't what you asked but how you asked it. Different prompt structures focus on different types of thinking. A direct question might get surface answers when a scenario-based prompt would go deeper.

> **Situation:** A software product manager needed help prioritizing their company's features.
>
> **First prompt:** "Which features should we build first for our project management tool?"
>
> **Claude's response:** It suggested starting with core functionality, specifically task creation, assignment, deadlines, and notifications.
>
> **Result:** Claude provided obvious necessities, not strategic choices. The product manager needed a scenario-based approach instead.
>
> **Second prompt:** "Our project management tool targets creative agencies frustrated by rigid, structured systems. Three agencies told us 'We need flexible workflows that match how creative projects actually evolve' and 'Stop making us fit our work into your structure.' Based on this feedback, which features differentiate us from the structured workflow approach?"
>
> **Claude's response:** It suggested customizable workflow states (not fixed to do/in progress/done), project templates that branch based on decisions rather than linear paths, and a parking lot feature for ideas that don't fit the current structure.
>
> **Result:** These features directly addressed the gap in creative flexibility.

When one approach gets weak results, try reframing it. Ask for examples instead of principles, and describe a scenario instead of asking a direct question. Different structures tap into different reasoning.

Recognizing When Claude Seems Wrong or Confused

Sometimes Claude sounds confident but something feels off. The facts seem questionable, or the advice contradicts what you know. Confident-sounding mistakes are more dangerous than obviously uncertain responses because they're easy to miss.

WARNING

Learning to spot these moments and verify them protects you from acting on bad information. The key is recognizing the patterns that indicate problems.

Spotting mistakes of confidence

Confidence doesn't equal accuracy. Claude can state incorrect information with the same authoritative tone it uses for correct details. You need to develop an instinct for when confidence needs verification.

Watch for these signals:

- **Suspiciously specific numbers without sources:** If Claude states that "The average conversion rate for SaaS companies is 2.87 percent" but doesn't cite a source, that statistic might be inaccurate or unsupported. Real statistics come from studies, reports, or research. Made-up statistics can sound equally confident.
- **Definitive statements about changing fields:** Technology, regulations, current events, and market conditions change constantly. If Claude says, "The current FDA guidelines require X," verify it. Claude's training has a cutoff date, so "current" information might be outdated.
- **Advice that contradicts domain expertise:** If you have experience in an area and Claude's advice feels wrong, trust your instinct. A financial advisor noticed Claude suggesting tax strategies that violated recent rule changes. Claude sounded confident, but the advisor was right to verify.
- **Perfect solutions to complex problems:** Real business, technical, and organizational challenges involve tradeoffs. If Claude presents a solution with no downsides or complications, it might be oversimplifying. Look for "This approach works, but you'll need to accept [tradeoff]" rather than "This approach solves everything."

These signals don't mean Claude is wrong. They tell you to always verify the information before acting on it.

Asking for sources and reasoning

When something feels off, ask Claude to explain its thinking or provide sources. This approach often shows you whether the answer is real or based on false assumptions.

Here's an example:

Situation: A business researcher questioned a statistical claim.

Claude's response: "Studies show that remote workers are 35 percent more productive than office workers."

Result: The researcher felt this answer was too simple. Productivity is complex and depends on the measurement methods used.

Prompt: "What studies are you referring to? What definition of productivity did they use and in what context?"

Claude's response: It acknowledged it couldn't cite specific studies and that productivity research shows mixed results depending on job type, individual work styles, and how productivity gets measured.

Result: The "productive" claim was exposed when the researcher questioned it.

TIP

Asking for reasoning works the same way. "Walk me through why you recommend this approach" often reveals whether Claude is applying sound logic or making it up.

For example, a software manager questioned a hiring recommendation. Claude had suggested hiring senior developers over junior developers for a tight-deadline project. When asked to explain the reasoning, Claude laid out assumptions that failed to account for the team's unique skills. The recommendation sounded right but was based on incomplete logic.

TIP

When something feels off, asking "why" or "what's your source" helps separate reasoning from plausible-sounding mistakes.

Knowing when to verify externally

Some questions require verification beyond what Claude can provide. You should always confirm current facts, specialized technical details, legal requirements, and medical information through authoritative sources.

For example, a small business owner asked about employment law requirements. They asked, "Do I need to provide health insurance for part-time employees in our company?"

Claude provided an answer about general employer requirements, but employment law varies by business size, employee hours, and legislative changes. The owner was right to verify this with their legal advisor rather than relying on Claude's response.

Always verify externally when:

- **Your decision has legal, financial, or safety implications:** Laws change, regulations vary by jurisdiction, and getting it wrong can have serious consequences.
- **The information is time-sensitive or frequently updated:** Current drug approvals, software version features, tax code changes, or market data might have changed since Claude's training.
- **You need domain-specific expertise:** Medical symptoms, legal strategy, structural engineering, or tax optimization require licensed professionals with current knowledge and liability.

WARNING

The cost of being wrong is high. If acting on incorrect information could harm your business, health, or legal standing, verify it with authoritative sources.

Claude helps you think through problems, draft content, and analyze situations. It doesn't replace professional expertise or authoritative sources for high-stakes decisions.

Understanding the Pattern Behind Problems

Most problems with Claude's responses follow predictable patterns:

- Misunderstandings can trace back to missing context or vague framing.
- Generic responses come from vague requests without constraints.
- Quality issues stem from overloaded prompts or insufficient information.

TIP

Recognizing these patterns helps you diagnose problems quickly and apply the right fix. Instead of mindlessly regenerating responses or abandoning the entire conversation, you identify the issue and adjust your approach.

When Claude misses the mark, ask yourself:

- **Did I give Claude enough context to interpret my request correctly?** If not, add the background details, constraints, and goals that guide accurate interpretation.
- **Was my request too vague to get specific answers?** If yes, add examples, constraints, or format requirements that force specificity.
- **Did I ask for too much at once?** If the quality feels thin, break your request into focused parts.
- **Does this need verification?** If the answer involves current facts, specialized expertise, or high-stakes decisions, confirm through authoritative sources.

TIP

This thinking turns frustrating interactions into productive ones. You stop treating every problem as arbitrary and start fixing the cause.

The goal is not to have perfect prompts every time but to develop the judgment to recognize what went wrong and the skills to fix it.

5 The Part of Tens

IN THIS PART . . .

Find ten ways to save time with Claude every day.

Spot ten signs that your prompt needs a fresh start.

IN THIS CHAPTER

» Writing and editing faster

» Learning and researching in minutes instead of hours

» Making decisions without overthinking

Chapter 21
Ten Ways That Claude Saves You Time Every Day

You know Claude is helpful, but do you know how much time it could actually save you? This chapter highlights ten everyday situations where Claude can reduce hours of work to mere minutes or even seconds.

These scenarios aren't hypothetical. You see where you can fit Claude into your daily routine, whether you're writing emails or learning new skills, and save hours every week.

Write an Email in 30 Seconds

Sometimes answering emails can consume your entire morning. Every response needs the right tone, the right words, and the right level of detail. You want it to sound like you. You can use Claude to draft professional emails by simply telling it what you want. For example, "Politely decline this meeting but suggest an alternative" or "Thank this person for their help." Claude responds with a complete, ready-to-send message. And Claude remembers the context of each conversation so that follow-up email responses are even faster.

Never Stare at a Blank Page Again

Writer's block isn't just frustrating; it's expensive. You waste 20 minutes staring at an empty document, another 30 trying different openings, and you still haven't written anything useful. Claude can eliminate blank page paralysis.

TIP

Ask Claude for an outline, a first paragraph, or a structure for your document, and suddenly you have something to work with. You're editing and refining instead of agonizing over how to start. The time saved isn't just the minutes spent staring; it's the momentum you build by jumping straight into productive work. You can also ask for several possible approaches so you can choose the most promising.

Edit without the Pain

Editing your own writing is not easy. You know something's wrong, but you can't quite tell what needs fixing. Claude gives you an editing partner who can instantly spot clarity issues, awkward phrasing, and tone problems.

TIP

Paste in your draft, ask Claude to improve the clarity or strengthen your argument, and you'll get specific suggestions in seconds. What used to require multiple read-throughs and hours of revisions now happens in minutes. You're not only saving time but also producing better work.

Learn a Complex Topic in Minutes

Trying to understand a complex topic usually means clicking through multiple articles and watching lots of videos, but you might still feel confused about how it all connects. Claude breaks down complicated subjects into digestible explanations tailored to your level. Ask it to "Explain blockchain like I'm a marketer, not a programmer" or "Teach me the basics of financial statements," and you get clear, focused explanations without the jargon overload. What used to require an hour of research and frustration now takes 5 to 10 minutes of focused conversation.

Create a First Draft Instantly

First drafts used to mean sitting down for an hour or two, forcing yourself to push through, and hoping something decent emerged. Claude creates first drafts in seconds. Need a project proposal? A blog post? A presentation outline? Describe what you want, and Claude generates a first draft that you can refine. You start not from a blank page but from text that's good enough to edit. This shift from creation to refinement saves hours and removes the psychological barrier of starting a draft.

Make a Decision without Analysis Paralysis

Big decisions can trap you in endless loops of weighing options and second-guesses. Claude helps you systematically think through decisions. Ask it to compare options, identify pros and cons, or suggest factors you haven't considered. You get organized thinking instead of mental confusion. What used to require days of deliberation and spreadsheets now takes a focused 15-minute conversation.

REMEMBER

You can make better decisions faster because Claude helps you see the structure in complex choices.

Organize Information Effortlessly

You're drowning in information, emails, meeting notes, research articles, and random thoughts scribbled on sticky notes. Organizing all this used to mean hours of sorting, categorizing, and trying to find the patterns. Claude processes information and extracts what matters.

TIP

Upload a long document and ask for key takeaways. Paste scattered notes and ask Claude to organize them by theme. Turn a rambling brainstorm into a structured outline. What used to be an afternoon project becomes a 5-minute task.

Research in a Fraction of the Time

Research used to mean opening multiple browser tabs, reading through each article, taking notes, and trying to synthesize everything into something useful. With Claude's web search feature (available to all users), you can ask research questions and get synthesized answers that pull from multiple current sources. Instead of spending two hours gathering and organizing information, you spend 15 minutes having a focused conversation that gives you exactly what you need. Claude doesn't just find information; it understands it and presents it in a way you can actually use.

Generate Unlimited Ideas on Demand

Brainstorming alone is exhausting. You come up with several ideas, but they all seem terrible, so you're stuck. Claude is an infinite idea generator that never runs out of suggestions. Need 20 social media post ideas or 10 approaches to solve a business problem? Claude generates options instantly, helping you break through creative blocks and explore possibilities you wouldn't have considered. You not only save time in idea generation but also get past feeling stumped, which kills productivity.

Get Unstuck Immediately

Being stuck is the ultimate time-waster. You can't move forward on your project, you can't make a decision, you can't see the solution, and minutes turn into hours of frustration. Claude can get you unstuck immediately. Describe what you're struggling with, and Claude helps you see the problem differently, suggests approaches you haven't tried, or breaks the problem into smaller pieces you can tackle. What used to mean abandoning work until inspiration struck now means a quick conversation that gets you moving.

IN THIS CHAPTER

» Spotting common signs of unclear instructions

» Knowing when to start over instead of regenerating your prompt

» Learning from unsuccessful prompts

Chapter 22
Ten Signs That You Need to Rewrite Your Prompt

As you've probably discovered, not every prompt works perfectly the first time. Sometimes Claude delivers exactly what you ask for, but it isn't what you actually wanted. Other times, Claude seems confused or gives you something unexpected.

This chapter helps you recognize the warning signs that your prompt needs a rewrite. Learning to spot these signals will save you time and frustration. Instead of clicking "Retry" five times, hoping for a different result, you'll know when to step back and improve your prompt.

Each item in this chapter points to a specific problem you can fix, turning your unsuccessful attempts into learning opportunities that make you better at working with Claude.

Claude Asks Clarifying Questions

When Claude responds with questions instead of answers, your prompt is missing critical information. Claude is telling you that it doesn't have enough context to proceed. Maybe you asked it to "Write a proposal" without specifying what kind, for whom, or about what. Or you said "Fix this" without explaining what's wrong.

TIP

Questions like "What's your target audience?" or "What tone do you prefer?" indicate that Claude needs more detail to give you useful results. Don't answer the question and hope for the best. Rewrite your original prompt to include this information upfront. Your revised prompt should be so clear that Claude can start working immediately instead of playing twenty questions.

The Response Is Too Generic

Generic responses mean Claude doesn't understand what makes your situation special. If you asked for social media tips and got the same advice you'd find in any marketing article, your prompt wasn't specific enough. Generic output happens when you ask broad questions without context: "How do I grow my business?" or "What's a good email subject line?" These prompts could apply to anyone in any industry. Specific details transform generic responses into useful ones.

REMEMBER

Instead of writing "marketing strategies," try "marketing strategies for a boutique bakery in Portland targeting health-conscious millennials." The more specific your situation, the more tailored Claude's response becomes. If the output feels like it could work for anyone, it's because your prompt described everyone.

You Get Something Unexpected

When Claude delivers something totally different from what you expected, your prompt probably meant something other than what you thought. You asked for "a pitch," but you got a baseball explanation instead of a business proposal.

You requested "help with Python" (a programming language), but you got information about the snake instead. These misunderstandings happen when prompts contain ambiguous terms or missing context. The fix is straightforward: be explicit.

TIP

Add context that removes ambiguity, "a business pitch for investors" or "help with Python programming." If Claude misunderstood once, it will misunderstand again with the same wording. Rewrite the prompt to eliminate the confusion, using specific terminology that points Claude in the right direction.

The Length Is Wrong

Length problems expose unclear expectations. You wanted a detailed explanation but got two sentences. Or you asked for a quick summary and received three pages. If you don't specify the length, Claude makes a judgment call and guesses. A prompt asking to "Explain quantum computing" could reasonably be answered in one paragraph or ten pages. There's no way to know which one you wanted.

TIP

State your length expectations explicitly: "Explain quantum computing in three paragraphs for a blog post" or "Give me a comprehensive 1,000-word explanation of quantum computing." When length matters, make it part of your requirements, not something you hope Claude guesses correctly.

Claude Seems Confused or Uncertain

Confusion shows up in hedging language and a lack of confidence. Claude responds with phrases like "this might mean" or "you could be asking about" or offers multiple interpretations because it's genuinely unsure what you want. This often happens with vague requests or when you're asking about something unusual without enough context.

If Claude seems uncertain, your prompt is ambiguous and needs clarification. Look for words in your prompt that could be interpreted multiple ways. Check if you've provided enough background for Claude to understand your specific situation. A confused response means it's time to rewrite. Make sure to add context and specific details that remove doubt about what you're asking.

The Result Doesn't Match Your Vision

Sometimes Claude delivers exactly what you asked for, but it's not what you had in mind. You requested "a professional email" and got something technically professional but way too formal for your friendly workplace. Or you asked for "ideas" and got a list when you wanted a narrative. This disconnect means you didn't communicate the essentials you cared about. The problem isn't Claude. It's that your prompt didn't fully capture your idea.

TIP

Think about what's missing. If tone matters, specify it. If the format has issues, describe them. If you have a particular approach in mind, explain it. Don't expect Claude to read your mind.

The Tone or Style Misses the Mark

Tone problems are among the most common reasons for rewrites. Claude's response is informative, but it sounds like a textbook when you needed conversational warmth. Or it's casual when you need formal business language, or the tone doesn't automatically match your requirements. You have to specify it. Phrases like "Write in a friendly, conversational tone," or "Use formal business language," or "Make this sound excited but not over the top" give Claude clear direction.

REMEMBER

If the tone feels wrong, your prompt probably didn't mention tone or did so vaguely. Be specific about the feeling you want the writing to convey. Style includes not only tone but also sentence length and personality. Give Claude these details upfront.

Regenerating Doesn't Help

If you've selected Retry (synonymous with regeneration) three times and every response has the same problems, regenerating isn't the solution; rewriting is.

REMEMBER

Regeneration gives you variations of the same response based on the same prompt. If your prompt has fundamental issues, you'll get similar results no matter how many times you regenerate.

It's like asking someone to paint your house blue when you wanted it green. Asking them to try again won't magically change the color. Instead of hoping the fourth regeneration will be different, step back and identify what's wrong with your prompt. Are you missing details? Being too vague? Not specifying a format? Fix the prompt itself, and then start again. You'll get better results from one good prompt than from ten regenerations of a flawed one.

You Keep Getting Variations of the Same Thing

Every response you get is slightly different but shares the same main issues. You keep getting formal language when you need casual, or you focus on the wrong aspects of your question. Something in your prompt is steering Claude in a direction you don't want. This often happens when one part of your prompt contradicts another or when an early detail dominates Claude's interpretation.

REMEMBER

Check your prompt for signals you didn't mean to send. Did you say "quick overview" but also ask for "comprehensive coverage"? Did you mention something minor that Claude thought was the main point? Rewrite the prompt to emphasize what matters most and remove contradictory signals.

The Answer Sounds Like Guessing

When Claude's response feels uncertain, filled with qualifiers, or presents information as possibilities rather than answers, something about your question made it impossible to give a confident response. Maybe you asked about something too specific or your question was ambiguous enough that Claude couldn't commit to one interpretation.

Guessing-style responses include lots of "this might," "possibly," "it could be." If Claude sounds like it's guessing, you probably need to provide more context or verify that your topic is something Claude can help with. Don't accept a guessing-tone response. Rewrite your prompt to be more specific, add relevant context, or break your question into smaller, clearer parts.

Index

B

C

D

E

F

G

H

I

J

K

L

M

N

O

P

Q

R

S

T

U

V

W

About the Author

Stephanie Diamond is the author and co-author of more than 30 retail books, including *Writing AI Prompts For Dummies*, *Artificial Intelligence For Dummies*, *Social Media Marketing For Dummies*, *The Visual Marketing Revolution*, and *Facebook Marketing For Dummies*, as well as more than 35 custom ebooks for Fortune 500 companies. Writing at the intersection of business and emerging technology, she translates complex tools into practical guidance that readers can put to work. She spent eight years as a marketing director at AOL during its rise from 1 million to 36 million subscribers. She holds a degree in psychology from Hofstra University and two master's degrees from the University of Hawaii. She is a licensed Buzan Mind Mapping practitioner trained by Tony Buzan, with deep expertise in visual thinking and the cognitive strategies people use to organize information, make connections, and think more clearly.

Dedication

To Barry, who makes all things possible.

Author's Acknowledgments

Writing this book has been a privilege. My deepest thanks go to the wonderfully creative team at Wiley Publishing, Inc.: Associate Editor Jennifer Yee, who championed this project; my dream-team project and copy editor Susan Pink and technical editor Guy Hart-Davis, whose talent shaped every chapter; and the expert Wiley production team that turn manuscripts into books. A thank-you as well to Steve Hayes, former executive editor at Wiley, for his support over the years.

Thank you to my agent, Matt Wagner of Fresh Books, for his tireless work on my behalf over so many years.

And finally, thank you for choosing this book as your guide to Claude. I hope your AI journey is full of curiosity and happy discoveries.

Publisher's Acknowledgments

Associate Editor: Jennifer Yee
Managing Editor: Ajith Kumar
Project and Copy Editor: Susan Pink
Production Editor: Tamilmani Varadharaj
Technical Editor: Guy Hart-Davis
Cover Images: maximon4ik/stock.adobe.com, Icons-Studio/stock.adobe.com